The Tamara Coast to Coast Way
(Hyns Tamara Arvor dh' Arvor)

First edition published in Grea
Tamar Valley AON
Tamar Valley Centre, Cemetery R
Gunnislake, Cornwall P

ISBN: 978-1-3999-5

Designed and typeset by:
PED (Paul Eustice Design), Cornwall
e: paul.eustice@pauleusticedesign.com t: 07885 638022
Typeset in Robotto Light 9/12pt

Written and compiled by: Steve Church, Mark Owen and Sue Viccars

The authors would like to thank all those who have kindly agreed to contribute photographic images for this publication. All photos, unless credited underneath by Steve Church. Produced with support from the Heritage Lottery Fund.

All Ordnance Survey maps and content have been used by kind permission of Ordnance Survey and with written consent.

Printed and bound by:
St. Austell Printing Company Limited, St. Austell Business Park, Cornwall PL25 4FD

The Tamara Coast to Coast Way

The *Tamara Coast to Coast Way (Hyns Tamara Arvor dh' Arvor* in the Cornish language) is a walking route spanning Britain's southwest peninsula between its south and north coasts. It runs closely parallel to the boundary between Devon and Cornwall, which for most of the way follows the course of the River Tamar.

The route has many attractions which will appeal to walkers. First, because the River Tamar runs very nearly from coast to coast, walkers can experience the landscape of a significant river and its valley as it progresses from mouth to source. This is further highlighted by the fact that the Tamar passes through an Area of Outstanding Natural Beauty (AONB), which is a national landscape designation, and areas defined by the local authorities as Areas of Great Landscape Value. Another AONB is passed through on the approach to and at the north coast. In other words, walkers will be passing through a very scenic landscape. And those who complete the route will be able to experience the contrast between the two coasts – the wide and bustling estuary of the Tamar, flanked on one side by woodland and the other by the great naval city of Plymouth at its southern end, and the wild, remote and dramatic coast at the Devon–Cornwall border at the northern end.

Further, the route gives walkers the opportunity to experience a range of features of historic and cultural interest. These include whole areas which have been recognised internationally as of cultural importance by designation as part of a World Heritage Site. The Cornwall and West Devon Mining Landscape World Heritage Site covers much of the Tamar Valley in its lower reaches and recognises the unique contribution the area made to the development of the modern world. Walkers will pass numerous examples of formerly important mining sites, often now romantic ruins almost lost in woodland, plus riverside quays and the lines of old railways, inclined planes and miners' cottages, and even miners' smallholdings and places of recreation.

In addition, in the northern half of its route, the Way is closely linked to the Bude Canal. This 19th-century transport link – Cornwall's premier canal – helped open up the relatively remote Devon–Cornwall border areas before the railway arrived and has a fascinating story to tell, with its own inclined planes, a reservoir supplying water for the canal and features of heritage interest including wharves.

And there is one more very special attraction. The South West Coast Path follows the entire Cornish coast between Marsland Mouth, the little cove that marks the Devon–Cornwall border on the north coast, and the Tamar Estuary on the south coast. By linking these two points, the *Tamara Coast to Coast Way* provides the opportunity to walk the complete circuit of Cornwall – the *Kylgh Kernow*.

The Circuit of Cornwall – *"Kylgh Kernow"*

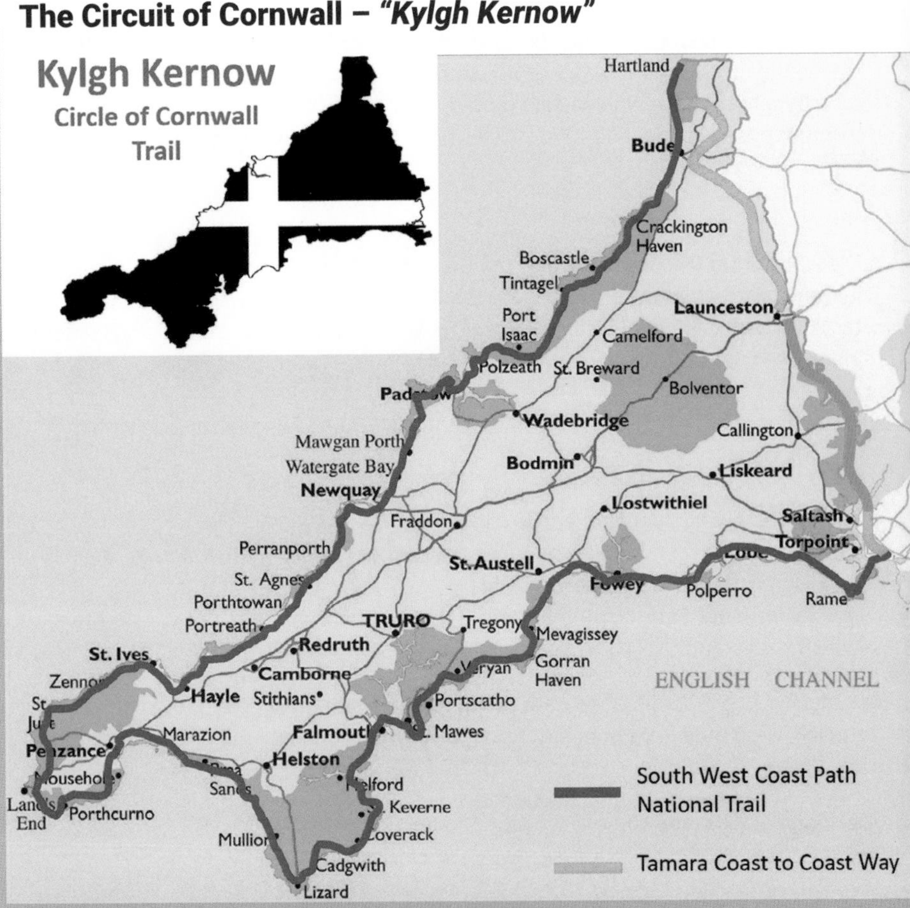

Map 1
The *Tamara Coast to Coast Way* completes the walking circuit of Cornwall (*Kylgh Kernow*) when combined with the South West Coast Path

The *Kylgh Kernow* is enabled by linking the *Tamara Coast to Coast Way* with the South West Coast Path. Many have already walked the coastline of Cornwall, and completing the circuit is an opportunity not to be missed by anyone with a connection to Cornwall, by birth, residence, historic background or just plain interest.

In recognition of this, the route offers specifically Cornish options over some lengths. The *Tamara Coast to Coast Way* is partly in Cornwall, but also partly in Devon. There are some generally short sections where geography and the existence (or not) of a safe walking route mean that there is no alternative but for the route to stay on the Devon side of the border.

But there are other stretches where what is recommended as the 'primary' route passes through Devon because the local geography means that views are better or because the route can follow footpaths rather than minor roads. For these sections, for the benefit of those who wish to remain on the west side of the Tamar for the maximum possible distance, alternative routes within Cornwall are available as a *Kylgh Kernow* option.

A Message from the Grand Bard of the Gorsedh Kernow
The Coast Path around Cornwall is known as a vast treasure of natural beauty. Now, after 2000 years, the circle is complete. The section that had been missing was the mighty River Tamar, from three-mile-wide ria to gorge to simple stream. The Tamar is:

- A body of water which was once the giantess Tamara, who fell in love with the wrestling giants Tavi and Taw;
- The border formed by the children of King Brychan c. 480CE;
- One of the oldest linguistic borders in Europe;
- The border between Wessex and Cornwall, agreed by King Athelstan of Wessex and King Hywel of Cornwall in AD936;
- A legal boundary, stated as the eastern bank in the Duchy of Cornwall charters, which was created in 1337.

At last, here is a long-distance path that encompasses the whole of the country of Cornwall. Here then is a chance to love it all 'in the round'. *Gwren ni kerdhes* – let's get walking!

Pol Hodge *Mab Stenek Veur*
Grand Bard of the Gorsedh Kernow *Bardh Meur Gorsedh Kernow*

Note: *The Gorsedh Kernow is the non-political body which preserves the history and culture of Cornwall. It comprises Bards, who are elected to the Gorsedh on the basis of having given exceptional service to Cornwall, its history and culture. The Gorsedh is headed by the Grand Bard.*

Route Overview

The total length of the route is 90.5 miles (146km). For convenience, the route has been divided into seven stages, each of which could be completed in a day by a good walker. Each stage begins and ends at an accessible location, with accommodation available locally and/or with public transport to a larger settlement.

In addition, cut-outs to public transport or other facilities in the course of each stage are described, as well as some recommended circular walks based on the Way for those who wish to stay in and experience a particular local area.

The seven primary route stages are numbered from south to north, and between Tamerton Foliot and Lifton these follow the Tamar Valley Discovery Trail:

Stage 1: Cremyll to Tamar Bridge (12.6 miles/20.2km)
Stage 2: Tamar Bridge to Bere Ferrers (9.8 miles/15.8km)
Stage 3: Bere Ferrers to Gunnislake (11.9 miles/19.2km)
Stage 4: Gunnislake to Lifton (13.5 miles/21.8km)
Stage 5: Lifton to Bridgerule (17.1 miles/27.5km)
Stage 6: Bridgerule to Upper Tamar Lake (13.8 miles/22.1km), or Kilkhampton for accommodation (extra 2 miles/3.2km)
Stage 7: Upper Tamar Lake (or Kilkhampton) to Morwenstow (11.8 miles/19.1km)

There are *Kylgh Kernow* alternatives for all or part of Stages 2, 3 and 4:

Stage 2K: Tamar Bridge to St Mellion (12.1 miles/19.5km)
Stage 3K: St Mellion to Gunnislake (6.1 miles/9.8km)
Stage 4K: Gunnislake to Launceston (25.6 miles/28.5km)

In addition, there is a short Kylgh Kernow option along part of Stage 7, described within that stage. There are also suggested links from the primary route to nearby places for accommodation or interest:

- Bere Alston Link – from Bere Alston station to village (Stage 3) – for facilities.
- Kit Hill Link – from Gunnislake (Stage 4) and Luckett (Stage 5) – for a superb viewpoint and historic location.
- Greystone Link – links the primary route and its Kylgh Kernow alternative at Greystone Bridge (Stages 4/4K) – creates circular walk options.
- Launceston Link – between Launceston and the primary route (Stages 4K/5) – this link is used by the Kylgh Kernow route but is also useful for accommodation and facilities for walkers on the primary route.
- Bude Link – from Marhamchurch (Stage 6) to Bude – for accommodation and facilities.
- Kilkhampton Link – from Upper Tamar Lake (Stages 6/7) to Kilkhampton – for accommodation and facilities.
- Kilkhampton and Coast Link – from Kilkhampton to the coast to create circular walks.

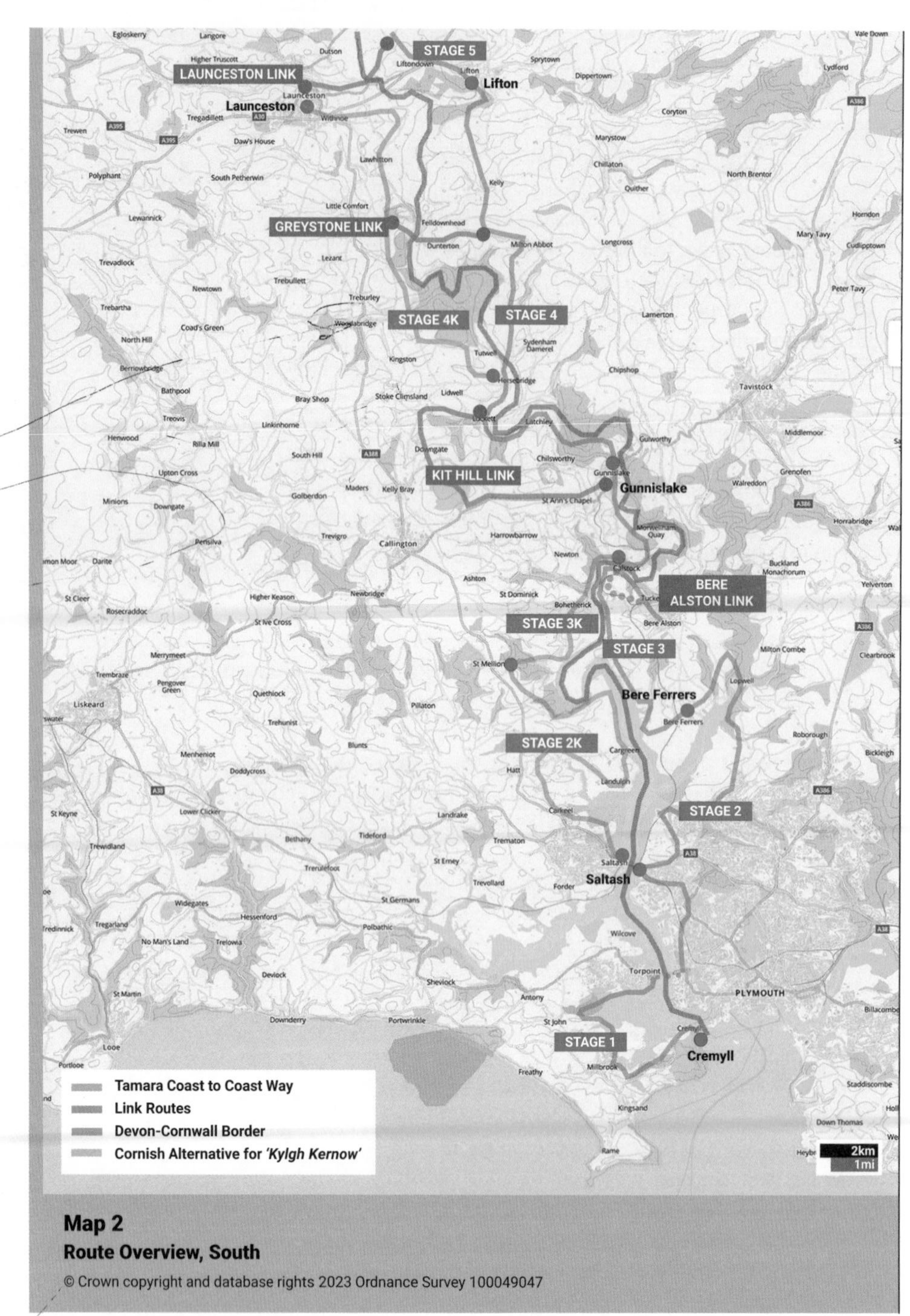

Map 2
Route Overview, South

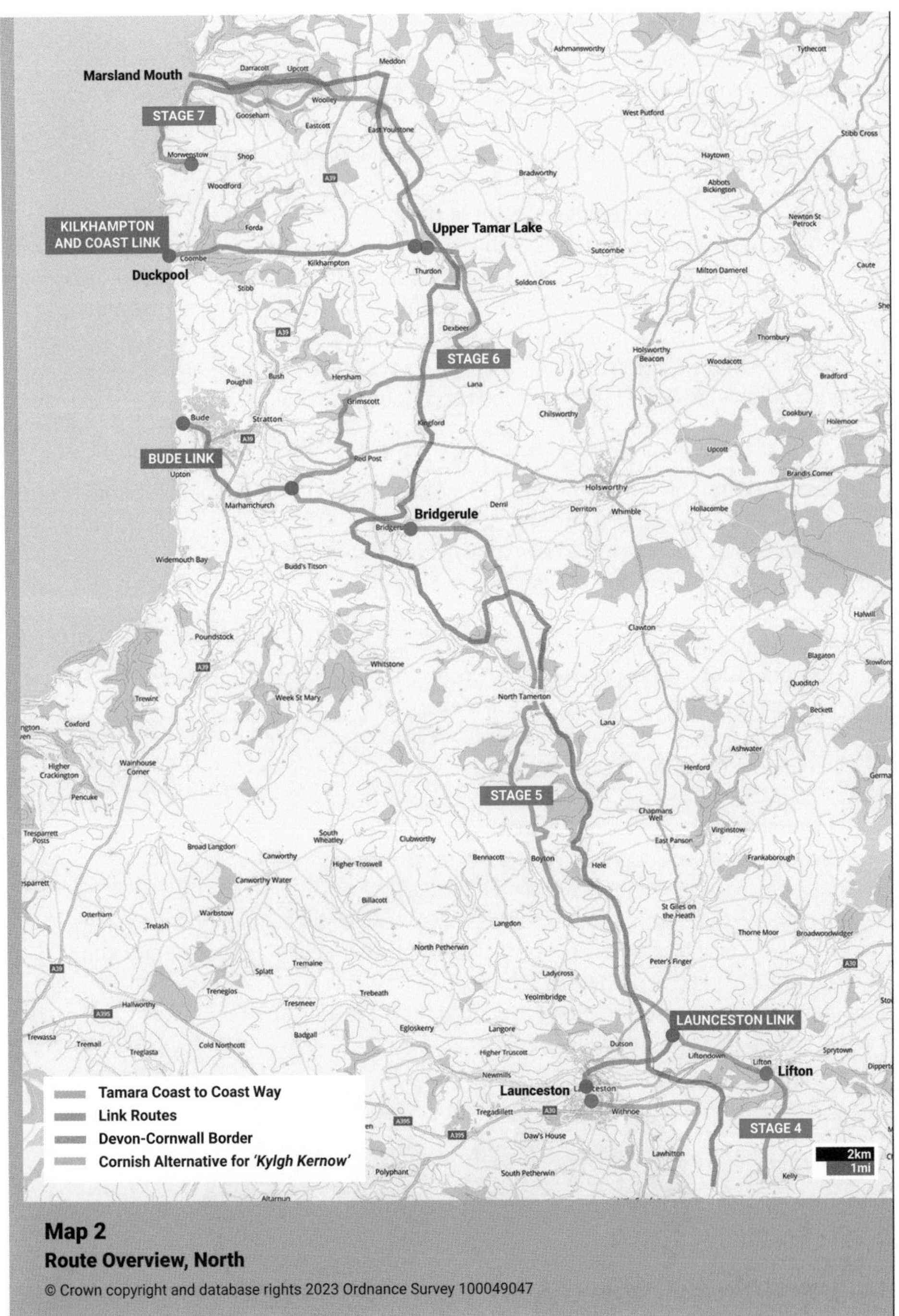

Map 2
Route Overview, North

Route Finding and Waymarking

In addition to the maps in the book, we recommend you download the free Ordnance Survey OS Maps app from the Apple or Google app stores onto your phone or tablet. Once you've done this, visit the website (www.tamarvalley.org.uk/tamarac2c) where you will find links to download each section of the route onto your phone.

The OS Map app is free, but if you want to view the 1:25,000 mapping, rather than the basic free mapping, and to save the map so it works when you are offline, there are a couple of options. The simplest is to subscribe to the premium version. This is currently £28.99 a year and gives you access to view and download up-to-date maps of the whole country. Alternatively, if you love paper maps, 1:25,000 OS Explorer maps now come with a scratch-off code, allowing you to download the map onto your phone or tablet to use while offline and keep indefinitely. For the entire route, the maps you need are:

- **Explorer 108:** Lower Tamar Valley & Plymouth. Covers from Plymouth to almost Milton Abbot (Stages 1, 2 and part of 3)
- **Explorer 112:** Launceston & Holsworthy. Covers from Milton Abbot to Boyton (part of Stage 3, Stage 4 and part of Stage 5)
- **Explorer 111:** Bude, Boscastle & Tintagel. Covers from Boyton to Dunsdon Nature Reserve (parts of Stages 5 and 6)
- **Explorer 126:** Clovelly and Hartland. Covers from Dunsdon Nature Reserve to Morwenstow (part of Stage 6 and all of Stage 7)

Alternatively, the 1:50,000 OS Landranger maps cover the entire route in two maps:

- **Landranger 201:** Plymouth & Launceston, Tavistock & Looe
- **Landranger 190:** Bude & Clovelly, Boscastle & Holsworthy

The primary route *Tamara Coast to Coast Way* is waymarked throughout its length with a bee inside a green arrow, using two slightly different waymarks. For much of the route, including at both ends, the Way uses the Tamara Coast to Coast waymarks; in the length between Tamerton Foliot and Lifton it follows the Tamar Valley Discovery Trail and so those waymarks are used.

The Cornish optional route of the *Kylgh Kernow*, described in Stages 2K, 3K and 4K, is not waymarked on the ground. There is no waymarking on any of the associated link routes: the Kit Hill Link, the Launceston Link, the Bude Link and the Kilkhampton and Coast Link.

The Name of the Route

The name *Tamara Coast to Coast Way* is generally used throughout the stage descriptions, but in places, for brevity and stylistic reasons, this is shortened to simply 'the Way'.

There are sections, as explained above, where there are alternative alignments on either side of the Tamar. Where the main route is on the Devon side, as well as being called the *Tamara Coast to Coast Way*, this may be referred to as 'the primary route' to distinguish it from the Cornish option. The alternative route on the Cornish side is referred to on such lengths as *Kylgh Kernow*.

Walking the Route

The route has been developed as a week-long walking trail, with each stage finishing at, or close by, places with accommodation. However, with a bit of planning it is also possible to complete it as a series of day walks; some circular, others there and back or using public transport to return to the start point.

Each stage has its own chapter, and there are also chapters describing the Cornish alternative stages. Each includes maps, information about local facilities and public transport, as well as points of interest on the way and, of course, walking directions. **Note that information regarding facilities (shops, pubs, and so on) is given in good faith but you are recommended to contact these in advance for up-to-date operating times if planning to use them.**

Accommodation

Accommodation provision varies along the length of the route. It tends to be concentrated in certain locations, especially on and near the two coasts, and at some inland towns, principally Launceston but also Calstock and Gunnislake. There is a large accommodation provider at St Mellion on the *Kylgh Kernow* option.

The first three stages between Plymouth and Gunnislake are easily accessed using the very scenic Tamar Valley Line, so an option is to stay close to one of the railway stations and use the train to get to the start or back home at the end of your day's walk.

For information on accommodation and luggage transfer services, visit the walk website (**www.tamarvalley.org.uk/tamarac2c**).

Public Transport

Each end and many of the villages and towns along the route can be reached using public transport, and details of where buses stop is given at the start of each stage. However, as timetables and services regularly change, you'll need to check online. While each bus company has its own website, one of the easiest ways is to use Google maps – enter the destination in the search box, click on directions, add your start point and – in the options – click on the train icon to bring up all the public transport options.

If you are thinking about using a bus to return to your day's starting point, it's a good idea instead to catch the bus out in the morning and then walk back to your car or accommodation. This means that you don't have to worry about rushing for, or waiting for, the bus, and if for some reason it doesn't turn up, you're not stuck.

Route Updates and Useful Information

Check the website (**www.tamarvalley.org.uk/tamarac2c**) for any route changes or updates to transport information, as well as information on short walks and links to OS map downloads, accommodation and luggage transfer.

Calstock viaduct

How to Use this Guide

Each stage is described using the following format:

Bold text, boxed – for route directions.

Italic text – **for information on facilities, links to public transport, points of interest, historical and cultural information etc.**

1 A Reference numbers in the descriptions, for example, (1), and reference letters in the information, for example, (A), relate to locations shown on the maps.

The directions and information relating to the various route options are colour coded as:

The main *Tamara Coast to Coast Way* (magenta/pink)

The section of the *Tamara Coast to Coast Way* that follows the Tamar Valley Discovery Trail (orange)

The *Kylgh Kernow* Cornish options (light blue)

The link routes (green)

So with that, off we go, to:

Trovya Tamar Teg

or

"Discover the Beautiful Tamar"

Stage 1
Cremyll to Tamar Bridge

The first part of this stage is spent walking around two large inlets on the Cornish side of the Tamar Estuary. It is rarely very far from the estuary complex and there are a number of unexpected views across the Tamar to Plymouth, often from unusual angles. The Way then uses the Torpoint Ferry to cross into Plymouth, continuing north parallel to the Tamar past part of Devonport Dockyard and through the western part of Plymouth.

Distance:	12.5 miles/20.2km between Cremyll and Tamar Bridge
Total ascent:	1017ft/317m
Estimated walking time (without stops):	5hr 35min
Car parks:	Cremyll, Millbrook, Torpoint, St Budeaux, Tamar Bridge

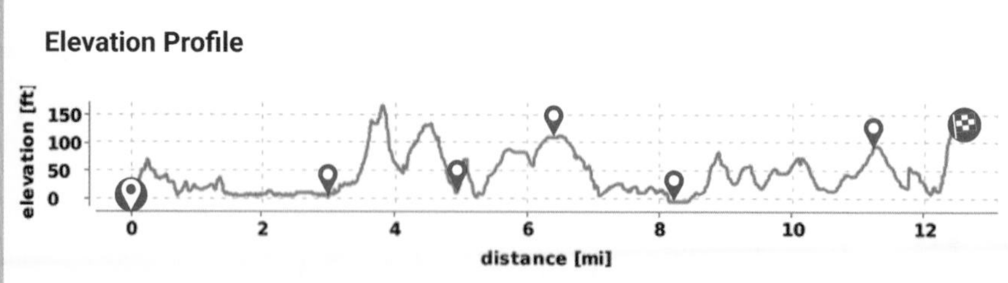

Start / 0m:	**Mount Edgcumbe**
3.5 miles:	**Millbrook**
5 miles:	**St John**
6.5 miles:	**Torpoint**
8.2miles:	**Torpoint Ferry**
11.2miles:	**St Budeaux**
End:	**Tamar Bridge**

Public transport & shorter options:
To reach the start you can catch a bus from Plymouth city centre (about 10 minutes' walk from the railway station) to St Paul's Church, Stonehouse. It is then a short walk to the pedestrian ferry that crosses the Tamar to Cremyll/Mount Edgcumbe. Options to shorten the walk are buses between Cremyll, Millbrook and Torpoint, and on the Plymouth side between Devonport and the Tamar Bridge.

The Devon–Cornwall border, at its southern end, runs along the centre of the Tamar at its narrow point between Plymouth Sound (where the Tamar meets the sea) and the Hamoaze, the name given to the broad middle part of the Tamar Estuary. At this narrow point a ferry crosses the Tamar between Cremyll on the Cornwall side and Stonehouse in Plymouth (**www.plymouthboattrips.co.uk**). Meanwhile, those walking around Cornwall on *Kylgh Kernow* will be approaching along the western shore of Plymouth Sound.

Cremyll Ferry

Cremyll is the starting point of the *Tamara Coast to Coast Way*.

Tamara Coast to Coast Way

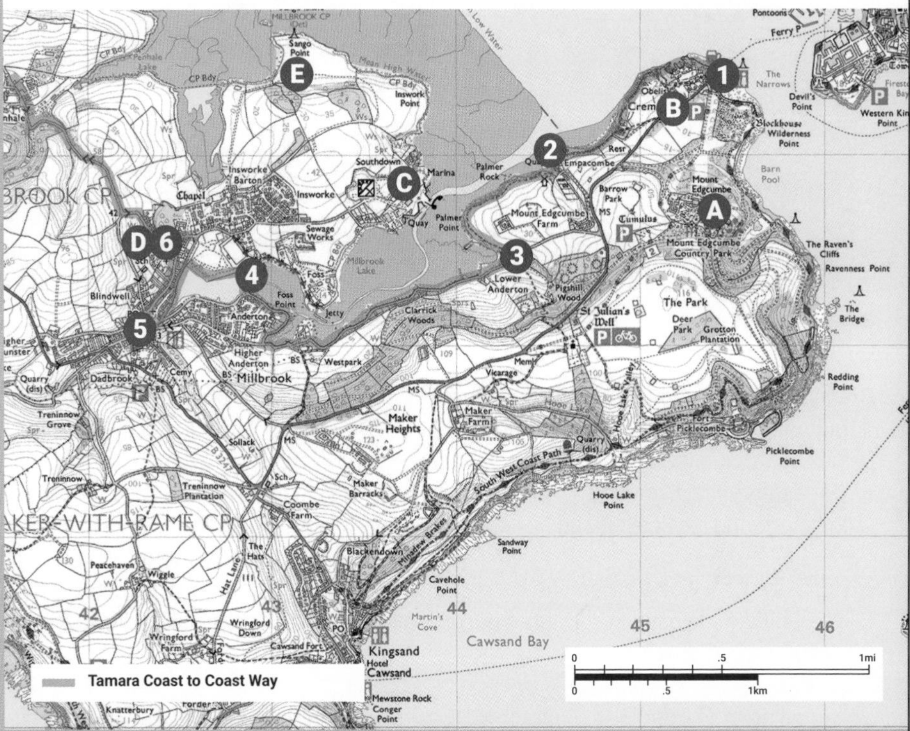

Stage 1, Map 1:
Cremyll to Millbrook

From Cremyll the Tamar continues downstream, past Drake's Island to Plymouth Sound, with the cliffs at Staddon Heights on the Devon side beyond. Directly opposite Cremyll are the impressive buildings and walls of the **Royal William Yard**.

The yard was designed by the eminent 19th-century architect Sir John Rennie, built between 1825 and 1831 and named after King William IV. It constitutes the largest collection of Grade I (or equivalent) military buildings in Europe. It was built as the victualling yard for the Royal Navy at possibly the height of its power. It was designed to bake 20,000 loaves of bread, produce 127,000 litres of beer and turn 100 cows into barrels of salted beef each day. The Royal Navy left the site in 1992 and it is now open to the public as a setting for restaurants, galleries, offices and apartments. On entering Devon via the ferry, the South West Coast Path passes through the yard.

Royal William Yard

Edgcumbe Arms, Cremyll

Cremyll's slightly odd-looking name is derived from the Old English crymel, meaning a fragment of land. It is first recorded in 1249. The buildings here are mostly 18th century, although the pub is a little later and has been completely rebuilt following a 21st-century fire. Cremyll has a long-established boatyard which still offers a full range of marine services. It can be seen a little way beyond the Edgcumbe Arms.

Historically there was a limestone quarry here. Among other uses, the limestone was taken upriver to be used in the numerous limekilns which will be passed later along the Way.

The focal point of Cremyll is the ferry. Note the crenellated ferry office, known as the Earl's Waiting Room. It was erected in the mid-19th century, when nearby Mount Edgcumbe House was being renovated. Nearby is the 'horse winch', used to help pull horse boats ashore – boats which ferried carriages with their horses. This would have been important for visitors to Mount Edgcumbe.

The ferry dates from at least the 11th century. It may date from as early as the Danish raid of AD997, when this western side of the estuary was incorporated into Wessex, and thereafter Devon, where it stayed until 1844.

Cremyll Ferry, 19th century (Photo courtesy of The Box, Plymouth)

Cremyll Toll House

Until the early 1800s the ferry was part of the main route into southern Cornwall. A description of the main routes in Britain in 1675 by John Ogilvie includes the ferry in the main route from London to Land's End, described in his work as *'Crimble Passage over the Tamer, which is here crossed by a ferry of 4 furlongs'*. A little later, in 1695, it appears in the diary of the early English travel writer Celia Fiennes. She followed this main route into Cornwall, but was not too happy about the crossing, writing *'I went to Cribly Ferry, which is a very hazardous passage by reason of three tydes meeting... I was at least an hour going over... those ferry boats are so wet and then the sea and wind are always cold to be upon, that I never fail to catch cold in a ferry boat, as I did this day.' She says she 'should not have been very willing to have gone it, but this is the constant way all people goe'.*

Any walkers who have come from Plymouth to start the Way will know that the journey now holds no such fears and is indeed very pleasant.

The ferry also meant that in time the road on into Cornwall needed improvement, and this was undertaken by the Liskeard Turnpike Trust after 1760. Their new and improved road bypassed the village of St John a little to the west and ensured that it remained the quiet place it still is. A Trust toll house was built just outside Cremyll in 1783.

Cremyll is also the gateway to **Mount Edgcumbe Country Park**, based on Mount Edgcumbe House (A) which was, for many centuries, the home of the Edgcumbe family. The Edgcumbes will be a presence for much of the southern half of the Way

– from here to Empacombe a little way up the estuary, then with their involvement in early mining on the Bere Peninsula, their grand Tudor house at Cotehele and their farm of origin near Milton Abbot.

The house was originally built as a villa for Sir Richard Edgcumbe between 1547 and 1553. It was regarded as revolutionary at the time, as it was built for its views out rather than facing inward defensively. Alterations and modernisations took place in the 17th, 18th and 19th centuries. It was badly damaged in 1941 by a stray incendiary bomb meant for Plymouth, but has since been fully restored.

As well as the house its parks and gardens have also been widely celebrated. The deer park was first enclosed in the 16th century and there are formal Italian, French and English gardens.

The house and its setting were so highly regarded almost from the start that the commander of the Spanish Armada in 1588, the Duke of Medina Sidonia, determined that he would take ownership of Mount Edgcumbe once England had been successfully invaded. It didn't quite work out like that and the Mount Edgcumbe family retained possession until 1971. At that time the family sold the house and estate to the local authorities, since when it has been jointly owned by Cornwall Council and Plymouth City Council. The grounds are open to the public as a country park all year round and the house is open to the public in the summer months (**www.mountedgcumbe.gov.uk**).

To visit the house, go through the park gates and follow the main drive ahead. Then either follow the drive as it bends right, then go left to the side of the house or, if the ground is dry, walk across the grass directly up to the house. The walk takes about 15–20 minutes – but it's all uphill!

Mount Edgcumbe House

There is a little accommodation at Cremyll. Alternatively, there is plenty in Plymouth, easily reached via the ferry. Cremyll has a pub (www.edgcumbearms.co.uk), toilets, refreshments and buses to and from Millbrook, Torpoint and Plymouth (locations further along the Way).

Start the *Tamara Coast to Coast Way* by leaving the road almost next to the information boards, walking along the path by the car park of the Edgcumbe Arms and passing the toilets (1). Pass the Old School Rooms and at a fork bear right.

The **Old School Rooms** date from 1867 and began as a 'chapel of ease' for Cremyll – an alternative place of worship for the parish church at Maker, some way away at the top of a hill. It then also served as the school rooms for Cremyll.

The path passes behind a boatyard, passing some discarded marine equipment, including an old boiler. A little further on a large obelisk will be seen in a field on the left (B).

This was erected by the Admiralty in the 18th century as one of a number of navigation markers around the estuary.

The path continues past some old reservoir buildings.

Along this stretch there is an engraved arrow in a stone in the path. The arrow symbol was used by the War Department, who presumably had an interest in this area.

The path then arrives at Empacombe (2). Continue ahead along the track with Empacombe House on the right and the stables of Edgecumbe Street on the left.

The house, which is partly hidden in its private grounds, is largely 18th century in origin. In 1987 the then Earl of Mount Edgcumbe moved here and it remains the family seat. The Edgcumbe family will be encountered further on the Way, particularly on the *Kylgh Kernow* route at Cotehele – also seen across the river from Devon on the primary route.

Follow signs ahead at the gate and through the gap in the wall, then left on the grass above the foreshore.

Empacombe

Empacombe: garden wall and gate

Empacombe is an attractive little spot, with its own harbour on the Tamar. Notable are the almost castle-like walls and gate on the left after the cottages. Surprisingly, this substantial wall only encloses the kitchen garden and was built in 1788 to protect the soft fruit, flowers and vegetables which were grown in its shelter, and which were produced for Mount Edgcumbe House.

Continue past the stone stile and on the path ahead.

Much of the land on the west side of the mouth of the Tamar was once in Devon. This seems to go back to Saxon times, and a tradition has it that it originated with the Danish Viking invasion up the Tamar in AD997, and a determination that it would not be repeated. Another tradition says that it was granted by Geraint, King of Cornwall, to Sherborne Abbey in the 8th century, the abbey holding much land on behalf of the West Saxon kings. In Norman times the situation changed slightly when the manor and parish of Maker was divided into two – the southern and higher part was held by William I and was included in Devon, while the lower part facing inland went to the de Valletort family and was allocated to Cornwall. The boundary between the two came on this next stretch, where the Way moves from historic Devon into historic Cornwall. These variations were ironed out in 1844 when all this land west of the mouth of the Tamar became Cornwall.

Continue alongside a field to arrive at a road. Turn right here (3).

The *Tamara Coast to Coast Way* is no longer alongside the main Tamar but on a tributary known as **Millbrook Lake**. The name here does not denote a lake in its modern sense of a standing body of water, but comes from the Old English *lacu*, meaning a watercourse, including a tidal one. Millbrook Lake is the first of a number of such 'lakes' encountered on the Tamar Estuary.

On the opposite side of Millbrook Lake can be seen the boatyards and marina at **Southdown** (C). In the 18th century an Admiralty victualling yard was established at Southdown. An early 19th-century map refers to the site as 'King's Brewhouse'.

Keep following the quiet and attractive waterside road.

Above and on the left are the wooded slopes of **Maker Heights**. These were a strategic vantage point, giving views both out to sea and inland over the estuary towards Plymouth. As a result, in the 19th century a number of batteries, barracks and other military buildings were constructed to face the threat of a possible French invasion or attack on Plymouth's dockyard. Around the perimeter were a number of low granite boundary posts engraved WD for War Department. (This might give a clue as to the origin of the engraved arrow stone earlier on the path.)

The route passes attractive cottage-type properties – Dexter's Cottage, Stable Cottage, Wood Park Cottages, Wood Park House – then follows round to the right by Higher Anderton House.

Higher Anderton House is an attractive 19th-century property; this and others passed immediately afterwards such as Tregenna House, St Elmo's and the Round House (originally built as a gazebo for Tregenna) were built as the village of Millbrook a little ahead was becoming popular among those with money.

Reach the dam across Millbrook Lake and cross over (4).

The **dam** was built across Millbrook Lake in 1977 as a flood prevention measure; the inland side of the dam is the only lake in the modern sense among the various Tamar Estuary 'lakes'. There can be quite a contrast between the two sides, especially at low tide. The dam includes tidal flaps which prevent ingress of tidal water while allowing the outflow of stream water from the upper lake.

On the far side of the dam follow the path to the left.

Millbrook Lake Dam

Millbrook from the lake

There are numerous benches and some picnic tables along this length which, combined with the pleasant views, makes this a good spot for a break. There is a lovely view up the lake to the village of Millbrook at its head.

The path arrives at a road on the outskirts of Millbrook. Turn left alongside the non-tidal part of Millbrook Lake to reach the village centre (5).

The Way arrives at what used to be Millbrook's quay at the head of the then tidal lake, identified by the names Quay House and Quay Garage.

Millbrook has all facilities – shops, pub (www.thedevonandcornwall.co.uk), coffee lounge, chemist, toilets – and buses to and from Cremyll, Torpoint and Plymouth.

The first reference to **Millbrook** is in 1342. The site of the original mill is unknown, but it is known that there was a tidal mill at the head of Millbrook Lake in the 16th century. By this time Millbrook had become a thriving settlement, with a large fishing fleet, a gunpowder factory, limekilns, a brewery and a boat-building industry. It had its own corporation and seal. Millbrook also had a slaughterhouse and a tannery as well as three brickyards; sailing barges took bricks from Millbrook all over the country.

Most of the industry has now gone, but a flavour of the old town may be glimpsed in the narrow streets of small houses and some former industrial buildings around the infilled quay.

An atmospheric touch, also found in some other Cornish towns, is the dual naming of streets in English and Cornish. The village also features the Cornish version of its name, *Govermelin*. This is a literal translation of 'mill brook', and there are no early examples of the use of this Cornish version, the first mention in 1342 being *Milbrok*.

Millbrook Lake

To continue on the *Tamara Coast to Coast Way*, from the centre turn along the road next to Millbrook Village Stores (Fore Street) and follow this road round to the right, signposted to Southdown. Continue along the road, passing some attractive 18th- and 19th-century buildings, to reach Millbrook's All Saints Church (D).

The **church** is Victorian, dating from 1867. Until that time Millbrook was in the parish of Maker, which covers the extreme southeast corner of Cornwall, but a separate parish was created which the church was built.

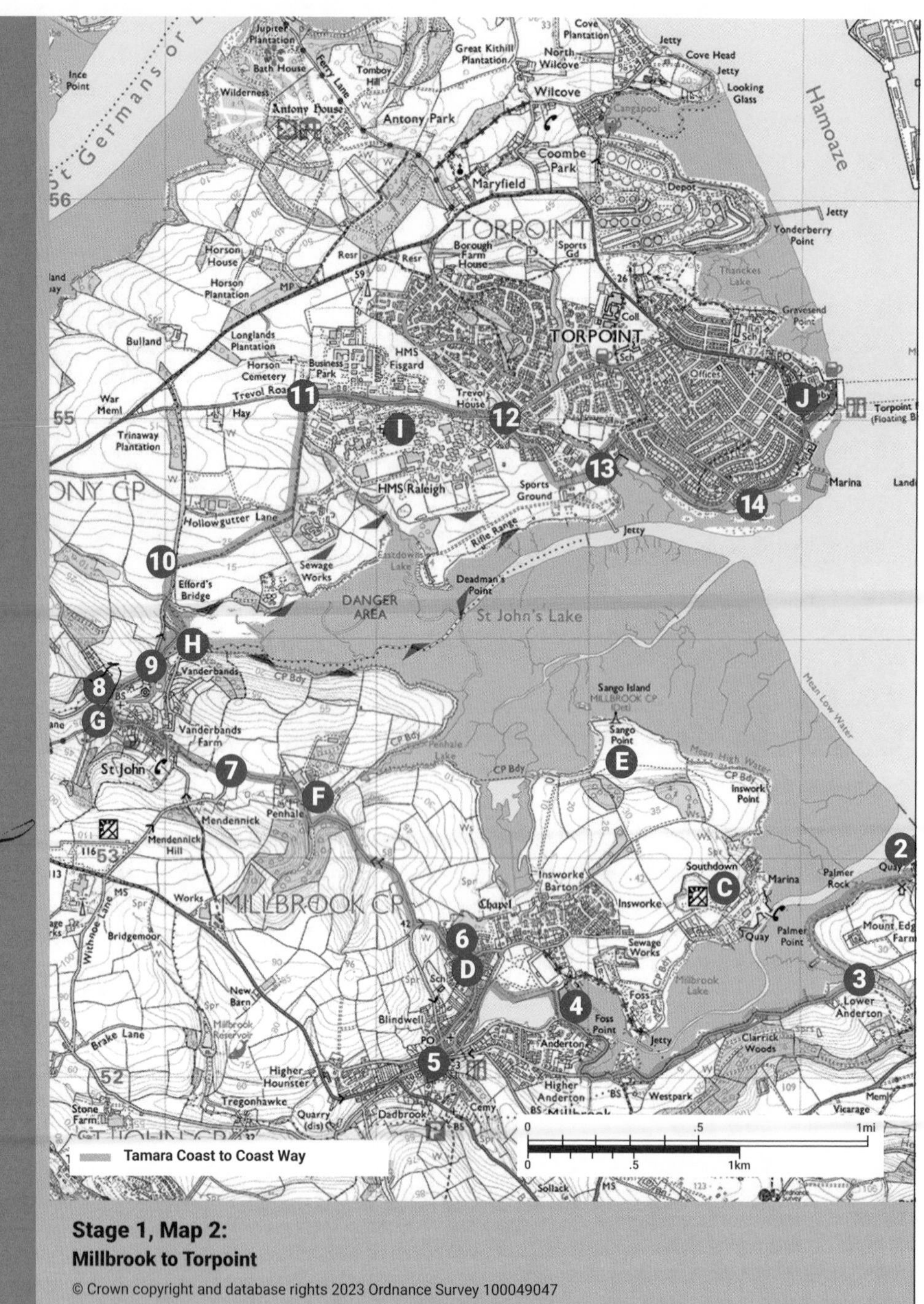

Stage 1, Map 2:
Millbrook to Torpoint

At the junction at the end (6) turn left (St John's Road) and climb out of the village.

Looking to the right and back nearing the top of the climb can be seen the distinctive red and white stripes of the navigation light at **Sango Point** (E). This will be seen later from Torpoint from a greatly different angle across the water. The Way has now left Millbrook Lake behind and is embarking on the next Tamar tributary, St John's Lake, which must be negotiated before reaching Torpoint.

A steep descent follows and then leads to a right-hand bend where the road goes round the head of a tributary of St John's Lake (unseen). The road then climbs.

Here at the valley bottom would have been a wet and marshy area: the location is called **Penhale**, Cornish for 'head of the marsh'. On the following climb is a short length which was traditionally another part of Devon's territory on the western side of the estuary which became Cornish in 1844 (F).

At a left-hand bend, just before a wooden field gate on the left leading into a domestic garden, look out for a narrow path on the right into trees (7). Follow this to a stile, then along the edge of a field to another stile and then on to a road. Turn right to a road junction at the edge of the village of St John and continue straight on into the village.

The route through the village passes the St John Inn and its attached village shop (check opening times – www.stjohninn.co.uk).

St John and its inn

St John Church

Historically this was referred to as **St John in Cornwall** (until 1844 part of St John parish was in Devon). Consequently, when crossing the mouth of the Tamar by ferry, St John was the first parish church in Cornwall the traveller would encounter. The village has an inn and attached shop, but these are only generally open at weekends.

St John was once a place of trade, with shipping reaching the village via the estuary of St John's Lake. Legend has it that local sailors gave the name of the village to St John's, the capital of Newfoundland, although it is more likely that city got its name from the landing of John and Sebastian Cabot there on the feast day of St John the Baptist.

At the bottom of the village, almost hidden away on the right, is St John Church (G).

By the 11th century there was a church here, but the origins of the present building are in 1150. The original Norman tower still stands, but most of the church was later rebuilt, especially in the 15th century. A date of 1605 on the porch could indicate a rebuilding at that time, but it is possible that this is a mis-carving for 1905, the date when the new churchyard was being developed. The church and its setting are very atmospheric. There is a handy bench here for a rest and snack.

At the junction just past the church (8) follow the road round to the right, signposted to Torpoint. Follow this road to the top of the hill, to a sign indicating a 17% steep hill back towards St John. Just after the sign is a wooden gate on the right leading to a permissive path through the Woodland Trust's Benskin's Wood (9). Follow this path then at a fork bear right to a bench with a super view down St John's Lake. From here go right and down steps to the waterside at St John Ford.

Benskin's Wood is partly ancient semi-natural woodland and partly younger woodland, planted in the 1980s.

St John's Lake is a Site of Special Scientific Interest, designated particularly for its birdlife. Large numbers of wildfowl and waders overwinter on its mudflats. A more macabre tradition is that prisoners who had died on prison ships moored in the Tamar would be buried in the mudflats. A headland on the north side is called Deadman's Point.

There is a fascinating clash of landscape character here. St John's Lake and its ford are quiet, rural and almost remote in character, while in the background across the Tamar can be seen Plymouth, its dockyard and even high-rise buildings. Note just before the ford the Admiralty bound stone with its anchor motif, marking the limit of the Navy's control of the Tamar and its tributaries (H).

St John's Lake from Benskin's Wood

Follow the road left away from the ford and at the junction at the end turn right. Start climbing the hill and a little way up look out for a stile to a public footpath on the right (10). Follow this path along the field edge, then cross a stone stile on the left and turn right to continue on the next field edge in the same direction. The path bears left and continues next to a metal security fence and then arrives at a road (11). Turn right here and pass HMS Raleigh.

HMS Raleigh (I) is the largest Royal Navy training establishment in the southwest. Situated on the edge of the town of Torpoint, the naval shore establishment is the only training centre for new recruits to the Royal Navy or the WRNS. It was first commissioned in 1940 and now covers some 240 ha (593 acres). Its establishment has helped Torpoint to grow, and it remains an important element in the town's economy and culture.

After passing HMS Raleigh the road begins to descend. Look out for Trevorder Road on the right and walk along here (12). Follow to the left at Trevorder Close, then go left down a tarmac path just before the end of the road. Turn right along the path at the bottom and follow this to a footbridge over a creek (13). Cross the bridge and continue on the track ahead then turn right at Millhouse Park, continuing on the path ahead at the end to a grassy area then on the road ahead (Chapeldown Road).

There are excellent views over the water from here and there is also a series of benches, ideal for a picnic. The views are over St John's Lake with the Tamar ahead. They include, on the far side and ahead, as the Tamar disappears, a collection of buildings. This is a view back to the start of the Way, Cremyll, and above on the skyline the church tower at Maker, the parish church for the western side of the mouth of the Tamar. The prominent red and white navigation light on the far side is at Sango Point (E), seen earlier on leaving Millbrook.

Chapeldown Road arrives at a T-junction (14). Turn right here, back to the waterside, along Marine Drive.

Towards the end of Marine Drive is the **Torpoint Yacht Harbour**, which incorporates the Ballast Pond, or Pound, which was built by the Admiralty in 1783 to load and unload ballast for naval ships.

A little further along are some late 18th-century warehouses (Carew Wharf), converted to housing c. 2000. The two-storey warehouse jutting into the river was the stores of the Western Counties and General Manure Company, who supplied fertiliser to the Tamar Valley market gardens.

Continue to the end of Marine Drive and at the junction go ahead to the ferry point on the right.

Buses cross the ferry to and from Plymouth and also link from Millbrook and Cremyll. There are toilets on the opposite side of the road. The town centre has a variety of shops.

The landing area has a genuine ferry terminal atmosphere – almost like travelling abroad!

For the town centre turn left up Fore Street, next to the Kings Arms. **Torpoint** is a 'new' planned town. There is no mention of it as a town before 1700, and even by 1787 it had only 44 houses. It seems to have been named after the headland on which it stands, originally 'Stertpoint', where 'stert' means tail, first mentioned as the local headland in 1608, and then later 'Torpoint', with 'tor' meaning rocky crag.

Torpoint Ferry and Devonport Dockyard

The town developed with the ferry to Devonport and the establishment and growth of Devonport Dockyard in the 18th century. It was planned and built in a grid pattern commissioned by the local landowner, Reginald Carew-Pole of Antony House, in 1787. Although modern development of the town centre has partly obscured this pattern, it can still be identified immediately behind the ferry (J).

The *Tamara Coast to Coast Way* has now reached the first of its crossings of the Tamar, this one using the Torpoint Ferry (www.tamarcrossings.org.uk).

One of the Way's appeals is that it offers the opportunity for a walk around Cornwall, *Kylgh Kernow*. At various points along the Way what is regarded as the 'primary' route crosses into Devon, so, in these instances a *Kylgh Kernow* option (staying within Cornwall) is also offered.

The section between Torpoint and Saltash, however, is an exception: *Kylgh Kernow* walkers have no option but to cross the Tamar into Plymouth. Progress north along the Tamar from Torpoint is blocked by the largest of the Tamar's Cornish tributaries, the Lynher; there is no safe feasible walking route between Torpoint and Saltash, and no bus between the two that stays on the Cornish side of the river.

***Kylgh Kernow* walkers need to cross the Tamar on the Torpoint Ferry and follow the primary route on the Plymouth side as far as the Tamar Bridge. This involves walking 4.25 miles/6.75km through Plymouth, or catching a bus. At the bridge *Kylgh Kernow* crosses back into Cornwall, while the Way's primary route continues on the Devon side, the two meeting again at Calstock.**

All this could be avoided if there was a ferry across the Lynher. Historically, this could have been done by using the Antony Ferry over the river between Jupiter Point behind Antony House, near Torpoint and Antony Passage, a little south of Saltash. The ferry here is first mentioned in 1324 and although strictly speaking it still exists – as only an Act of Parliament could end it – it has not been used since the 1950s. Unfortunately there are no current plans to reinstate it.

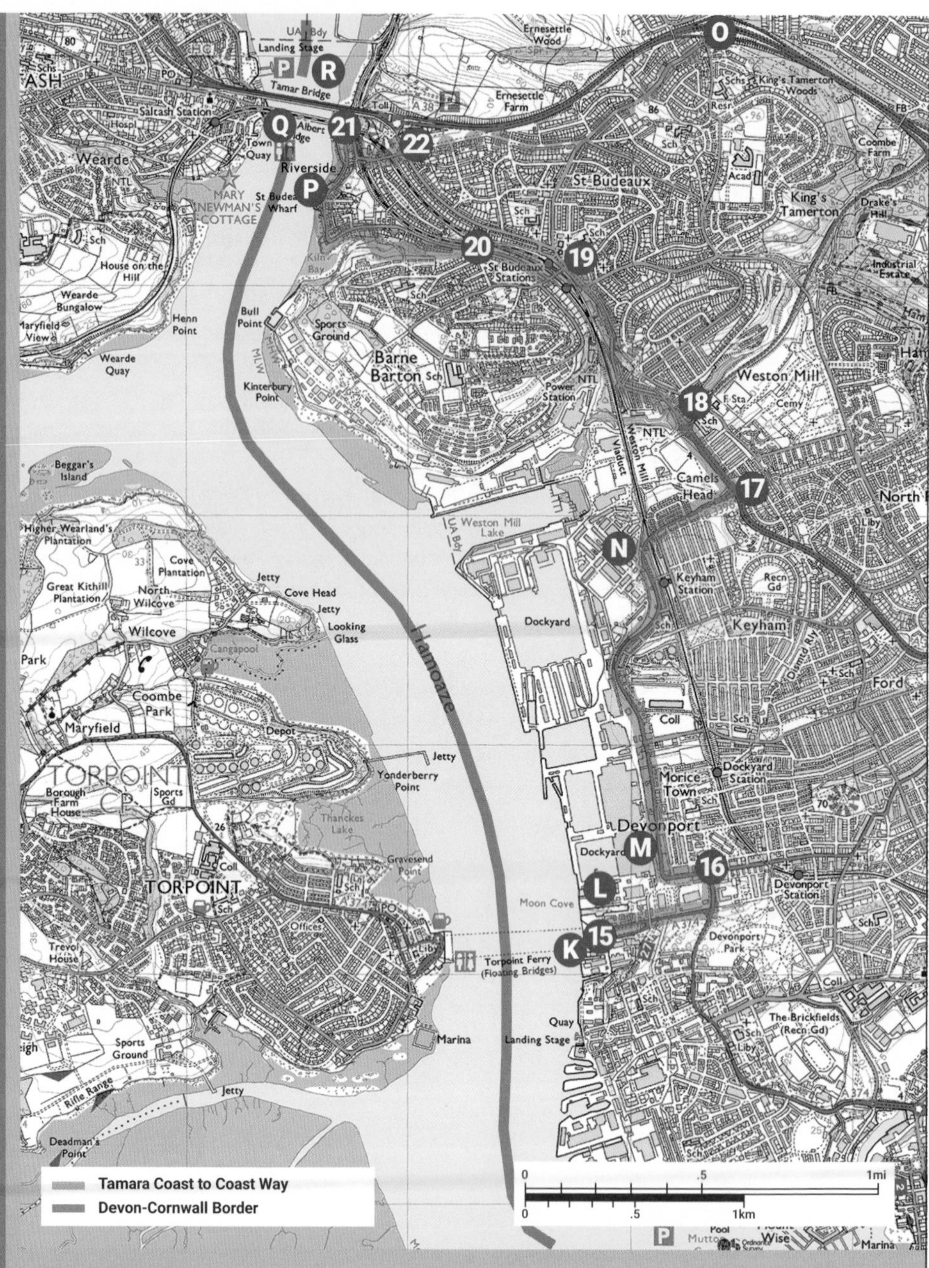

Stage 1, Map 3:
Torpoint Ferry to Tamar Bridge

From Torpoint take the ferry to Devonport (K).

The **ferry** between Torpoint and Devonport began when two local major landowners were granted permission to set up a ferry service in 1791, probably prompted by the growth of the dockyard at Devonport. Originally it was operated by conventional boats but in 1831 it was redesigned as a 'floating bridge', or chain ferry. Chains are fixed to both banks and the vessels haul themselves across the river on vertical wheels attached to the chains. After the ferry has passed the chains sink to the bottom of the river to allow for passage of boats. The ferries were steam driven until 1960; the current three vessels date from 2005 and the current service was officially opened by the Princess Royal in 2007.

Torpoint, Steam-powered Ferry, 19th century (Photo courtesy of The Box, Plymouth)

The service is said to be the busiest estuary vehicle crossing in the UK, carrying nearly 2 million vehicles each year. The crossing is free to foot passengers and gives excellent views up and down the river. Especially impressive is the covered frigate yard immediately north of the ferry landing on the Devonport side, developed in the 1970s to enable works to be undertaken on frigates in a controlled environment (L).

This part of the Tamar Estuary is often referred to as the **Hamoaze**. Originally this name seems to have applied to a tributary of the Tamar, probably Weston Mill Creek which will be passed a little later, and then extended to the main estuary between Saltash and Plymouth Sound.

(Left) Torpoint Steam Ferry, 19th century (HMS Powerful in background) (Photo courtesy of The Box, Plymouth)

The ferry is used by a bus route which crosses the Tamar to Devonport then continues to the city centre, and which meets the Tamara Coast to Coast Way at Millbrook and Cremyll.

On the Devonport side (15) walk up the road away from the river, under a bridge, to traffic lights at the top. Turn left here.

There are buses to the city centre from here. One route connects this spot with the Tamar Bridge, overcoming the need for the urban walk between the two Tamar crossing points.

Go down to the traffic lights at the bottom and turn left, signposted A38 Liskeard (16). The route is now alongside Devonport Dockyard. Pass the dockyard's Albert Gate then follow the road round to the right and alongside the imposing dockyard wall at Keyham Road (M).

(Left) Torpoint Ferry, 21st century

Devonport was first so-called in 1824. Previously it was known as Plymouth Dock or just Dock. The dockyard was first developed on what had been mudflats and marshes from 1692 by William III, although a proposal to build a naval dockyard on the lower Tamar had been made by Sir Walter Raleigh in the 1590s.

What is now the South Yard is the site of the original dockyard, but this is actually south of the Way, behind us. The dockyard expanded northwards to this area in the 19th century to cater for the larger warships of the time. The most northerly part of the yard was developed in the 1970s to service modern warships, and includes the submarine complex.

Pass the St Levan Gate and then, a little further on, Keyham Station on the right and the entrance to HMS Drake on the left.

HMS Drake, the Royal Navy's shore-based barracks on the dockyard site (N), was developed in the 19th century and is between the road and the docks. It includes a number of grand listed buildings, inaccessible to the public but glimpsed over the dockyard wall a little further on.

The wall becomes less forbidding and the dockyard is left behind as the route continues along Saltash Road. The road then arrives at a junction (17). Turn left here, signposted A38 Saltash and Liskeard (Wolseley Road).

This area has the unusual name of **Camel's Head**. It is recorded as early as 1286 as 'Kemel' and seems to have no connection with the ship of the desert. It is probably a name of Celtic origin, perhaps meaning 'neighbourhood' or 'district'.

Keep ahead at the next junction (18) – opposite the Weston Mill Community Academy.

Just after the lights a small creek can be seen on the left. This is **Weston Mill Creek**. Until the 19th century this was a large creek, a tributary of the Tamar extending some way inland. The mouth of the creek was adapted and absorbed into the dockyard in the 19th century, the creek reclaimed and its valley developed.

The road (still Wolseley Road) bends right then left then arrives at the shopping centre for the suburb of St Budeaux.

This French-looking name is actually a corruption of 'St Budoc's'; early versions suggest it used to be pronounced 'St Buddocks'. The name comes from an early Celtic saint who landed on the banks of the Tamar at some point around the 5th to 7th centuries. Budoc is supposed to have been born in a cask at sea off Brittany, after family enemies had cast his pregnant mother adrift. They landed in Ireland or Cornwall, depending on which legend is believed. In time he returned to Brittany and became Bishop of Dol-de-Bretagne. He then sent monks to Britain, later accompanying them, to spread Christianity. He seems to have established an early Christian site by the Tamar. He also established a religious site near what is now Falmouth, at St Budock.

Budoc's original settlement was presumably at the waterside, but later a medieval church was built on higher land away from the estuary and creeks. The church (O) is near the Way's crossing of the A38 later, but out of sight. It is where Sir Francis Drake married his first wife, Mary Newman of Saltash. The settlement's main centre then moved here, southwest of the church, possibly prompted by the arrival of the railways.

In the 19th century **St Budeaux** was absorbed into the jurisdiction of the dockyard town of Devonport, although it remained largely separate as a settlement. Following World War I, Devonport, including St Budeaux, became part of Plymouth and large housing areas were built between the church and the Tamar.

St Budeaux has all the usual facilities.

Immediately after the bus stands turn left (still Wolseley Road) to pass between the two St Budeaux railway stations: Victoria Road on the right and Ferry Road on the left (19).

The two adjacent stations are the result of the two railway lines here. **Ferry Road station** was built in 1904 for the old Great Western Railway (GWR) main line to Cornwall, over the Royal Albert Bridge. It is still in use for occasional stopping trains on that line. **Victoria Road station** was built in 1893 for the old London and South Western Railway main line to London Waterloo. This line was closed during the Beeching era of the 1960s but a branch line up the Tamar Valley was retained, with Victoria Road station on that line.

Follow Wolseley Road round to the right. Take the path on the left (20) leading into Kinterbury Creek Nature Reserve, keeping the stream on your left-hand side.

About 50m before you reach a boardwalk section at the head of the creek (if you've time, it is well worth the detour to walk down to the end), take the steep path on your right which will take you back onto Wolseley Road. When you reach the road turn left.

The **nature reserve** is important for its maritime habitats, giving rise to numerous notable plant species, butterflies and birds. Continuing down the road, it is difficult to believe that until the new road bridge was built in 1961 this was the main road from Plymouth into Cornwall via the Saltash Ferry.

The route descends to come alongside the Tamar, the river now seen for the first time since leaving the Torpoint Ferry.

This is **Saltash Passage**, named after the ferry which preceded the road bridge. The ferry is said to have operated since Norman times, although the first real record is from the 1300s. It was important as there was no road crossing of the Tamar below Gunnislake, many miles upstream. In 1833 it began to operate as a chain ferry, or 'floating bridge'. By 1961 it was being operated by a ferry which could take 24 vehicles at a time, and this was nothing like enough to satisfy demand. It created a considerable bottleneck, hence the need to build the bridge.

Saltash Ferry and Bridge, 1930s (Photo courtesy of The Box, Plymouth)

Royal Albert Bridge from Saltash Passage

The ferry slipway still exists on the riverside and opposite is the ferry office building.

Saltash Passage has two pubs, the Royal Albert Bridge Inn and the Passage House Inn, and a little café. On the left is a little park with an information board showing some photographs of both bridges being built and the operation of the ferry (P).

Until the 1800s this area around the ferry on the Devon side was part of the manor of Trematon in Cornwall, since the manor held the rights to operate the ferry. This had been the case since the Norman Conquest. Although by the 19th century for most purposes it was considered part of Plymouth, formally it was part of Cornwall and was not transferred to St Budeaux parish in Devon until 1895. This eastern bank of the manor was known as Little Ash; it is possible that the name was based on that of the much larger Saltash, the ferry terminus on the opposite bank. Its original name was simply 'Ash', with the 'Salt' added in the 1300s in recognition of the production of salt there. The *Tamara Coast to Coast Way* passes Little Ash Road and Little Ash Gardens on the way down, named after the earlier manorial holding.

There is one of the best views of the **Royal Albert Bridge** from here.

At the end of Saltash Passage (21), when you are almost underneath the railway bridge, follow the road round to the right, and up Normandy Way, crossing both the railways (first the Cornwall main line then the Tamar Valley branch) to reach a little roundabout close to the Tamar Bridge car park and Visitor Centre.

Normandy Way was originally called Tamar Terrace. It was renamed in honour of American troops who were stationed nearby then set sail from here for D-Day in 1944.

The top of Normandy Way marks the end of Stage 1. From here there is a choice of routes. The primary route, Stage 2, continues on the Devon side of the Tamar to Calstock. This option involves a tidal crossing of the tributary River Tavy and use of the Tamar Valley branch line to cross the Tamar between Bere Alston and Calstock.

The alternative *Kylgh Kernow* route crosses the river then stays in Cornwall to Calstock, where it re-joins the primary route. For walkers wishing to follow this Cornish option the details are set out as Stages 2K and 3K (see page 52 and page 94).

Even those continuing on the primary route, Stage 2, will probably wish to go to the bridge, where there is a Visitor and Learning Centre and toilets (22). For the bridge turn left on the footpath along the top of the car park.

Erection of Royal Albert Bridge, 1857 (Photo courtesy of The Box, Plymouth)

The **Visitor and Learning Centre** has exhibitions, old photographs and interactive displays relating both to Brunel's 19th-century Royal Albert Bridge, the historic bridge carrying the railway to and from Cornwall, and also the mid-20th-century road bridge. For more information visit www.bridgingthetamar.org.uk.

The railway bridge, the **Royal Albert Bridge** (Q), is one of Isambard Kingdom Brunel's most famous works. Its construction was started in 1854 and it was opened by Prince Albert in 1859. Brunel had his first and last look at the completed bridge a little after its opening, when he was taken across as a dying man on a specially prepared truck. He died later the same year and his name was added to the bridge portals as a memorial. Its design is unique for a large railway bridge, a bowstring semi-suspension bridge with the floor carrying the track being slung below tubes on vertical members connected by chains. There are two main spans of 455ft/138m, each with seven additional arches on the Devon side and 10 on the Cornish side. The design was prompted by the need for a high clearance – 100ft/30.5m – above the waters of the Tamar demanded by the Admiralty. In addition, the design means that there is no horizontal thrust exerted on the piers, crucial because of the need for a curved approach track on both sides.

It is difficult to exaggerate the impact the bridge had on Cornwall as a result of the arrival of the railway. No longer was Cornwall a virtual island, remote and inaccessible. Journeys which had taken days could now be completed in hours and the market for Cornish goods – minerals, agricultural and horticultural products, fresh fish – opened up enormously, while the landscape and culture of Cornwall attracted visitors in search of the accessible exotic.

Next to the Royal Albert Bridge is the A38 Tamar road bridge (R). Work started on the bridge in 1959 and it was opened in 1961. A formal opening was performed by the Queen Mother in 1962. The bridge replaced the Saltash Ferry, which by the mid-20th century had become woefully inadequate for the volume of traffic. The bridge walkway offers one of the best views of the Royal Albert Bridge alongside, as well as being a superb experience in its own right.

There is accommodation in Saltash, just across the river via the bridge walkway. Alternatively, there are numerous bus services into Plymouth, where there is plenty of accommodation.

Stage 2
Tamar Bridge to Bere Ferrers

Stage 2 starts through a mainly urban environment on the western fringes of Plymouth, becoming semi-urban until it reaches the old village of Tamerton Foliot at the edge of the city. It then heads for the River Tavy, the main tributary of the Tamar on the Devon side, crossing into the quiet Bere Peninsula, the area between the Tavy and the Tamar, to the picturesque village of Bere Ferrers.

Distance:	9.8 miles/15.8km between Tamar Bridge and Bere Ferrers
Total ascent:	1024ft/310m
Estimated walking time (without stops):	4hr 30min
Car parks:	Tamar Bridge, Lopwell Dam

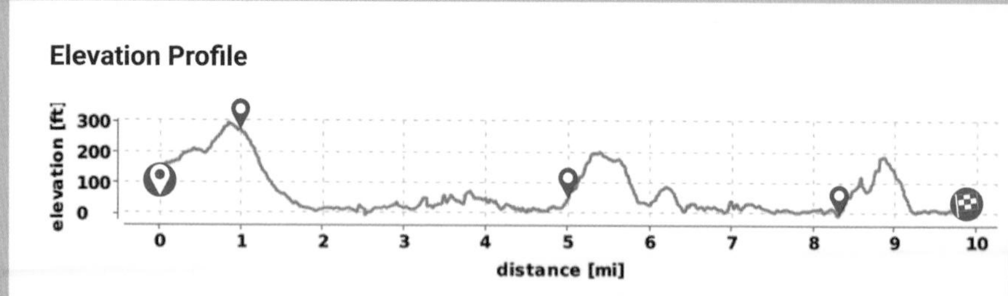

Start / 0m:	**Tamar Bridge**
1 mile:	**A38**
5 miles:	**Tamerton Foliot**
8.3 miles:	**Lopwell Dam**
End:	**Bere Ferrers**

Public transport & shorter options:
The start can be reached by bus from Plymouth city centre; buses return to the city centre from Ernesettle and Tamerton Foliot. From Bere Ferrers there is the option of catching the train back to Plymouth.

NOTE The crossing of the River Tavy is tidal, and is unavailable within two hours either side of high tide. Visit **www.tidetimes.co.uk**: tide times are given for Plymouth (Devonport), which is suitable for the crossing.

Stage 2 starts from the Visitor Centre (1) along the footpath above the car park to the little roundabout. Cross the road above the roundabout and follow a path which leads to a residential road signed as a cycle route to Crownhill, Tavistock and Plympton.

At the junction at the end (2) bear left, still signed as the cycle route, up Victoria Road. After a steady climb the road descends slightly towards a roundabout. Just before the roundabout turn left into Ernesettle Road (3) and at the bottom turn right along the footpath which crosses the A38 dual carriageway.

Buses along Victoria Road link to the city centre.

When the Tamar road bridge was built in 1961 existing roads around the northern edge of Plymouth were improved to provide the link between the bridge and the road to and from Exeter. These soon proved inadequate for the traffic and the new dual carriageway, now known as the Parkway, was constructed and completed in the 1980s.

On the far side continue straight ahead, downhill.

Royal Albert Bridge with Tamar Bridge adjacent

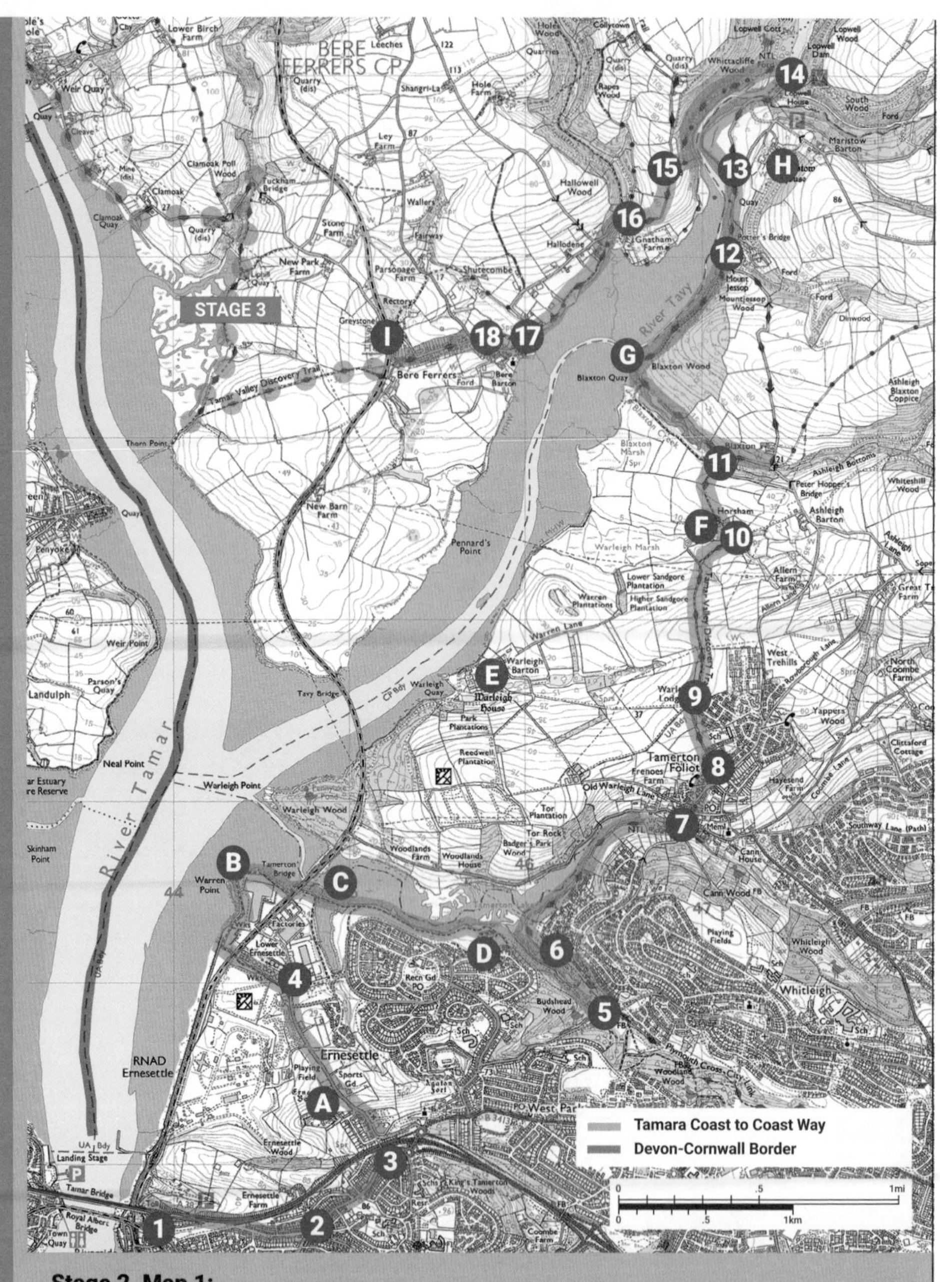

Stage 2, Map 1:
Tamar Bridge to Bere Ferrers

This area is **Ernesettle** (normally pronounced 'Erney-settle'). There was an early settlement here; the name interprets, rather romantically, as 'eagle's seat' (possibly on account of its relatively high location). in the 15th century there were just two farms here, and for a while Sir Francis Drake lived in the area. The area lower down on the right was developed as a fairly extensive housing area during the 1950s.

Descending the road, on the hillside on the left is the site of **Ernesettle Battery** (A). This was built in 1863 as the westernmost of a line of forts defending Plymouth's dockyard from attack from the north. Its use was discontinued by 1900.

Continue down the road, the Tamar now visible again ahead. Pass the entrance to the Defence Munitions Depot on the left and then past Northolt Avenue on the right. Then look out for a public footpath leaving the road on the left and follow this (4). The path passes a water treatment works then goes beneath a small railway arch (the Tamar Valley branch line) to arrive alongside the Tamar.

There are numerous viewpoints over the river along this stretch as it rounds the area known as **Warren Point**. Its name indicates its early use as an area for the raising of rabbits as food. Somewhere in this area is the location of St Budoc's early site (B), possibly even his original landing place (see Stage 1 – St Budeaux).

As the route bends to the right at a little triangle in the path there is a particularly good viewpoint on the left by a rocky cliff. This shows a broad area of water, where the Tamar is joined by two major tributaries. The one immediately next to the path is **Tamerton Lake**, occasionally referred to as Tamerton Creek. The 'lake' in the name is from the Old English *lacu*, meaning a stream or river, and does not refer to a lake in the modern sense. Behind the wooded headland towards the right the Tamar is joined by the River Tavy, the Tamar's major tributary on the Devon side.

Rivers meet – Tamar, Tamerton Lake and Tavy

Tamerton Bridge

Continue along the path, now alongside Tamerton Lake. The Way now leaves the Tamar for some time to get around this estuary and that of the Tavy. It soon passes under Tamerton Bridge.

Tamerton Bridge was built in 1889 by the Plymouth, Devonport and South Western Junction Railway to carry the London and South Western's main line between Plymouth and London Waterloo over Tamerton Lake. The main line is now closed but it continues to carry the Tamar Valley branch line. It is of some importance as an example of Victorian railway engineering and is a listed building.

A little further on the path reaches the tributary Ernesettle Creek and crosses its mouth on a causeway.

On the far side of Ernesettle Creek is the site of an old **tide mill** (C). The tide coming in and going out of the tributary creek drove two waterwheels which in turn powered six pairs of grinding stones, milling flour from local farms. There is an information board here.

Ernesettle Creek

Keep ahead on the main path.

At the top of the grassy area on the right is a bus route to and from the city centre.

After passing the open grassy area the path passes some old walls and ruins on the right.

These are the remnants of **Budshead Manor** (D). The early 15th-century foundations were added to in the 16th to 18th centuries, but by the 19th century the house had been largely abandoned and it was demolished in the 20th century. Its most important period was the 17th century when it was the seat of Sir Ferdinando Gorges, Governor of the fort of Plymouth. He founded two companies to colonise New England, founded the settlement of New Plymouth and became the first Governor of Maine in 1635. The site therefore has a close relationship with the settlement of America.

Continue on the path ahead then take a narrower path on the left, at the 'Welcome to Budshead Wood' sign.

Budshead Wood is regarded as 'ancient woodland', meaning it has been woodland non-stop since at least 1600. It is maintained as a Local Nature Reserve by Plymouth City Council and includes a number of walks. The woodland path is parallel to the watercourse of Budshead Creek, a tributary of Tamerton Lake, occasionally glimpsed through the trees.

At the end of Budshead Wood pass an information board and follow the path round to the left then take the concrete path ahead, which crosses the head of Budshead Creek, though this is largely unseen. Go to the road junction and turn left alongside Milford Lane (5).

This area is **Budshead**, an old settlement now absorbed into Plymouth. The earlier version of its name is *Budocshide*, which means the land of St Budoc (see Stage 1). This early Celtic saint is said to have arrived in the area in the 6th or 7th century, and presumably sailed up Budshead Creek from the Tamar. He seems to have established a religious site somewhere around Warren Point, and Budshead probably represents an early farmstead associated with this.

There are buses from here to Plymouth's Derriford Hospital and to Saltash and to the city centre.

Walk up alongside Milford Lane then take the first left, Truro Drive. Walk as far as a postbox on the left as the road rises to the right. Fork left here along a footpath and follow the path over a grassy area (6) until it arrives alongside a tidal creek.

This is Tamerton Lake again, now much further upstream and no longer an estuary.

Continue to the end then along a residential road to arrive at Tamerton Foliot (7).

Tamar Valley Discovery Trail

Between Tamerton Foliot and LIfton, the *Tamara Coast to Coast Way* follows the route of the Tamar Valley Discovery Trail. This 31 mile long trail links Plymouth, with its maritime associations, in the south (in conjunction with the Two Castles Trail / Launceston link at the northern end), with Launceston, the ancient capital of Cornwall, just over the county boundary.

To save duplication, this stretch of the route is only waymarked with the Tamar Valley Discovery Trail discs – so continue following the bee northwards.

Tamerton Foliot, now on the northern edge of Plymouth, is an ancient settlement in its own right. In the 6th or 7th century the Celtic saints Indract and Dominic (or Dominica), Irish siblings, landed at a place recorded as Tamerunta, which is usually identified as Tamerton Foliot. They presumably sailed up Tamerton Lake, which is still navigable by small craft virtually to Tamerton Foliot. They also landed on the Cornish side of the Tamar and St Dominica established a religious settlement at what later became the village of St Dominick. This is likely to have been at a similar time to St Budoc's arrival at Budshead.

Tamerton Foliot got the second part of its name from the Foliot family, who were given the land here following the Norman Conquest, John Foliot being said to be a half-brother of William I. They established their base at Warleigh, a little beyond the present village. From medieval times it was a prosperous farming area then from the 19th century became important as a market gardening centre, supplying Plymouth.

Tamerton Foliot has pubs, a general store and a post office. There are buses to and from the city centre.

Turn left at the T-junction at the end of Riverside Walk, up Fore Street and past the post office and village stores. Keep going to the mini-roundabout and bear left here, up Horsham Lane. At the first junction up the hill, by a school sign, fork left (8) and climb into what now becomes a rural environment, Plymouth being left behind.

Don't forget that the crossing of the River Tavy at Lopwell Dam ahead is tidal; the crossing is unavailable within two hours either side of high tide. It is about 3.25

miles/5.25km from Tamerton Foliot to Lopwell Dam, taking about 90 minutes to walk at a good steady speed.

Tamerton Foliot

Rising out of Tamerton Foliot the *Tamara Coast to Coast Way* enters the **Tamar Valley Area of Outstanding Natural Beauty** (AONB). Although the landscape of the whole Way is extremely attractive, only part of the route is within an area recognised nationally for its landscape quality. These lower reaches of the Tamar, from the outskirts of Plymouth to south of Launceston, are included within the Tamar Valley AONB, while the north coast and its hinterland is included as part of the Cornwall and North Devon AONBs. AONBs are regarded as the finest landscapes in the country, on a par in landscape terms with the National Parks (for more details see page 242).

Follow the lane up to arrive at Warleigh Lodge (9).

The lodge is probably 19th century in date, built as the entry lodge to **Warleigh House**, which is down the private drive to the left (E). The unseen house is mostly Tudor (16th century) on medieval origins. In early medieval times it belonged to the Foliots, the major local landowners. Gilbert Foliot, born here, was influential with Henry II in the 12th century and a great opponent of Thomas à Becket. After the medieval period Warleigh was owned by a variety of notable Devon families: Gorges, Bonvilles, Coplestones, Bampfyldes and Radcliffes.

At the Warleigh Lodge bear right on the footpath. The path slowly descends then joins a farm track.

The path is shown on old maps as a road, the main access from the south to Horsham Farm ahead. It is a hedge-lined sunken lane, showing that it is likely to be of great age.

Follow the track to pass through the yard at Horsham Farm (10) (F).

Many of the buildings here are no longer in use, but the farm is an ancient establishment, being recorded as early as 1270.

Continue on the surfaced track ahead.

Soon there are excellent views to the left over the River Tavy. This is the Tamar's major tributary in Devon, rising high on Dartmoor and draining much of the west side of the moor before reaching its tidal and navigable limit at Lopwell Dam, where the Way crosses the river. Seen on the opposite side of the river is the Bere Peninsula and the village of Bere Ferrers.

When the track meets another coming in from the left (11), turn sharp left (almost back on yourself) and follow this other track downhill, past a 'Road Closed' sign – this only applies to traffic. At the bottom ignore the public footpath through the gate ahead and turn sharp right up the lane. A little way up here the route crosses Blaxton Creek, a tributary of the Tavy; a short way after the crossing look for a permissive path which enters the woods on the left.

The permissive path goes along the edge of Blaxton Wood, parallel to Blaxton Creek, until it reaches the Tavy at a mock fortification (G), a folly built in the 19th century by the local Maristow Estate (and a superb picnic spot).

This location gives great views across the Tavy to the Bere Peninsula and Bere Ferrers, passed a little further on the Way. Looking downriver can be seen the **Tavy Viaduct**. This is a very handsome viaduct and, like Tamerton Bridge, was built in 1889 by the Plymouth, Devonport and South Western Junction Railway to carry the London and South Western Railway's main line between Plymouth and London Waterloo. It now carries the Tamar Valley branch line.

Bere Ferrers from Blaxton Wood

Tavy Viaduct from Blaxton Wood

On the opposite side of the tributary **Blaxton Creek** are the remains of Blaxton Quay. It includes an unusually large 18th/19th-century limekiln, used to supply lime to a large local area.

Much of Devon and Cornwall has relatively poor soil, which needs the addition of a fertiliser to make it productive. One such fertiliser was burnt lime, and limekilns are a feature of many parts of the coast of Devon and Cornwall and also, as here, of the navigable rivers. In this part of the country lime may have been first used as a fertiliser about 1600, following which its use grew rapidly, although there are claims it was used as early as the 15th century. The high cost of transporting the lime meant a coastal or estuarine location was favoured for the kilns.

Coal was fed into the bottom of the kiln and limestone into the top. Once the burning coal had brought the limestone to a sufficiently high temperature – about 550 degrees C – it began to decompose and turn into quicklime. When spread onto the land it absorbed water and produced slaked lime, a fine, soluble alkaline powder which neutralises the soil's acidity. The *Tamara Coast to Coast Way* passes numerous further limekilns on its southern half.

Continue on the path, now parallel to the Tavy, past a little ruined building and, a little further on, passing above a ruined boathouse on the foreshore. The path then emerges at a lane, where the Way turns left (12).

Continue ahead alongside the Tavy to pass Maristow Quay.

Maristow Quay was developed in the 19th century by the local Maristow Estate from earlier jetties here. It was used to export ore from the silver and lead mines on the opposite side of the river. Just after the quay note the apparently incongruous 'Unsuitable for Motor Vehicles' sign in the river. This marks the line of an old ford, unusable for very many years by walkers, let alone cars, but still remaining a legal road.

Beyond this take the permissive path on the left – however this may only be used from 2 February to 30 September inclusive (13).

The permissive path follows an embankment next to the Tavy as the river quickly narrows from an estuary to a medium-sized river.

During winter simply follow the road, which is re-joined by the path a little further on; almost immediately reach a road junction. Go left here.

Up to the right through the trees can be seen **Maristow Hous**e (H). This large mansion was built in 1760 in a landscaped park. Over the years it has been badly damaged by fires, the latest in 1982. The location was earlier associated with Plympton Priory, until Henry VIII dissolved the religious houses. In 1798 it was acquired by the Lopes family who made it their family seat until the early 20th century. The house has now been converted into flats. Its original name seems to have been Martinstow, from a medieval chapel dedicated to St Martin. The change of name came with its falling into the ownership of the priory, which was dedicated to St Mary.

Continue on the road to arrive at Lopwell Dam, the tidal limit of the Tavy and its lowest crossing point (14).

The dam was built in 1953 by Plymouth City Council to create an additional water supply for the city. The pump house still exists by the quay. Adjacent to the car park is the granite stone base from a cider press, set into the perimeter wall, and two small granite farm rollers, set into the ground beside the perimeter fence.
Today **Lopwell** is chiefly important for its wildlife. The area is a mix of woodland, some of it semi-natural, marshes and mudflats, giving a range of habitats. Lopwell is both a formal Site of Special Scientific Interest and a Local Nature Reserve.

Lopwell Dam

Bere Ferrers Quay

Access across the river is by the raised walkway but alongside is the older ford, still a right of way. Previously there had been a ferry crossing here, and the remains of the ferryman's cottage of the early 20th century still exist in the woods.

Assuming the timing is right, cross the causeway and on the far side turn left on the track.

In medieval times there were silver and lead mines in the woods here, one of which, **Wheal Maristow**, was reused in the 19th century and its ores exported from the predecessor of the quay on the opposite side of the river. This is the first example on the Way of the use of the name 'Wheal', from the Cornish word for a place of working.

The *Tamara Coast to Coast Way* has now entered the quiet and atmospheric Bere Peninsula, between the Tavy and the Tamar.

Climb through the woods and at the T-junction at the top (15) turn left.

Descending this lane there are superb views ahead down the Tavy estuary.

At the junction near the bottom of the hill (16), with a signpost to Hallowell and Bere Ferrers, continue straight ahead and you will shortly reach the creek. At the creek, turn right and follow the track alongside the foreshore through to Bere Ferrers Quay (17).

(If the track to the creek is too muddy, bear right, away from the river and round to the left at a sharp bend. A little beyond fork left on a track. Reaching a junction next to the Tavy bear right, then round to the left, parallel to the river, and join the foreshore track to the quay.)

Nearby is the farmstead of **Hallowell**, a 17th-century house on a 16th-century core. It is possible that the name may commemorate an early 'holy well' in the area. The quay gives lovely views up the Tavy and over the estuary.

Pass the quay and walk up the road into the village. The route passes the village pub, the Olde Plough (18).

Bere Ferrers has its pub, the Olde Plough (www.theoldeploughinn.co.uk), with public toilets behind, and buses to Bere Alston and Tavistock. Trains go to Gunnislake, Bere Alston and Plymouth on the Tamar Valley branch line.

There is no shop in the village. Accommodation is in short supply here and it is recommended to use public transport to larger nearby centres. For public transport options, from outside the Olde Plough walk up the road then turn left opposite 'The Club', signposted Station, Clamoak and Hole's Hole. Buses go from this junction.

For the station, turn left here, then at the top follow the road round to the right; the station is found a little way on, on the left. Buses also go to and from Bere Ferrers Station (I).

Bere Ferrers, late 19th century (Photo courtesy of The Box, Plymouth)

For some brief details of the medieval Ferrers family who gave their name to the village, as well as a note about the 13th-century church, see the start of Stage 3, page 70.

Celtic cross, Saltash

Stage 2K (Cornish Option)
Tamar Bridge to St Mellion

From the Tamar Bridge, Stage 2 of the *Tamara Coast to Coast Way* continues through Plymouth before crossing the River Tavy and the Bere Peninsula, all in Devon. It continues (Stage 3) on the riverside to Bere Alston, where the train is used to cross into Cornwall at Calstock.

For those wishing to complete *Kylgh Kernow* – a circuit of Cornwall – an alternative option stays on the Cornish side of the river from Saltash to Calstock. This avoids the tidal crossing of the River Tavy at Lopwell Dam (primary route Stage 2) and taking the train between Bere Alston and Calstock (primary route Stage 3).

This Cornish route is divided into two lengths: Stage 2K from Saltash to St Mellion and Stage 3K from St Mellion to Calstock, where the primary route Stage 3 to Gunnislake is joined. Measuring from the end of Stage 1, Stage 2K is 18.2 miles/29.3km to Calstock, whereas the primary route on the Devon side is 17.4 miles/27.9km (to Bere Alston Station for train to Calstock).

Stage 2K crosses the Tamar to Saltash on the 20th-century road bridge, where there are excellent views of Brunel's iconic 19th-century railway bridge alongside. Leaving Saltash the route then deviates away from the Tamar to cross a tributary. After returning alongside the Tamar the route climbs away again for a while, before arriving at St Mellion.

Distance:	12.1 miles/19.5km between Tamar Bridge and St Mellion
Total ascent:	1790ft/545m
Estimated walking time (without stops):	5hr 50min
Car parks:	Saltash (centre, riverside)
Public transport:	Saltash (bus, train), Carkeel (bus), St Mellion (bus)
Public transport & shorter options:	Saltash is easily reached by bus or train from Plymouth; there are regular bus services between Saltash, Carkeel, Paynter's Cross and St Mellion.

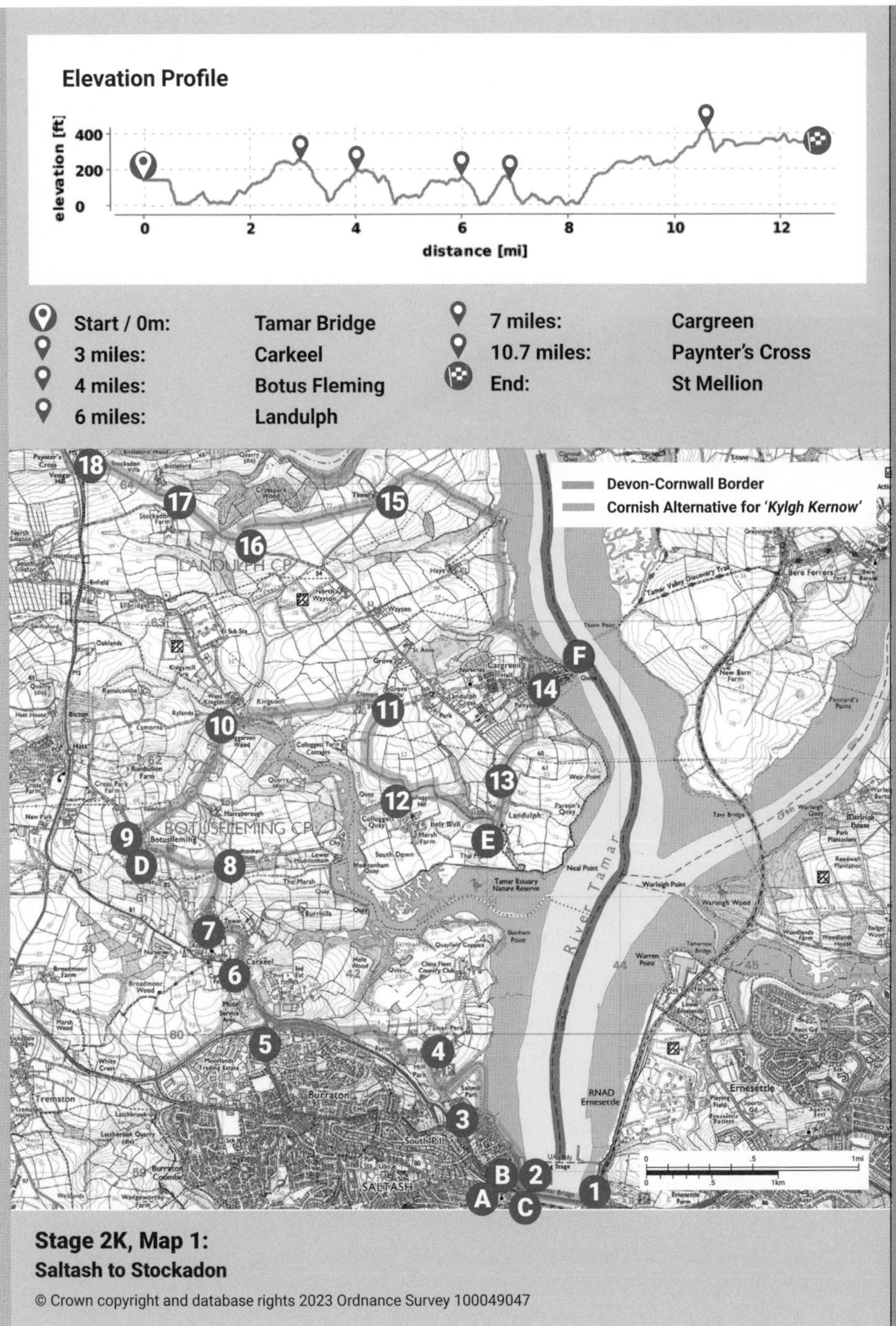

Stage 2K, Map 1:
Saltash to Stockadon

From the end of Stage 1 at the Tamar Bridge Visitor Centre (1), follow the walkway over the bridge to arrive at Saltash on Lower Fore Street (2). Turn left down the hill for the main route, or turn right to visit the town centre.

If you are going to the town centre further up along Fore Street, you pass the town's Guildhall, a handsome building dating from 1780.

Saltash Guildhall

The original settlement here was simply called 'Ash', presumably from a prominent ash tree. Later, probably in the 13th or 14th century, 'salt' was added to distinguish it from other 'ashes', probably from the production of salt from the estuary (the *Kylgh Kernow* option passes Saltmill Creek on the edge of the town). Incidentally, it is sometimes said that the old Cornish name for Saltash was 'Esse' or 'Essa', but these are only the Norman spellings of 'Ash'.

Saltash had achieved borough status by 1201 following its redevelopment the previous century, perhaps based on the ferry point. Much of its old centre was destroyed by bombing during World War II and by modern development, but the church (A), behind the Guildhall between the riverside and the town centre, is of considerable interest. It dates back to Norman times, with much early work remaining, even though it was not strictly a parish church until 1881, but a chapel of the official parish church at St Stephen, now a Saltash suburb. Another notable old building, behind and below the church, is Mary Newman's cottage, dating from the 17th century, and said to be the home of Sir Francis Drake's first wife.

Saltash has all facilities, including buses to and from Plymouth and also north to and from St Mellion, Callington, Launceston and Bude.

From the town centre return down Lower Fore Street. Pass the path from the bridge and a little way further down the hill, after passing some handsome 18th- and 19th-century buildings, is another path off to the left. This leads to the Celtic cross erected as a welcome into Cornwall (B). Pass the information board giving some details about the road bridge and follow the path under the bridge and up to the cross.

The **cross** is 62ft/19m high. It was erected in 2013, and represents a welcome to Cornwall and its culture to visitors crossing the Tamar. It was constructed under the direction of sculptor Simon Thomas, assembled from 6000 individual pieces over three years. It is designed to look like weathered copper, mined nearby on the edge of Bodmin Moor in the 19th century, with the cost of £650,000 funded by the Big Lottery and local contributions. Inspired in part by the Angel of the North, it is a similar height.

Return along the path under the bridge to Lower Fore Street. Turn left and continue down the hill to the bottom.

The scale of the bridges is really impressive from here at their base.

There are toilets here, underneath the railway bridge, and refreshments just beyond.

Just beyond the bridges to the right is **Saltash Town Qua**y (C). Next to the quay is the slipway for the old ferry, which linked to Plymouth before the road bridge was built in 1961. It may have originated in pre-Norman times, as a link to and from St German's, which was Cornwall's cathedral from AD930 until 1050, when the bishopric was merged with Exeter. Another story is that it originated when Edward the Black Prince gave the right of a ferry to a soldier who had been wounded fighting with him in France in the 14th century. In any event it had a long history and it remained important as there was no road crossing of the Tamar downstream of Gunnislake. By 1961 it was being operated by a chain ferry, or 'floating bridge', which could take

24 vehicles at a time (nothing like enough to satisfy demand, hence the need for the bridge).

Of interest on the quay are two Victorian figures, Isambard Kingdom Brunel and Ann Glanville. Brunel is celebrated here because of his building of the railway bridge above, the Royal Albert Bridge. Ann Glanville was, unusually for a Victorian lady, a champion rower who formed her own female crew of rowers. Her husband operated the ferry for a while in the 19th century. She had 14 children and was widely regarded as a local 'character'.

Most of the old buildings which existed on the quay have now gone, but what was the Boatman pub, now a wine and coffee lounge, has a date of 1595 on its wall and, although much altered, is based on a 16th-century core. Until the mid-20th century the quay would have been a bustling place.

Victorians at Saltash Riverside

Return to the bottom of Lower Fore Street and continue along the riverside, diverting onto the waterside path after the car park.

An information board here gives some background to this part of the riverside, **Sand Quay Beach**. As the name suggests, it once had a role landing sand, but it became important in World War II as a site for the repair of landing craft in preparation for D-Day.

Tamar Bridges from Saltash Riverside

The Tamar Bridges from Saltmill Park

The path returns to the road at some steps. Turn right and follow the road up to Lander Road (3) on the right, a little way short of the top. Turn down this road then at the bottom go left. A short way along, turn right to enter Saltmill Park and follow the riverside track.

Originally this was a tidal inlet, **Saltmill Creek**. Its name suggests an early use was the production of salt from the estuary. The inlet was partly reclaimed in the 19th century, then during the 20th century used as a waste tip. This was in turn reclaimed at the turn of the 21st century by Plymouth City Council and the Groundwork Trust as a park and sports centre.

There are superb views of the Tamar Estuary, downstream to the Tamar Bridges and over the river to a railway viaduct. This carries the old London and South Western Railway main line, and now the Tamar Valley branch line, over the River Tavy, the main Tamar tributary on the Devon side. Looking back down the river the outline of the Celtic Cross is clearly visible on the skyline.

Follow the track along the edge of the park, initially alongside the Tamar, then turning inland away from the river along a creek.

The original wide creek was reduced to this narrow tidal watercourse at the north end of the inlet and in the 19th century a tidal mill was established here. This is commemorated by an engraving on the fencing alongside the creek – 'They Used the Ebb and Flow of the Tides to Grind their Grain'.

Leave the park opposite the attractive Shute Cottage and turn right. Follow the road as it climbs (be aware of traffic here) then turn left along a side lane at the junction (4) where the China Fleet Country Club is signed ahead. At a fork by some old stone buildings go right, then bear left along the signed public bridleway, which loses its surfacing when passing 'Byeways'. Watch out for a few potentially muddy patches on this section.

It is not possible to continue directly north from Saltash next to the Tamar because of the existence of a sizeable tributary, **Kingsmill Lake**, and its own tributary streams; *Kylgh Kernow* has to divert to the west. Like earlier 'lake' features on the Tamar Estuary, Kingsmill Lake is a watercourse rather than a standing body of water.

The sound, and often the sight, of nearby traffic is noticeable as the path narrows and continues close to, and parallel to, the A38. This was built in 1986 to take traffic to and from the Saltash tunnel, the two features combining to form the Saltash bypass. Saltash is rare nationally, and unique in Devon and Cornwall, in being bypassed by means of a tunnel. This was built in the 1980s, becoming necessary as Saltash was increasingly overwhelmed by traffic following the completion of the road bridge.

The path arrives next to a pedestrian and cycleway bridge (5). Continue ahead, ignoring the bridge, passing the Waitrose car park.

Waitrose has refreshments and toilets and buses stop nearby on route to and from Plymouth, Saltash, Callington, Launceston and Bude.

At the end of the car park continue ahead across Edgcumbe Road and follow the footway to the left. Cross the next road next to the roundabout and turn right along the footway to another roundabout. Follow the footway alongside the A388 – be especially careful here – in the Launceston direction and continue the short distance to Carkeel. Here, very carefully, cross the A388 to the lane signed as 'Unsuitable for Heavy Goods Vehicles' (6), opposite Southdown Cottage.

Carkeel's Cornish name means 'fort on the ridge', indicating it could have been an important defensive vantage point overlooking the Tamar Estuary. It has a rather different character now.

Arriving at the A388 Saltash–Launceston road Kylgh Kernow enters the Tamar Valley Area of Outstanding Natural Beauty (AONB). AONBs are regarded as the finest landscapes in the country, on a par in landscape terms with the National Parks. Walkers on the *Tamara Coast to Coast Way* will surely soon agree that the often dramatic landscape of the lower half of the Tamar Valley deserves such a designation. The Tamar Valley AONB continues as far as a little way short of Launceston.

The *Tamara Coast to Coast Way* passes through another AONB at the north coast and its hinterland, which forms part of the Cornwall and North Devon AONBs. The landscape of the whole Way is extremely attractive, even if not all nationally recognised formally (for more details of the AONBs see page 242).

Follow the lane down through Carkeel, bearing left at the fork near the end of the village. At the next junction (7), turn right (signposted to Moditonham and Botus Fleming. This descends to cross a small stream.

This is **Clark's Lake** ('Lake' here has the same wider meaning as with Kingsmill Lake). Barely visible now, what was a wide tidal creek to this bridge was drained in the 1700s for agricultural land.

At the junction (8) immediately after the stream, follow the road round to the left, signposted to Botus Fleming and Hatt.

The lane to the right is a cul-de-sac which leads to **Moditonham**. This was the centre of a medieval, possibly Norman, manor and in medieval times there was a castle and later a fortified house there. There is now a house of 18th-century origin with later additions, but it is not public.

Follow the road to the left as it rises to the village of Botus Fleming.

Entering the village *Kylgh Kernow* passes the village pub, the **Rising Sun Inn**. The pub is the village's only facility for walkers, but check opening times in advance if planning to use it (01752 842792).

Continue past the pub to a junction (9). Go left for the village church (D), or for *Kylgh Kernow* follow the road to the right, uphill.

The **church** is attractively positioned overlooking the valley of a tributary of Kingsmill Lake. It is mainly 15th century. In the porch are the old village stocks. Possibly its main feature is a monument of a medieval knight carrying a shield, which may be as early as 14th century in date. It has been suggested that this is for Stephen le Fleming (see below).

The first part of the village's unusual name probably derives from the Old Cornish bod, meaning a dwelling, but the second part is obscure. The original form is recorded in the 13th century as flumyet, the meaning of which is unknown. It has therefore been suggested that Stephen le Fleming gave his name to the village, but there is no evidence for this. It is one of the Way's historical mysteries.

One oddity is found in a nearby field: a 12ft/4m **obelisk**, a memorial to William Martyn, a doctor in Plymouth who lived locally. His will set out that he 'knew no superstitious veneration for church or churchyard' and wished to be buried in unconsecrated ground. When he died in 1762 this was done, but with the addition of the memorial.

Also in the village is **The Bidwell**, a well-house possibly of 15th century date, with an added 19th-century gate and statue.

Historically, like so much of the lower Tamar Valley, the parish was famous for its fruit, in this case cherries.

A little way up the hill on the right is the old village pound.

At the junction a little further (9) on turn right, signposted Cargreen and Landulph. The route then descends steeply to a T-junction (10), where it turns right (again signposted Cargreen and Landulph).

Botus Fleming church

Landulph church

Here the route crosses the head of the Tamar tributary Kingsmill Lake, at its tidal limit – tidal on the right, not on the left.

Keep going past Kingsmill Farm and then at the junction at the top of a rise (11) turn right along a lane signed 'No Through Road', opposite 'Trelevans'. Follow this and after a while pass a wooden fence on the right.

Over the fence is a view on the skyline of the buildings at Saltash, still visible after this considerable diversion around the tributary.

A little further on there is a bend to the right and the road begins to descend ahead at another wooden fence. On the left (12) take the green lane track, signed as a public bridleway.

The route has now arrived at **Colloggett Hil**l. Its name is from the Old Cornish for 'mouse ridge'; whether the inspiration for the name came from the shape of the ridge or from an early rodent infestation will never now be known.

Note that this lane is a bridleway and therefore used by horses. Meeting a rider is unlikely, but horses' hooves can churn the surface so be aware that there can be mud on some lengths, especially in winter.

The path passes the attractive Lower Marsh Farm on the left then arrives at the farm entrance gate. Turn right here to reach Landulph church (E).

Landulph consists of the church and a scattering of buildings. Its name means the 'holy place of Dylyk' (or Delek or Dilp or Dilph – all these forms are found in the records). Whatever the form of the saint's name, nothing is known of him (or her), except for one story that suggests an Irish origin. As other saints of Irish origin landed on the banks of the Tamar in the 5th to 7th centuries, this must be a possibility.

There was a church here in early times, certainly by 1086. Little remains of any very early building, although there are elements of Norman work in the current church. In the 15th century Landulph became important as an embarkation point for pilgrims to Santiago de Compostela in Spain. It may have been the numbers of pilgrims passing through that led to the church being rebuilt at this time.

The *Tamara Coast to Coast Way* will encounter such pilgrims again towards its northern end, at Kilkhampton; some pilgrims would walk between the north and south coasts to avoid the potentially dangerous voyage around Land's End. Who knows – perhaps *Kylgh Kernow* walkers are following in the footsteps of these medieval pilgrims along the Tamar.

A little later, when it is said there was a village here, it was badly hit by the Black Death. Any survivors fled over the hill to neighbouring Cargreen, leaving the church all but alone among the marshes.

The church is mostly 14th and 15th century, with 15th-century bench ends. Of interest is a memorial to Theodore Palaeologus, a descendant of the medieval Christian emperors of Byzantium, who died in the parish in 1636. When the last emperor was killed by the Ottomans his successors escaped to Italy. Some generations later Theodore was born. By all accounts he led a colourful life, apparently including an occupation as a hired political assassin. He came to England, initially perhaps for an assassination job, but then settled down quietly, married and eventually died in this out-of-the-way parish: a Cornish villager with a very colourful past, who might have been an emperor.

For those interested in a short diversion, there is a cul-de-sac path over the marshes to the riverside, and the probable site of the pilgrims' embarkation point.

It is about 0.25 mile/0.4km each way, taking about 10 minutes. Go straight ahead past the church. A little way along turn right at the gate by the public footpath sign and continue to the river. Afterwards retrace your steps to Landulph church.

An information board at the start of the path gives some examples of what birds can be seen. Particularly notable are the avocets. In winter the lower Tamar is home to these attractive white waders with upturned beaks. These birds are not common in the west – they nest primarily in the east of England and some head west for the winter, most of them to the Exe, but some continue on to the Tamar. There is also an excellent view of Plymouth and Saltash and the Tamar Bridges.

Tamar Bridges from Landulph

To continue on *Kylgh Kernow*, turn left in front of the church (arriving from the Botus Fleming direction), or right (if returning from the foreshore). Climb the hill, passing Landulph Farm and then Landulph Rise. At a fairly sharp left-hand bend (13) there are two accesses on the right: a field gate, and to its left the start of a green lane with a sign saying 'Private Land – Please Keep to the Public Rights of Way'. Take this path, which is a public footpath. In time it turns left over a stile before passing between fields.

From the stile, there is a superb view over Cargreen and the Tamar. On the far, Devon, bank, where the yachts are moored, is Weir Quay. In the 19th century, this was where most of the ores mined locally were smelted, as well as imported ore. There would probably have been a pall of smoke over it in those days as 30 tons of ore a month was being smelted in 18 furnaces.

Over Cargreen

Descend the path until it arrives at a road (14) and here bear left and ahead.

This leads to a children's play area and benches overlooking the Tamar – a good spot for a break.

Follow the road ahead – Penyoke Lane (or Bownder Pennek, the Cornish language version, meaning 'the headland lane') – and go ahead to arrive at Cargreen. For the riverside and quays turn right and go to the end (F).

Originally the name **Cargreen** referred to a riverside rock, the name deriving from Cornish *karrek reun*, meaning 'seal rock'. Like many settlements in the lower Tamar Valley, it became important in the 19th century for the growing of soft fruit and flowers, especially daffodils. These were sent to Plymouth by boat or, more often, put on the ferry that then existed to Thorn Point on the Devon bank opposite, from where they were taken up the hill to Bere Ferrers railway station and then on to Plymouth or, by direct express, to London – Bere Ferrers was on the London and South Western Railway's main line between Plymouth and London Waterloo. The ferry continued into the early 20th century. In 1978 the remains of a boat were discovered on the river bed between Cargreen and Thorn Point. It contained late 19th-century pottery vessels from Bristol and perhaps Honiton. Perhaps it was on its way to Calstock. Fertiliser, in the form of sweepings from Plymouth's streets, dockyard and markets, was brought in by boat and spread over the fruit and flower fields. The old quay buildings and warehouses remain, now converted to residences.

There are no facilities for walkers in Cargreen. The earlier stores and the village's two pubs have all gone, the last pub closing in 2007.

(Left) Cargreen Quay

To continue on *Kylgh Kernow* from the quay return up the road and turn right along Coombe Lane. At the end of the residential road follow the narrow road ahead past Cargreen Yacht Club and then around a Tamar tributary creek to reach a gate. Follow through and on the old road, no longer maintained for vehicles. After more gates the route passes Salter Mill and Quay Cottages.

In the 19th century there was a tidal mill, a malthouse and a brewhouse at **Salter Mill**. Originally, the tidal mill may have been operated by damming water in a tributary – old maps show a tributary entering the Tamar here. Later, it may have used a tidal pool, probably where the marshes are, the water being released to drive the mill. The quay commemorated in the name of the cottages would have been used to import the materials needed for the brewing.

The reed beds alongside the Tamar are an important habitat and here are found reed and sedge warblers in summer and reed buntings all year round.

Another creek is passed and then the road climbs away from the river, although still shadowing its course as it meanders to the west here. After passing the farmstead of Tinnel the road forks (15). Bear right here. Keep going until the road bends to the left to meet a T-junction (16). Turn right here.

Note over the hedge on the left just after the junction the distant view of Plymouth, with the two Tamar bridges especially prominent. The Tamar, unseen hover to the right, now turns back north from its westward meander, but *Kylgh Kernow* continues to the west, away from the river, in order to get round the Pentillie Estate, which occupies the Cornish bank north of here.

Pentillie Castle was named after himself by Sir John Tillie, who acquired the land by marriage in the late 1600s, with the Cornish prefix *pen*, meaning head or, as in this case, hilltop. He built the house in 1698, but it was largely rebuilt in 1810. It passed to the Coryton family by marriage in the 18th century – the same family still operates the estate today. After a period of neglect in the 20th century it was restored in the early 2000s. It is now used as a hotel, a wedding venue and for corporate events. The surrounding gardens were enhanced by the famous garden designer Sir Humphrey Repton in 1810 and the land is now used for a shoot.

Follow the road past the Saltash turn (17) – take care on the stretch before the turn, as the road is used by local traffic to and from Cargreen – and pass Stockadon Villa on the left.

This handsome Regency style building was formerly the Pentillie estate office. It was built in the early 19th century, probably c. 1815.

A little further on the road arrives at the little settlement of Paynter's Cross (18).

The main features here relate to the main access to Pentillie Castle. Here is the main estate lodge with, nearby, a number of estate cottages. Next to the lodge are the entrance gates. All these date to the time of the major castle rebuilding in 1810.

Pentillie Lodge

Pentillie Lodge, Paynter's Cross

At the side of the road opposite the lodge is a **milestone** reading '4½ C'. This was erected by the Callington Turnpike Trust showing the mileage to Callington. The Trust was set up in 1764 to maintain the main roads to the town and provide signing. At the time the stone was erected the turnpike road looped past the entrance to Pentillie. During the 20th century the main road, now the A388, was realigned to bypass the hamlet. The stone dates from the late 18th or early 19th century.

Milestone, Pentillie

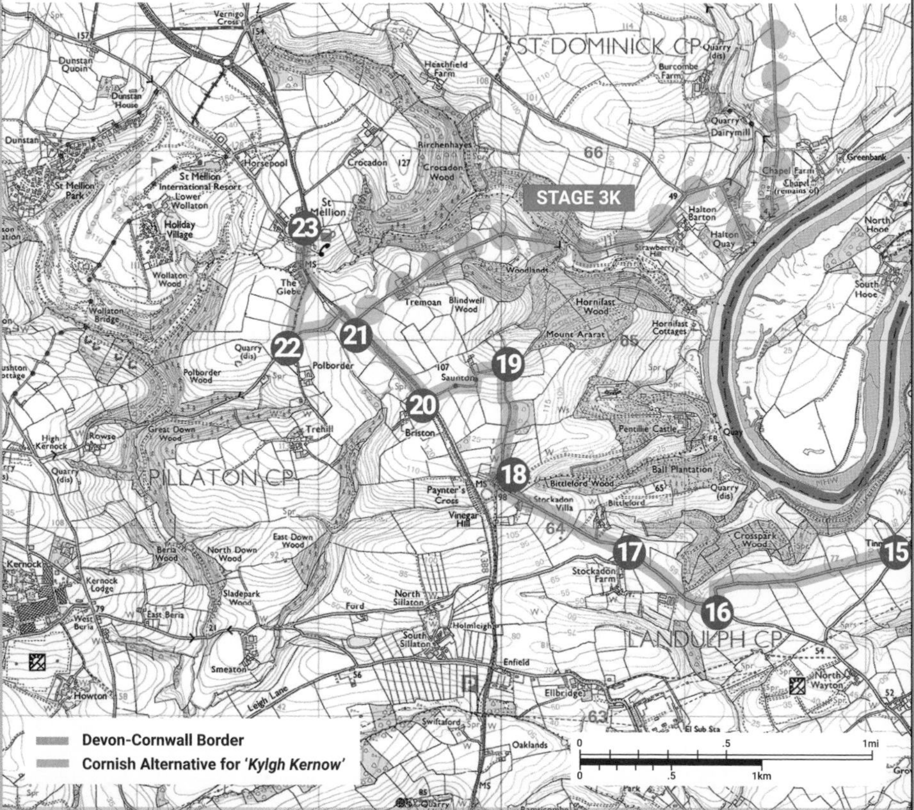

STAGE 3K

Devon-Cornwall Border

Cornish Alternative for *'Kylgh Kernow'*

0 .5 1mi

0 .5 1km

Stage 2K, Map 2:
Stockadon to St Mellion

There is an opportunity to pick up a bus nearby – there are bus services to Plymouth, Saltash, Callington and Launceston – note that it is another 6 miles/9.5km to Calstock. For the bus stops, turn left at the lodge, signposted to Plymouth and Launceston, to arrive at the A388 Plymouth–Launceston road. Take great care approaching this road which is fast and busy. Buses will stop on either side of the road.

Incidentally, note the name **Vinegar Hill** here. This name was often applied to locations where grapes were grown, so it could be that there was a 19th-century vineyard here.

To continue on *Kylgh Kernow*, at the lodge (18) bear round to the right and follow the lane as it climbs then descends to a junction.

On the descent, on the skyline ahead is a distinct dome shape surmounted by a chimney. This is **Kit Hill**, something of an icon of the southern half of the Way (see Kit Hill Link, page 122).

To the right at the junction, past the 'No Through Road' sign, is a private track into the Pentillie Estate. In the grounds here is **Mount Ararat**, built in 1712 as a monument to Sir John Tillie. He directed that on his death he should be entombed in the tower, sitting upright and looking over the Tamar. In 2013 archaeologists investigated the tower and found evidence that his wish was only partially carried out, as what are likely to be his remains were discovered in a vault beneath his mausoleum.

Turn left at the junction (19) and climb to reach the A388 Plymouth–Launceston road.

TAKE CARE APPROACHING THE A388 AS THIS IS A FAST AND BUSY ROAD. Make sure dogs and children are closely looked after.

Turn right at the gate immediately before the A388 (20) and follow the permissive path next to the hedge parallel to the A388. Go through the gate at the end (21). Here the *Kylgh Kernow* turns right down the lane, but to divert to St Mellion go alongside the A388 to the roundabout.

The end of Stage 2K is at the village of St Mellion, 0.6 miles/1km from here. St Mellion has accommodation and buses to Plymouth, Saltash, Callington and Launceston but no other facilities. Walkers who wish to give St Mellion a miss and continue directly onto Stage 3K to Calstock, which has more facilities, turn right down the lane on emerging from the gate. It is a further 6.5 miles/10.5km to Calstock. Follow the directions on page 94.

To continue to St Mellion, at the roundabout carefully cross the A388 and go down the lane opposite, signposted Polborder. About 200yd along the lane (22) turn right along a sometimes wet track. Go through a gate in the fence on the right and continue next to the hedge in the same direction to a kissing-gate at the end. Go through then left along the residential road, bearing right at the end to arrive at the A388 at St Mellion (23).

The bus stop towards Saltash and Plymouth is on the opposite side of the road, towards Callington and Launceston on the near side. Accommodation in St Mellion is mostly at the Holiday Village, reached by taking the first turning on the left off the A388 and passing the school and church (www.st-mellion.co.uk). The village no longer has a shop or pub.

St Mellion church

St Mellion gets its name from the dedication of its church to St Mellanus, a 5th-century Breton who was Bishop of Rennes.

Stage 3
Bere Ferrers to Gunnislake

From Bere Ferrers it is largely a riverside walk along the edge of the Bere Peninsula to Bere Alston, with the Tamar losing its estuarine character on this stretch. At Bere Alston the *Tamara Coast to Coast Way* crosses to the Cornish side of the river. Work is currently in hand to reinstate the tidal ferry across the river here but it may be necessary to take the train between the two stations on the opposite sides of the Tamar at Bere Alston and Calstock. The river crossing on the superb Calstock Viaduct offers excellent views. At Calstock Stage 3 is joined by the Cornish *Kylgh Kernow* alternative, Stage 3K (see page 103). The joint routes then continue generally close to the Tamar to Gunnislake, where the river's tidal limit is reached.

Distance:	11.9 miles/19.2km between Bere Ferrers and Gunnislake
Total ascent:	1630ft/500m
Estimated walking time (without stops):	7hr
Car parks:	Bere Alston, Calstock, Gunnislake

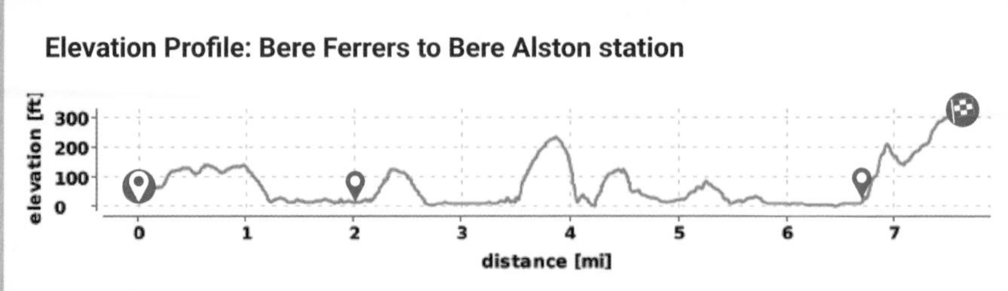

Start / 0m:	**Bere Ferrers**
2 miles:	**Hole's Hole**
6.8 miles:	**Ferry Farm**
End:	**Bere Alston station**

Public transport & shorter options:
The start can be reached by train (station at the top of the village), or by bus from Bere Alston or Tavistock. The easiest way to shorten the route, or return to the start, is to use the train (stations at Bere Alston, Calstock and Gunnislake).

Link routes: Bere Alston Link to/from Bere Alston Station; Kit Hill Link to/from Gunnislake.

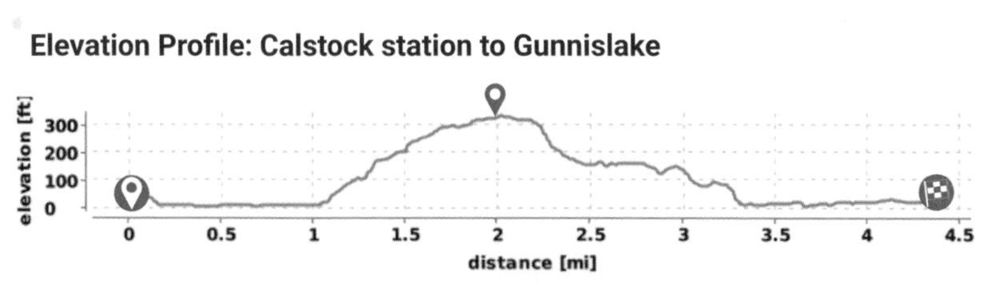

Start / 0m: Calstock station
2 miles: Calstock church
End: Gunnislake

Bere Ferrers has a pub, the Olde Plough (www.theoldeploughinn.co.uk), with public toilets behind. There is no shop in the village.

The Ferrers family acquired the manor in Henry II's time (12th century). The family seat was at **Bere Barton**, on the left above the church. The family gained a licence to build a fortified house here in the 14th century, but only a few medieval features remain in the rear of the current farm. There is also a battlemented wall which may have enclosed a medieval courtyard. The family's prosperity was based on the silver mines of the parish. The current house frontage is 18th century. There is no access to this historic building, but it is visible from the churchyard.

Coming from the quay, at the bottom of the village, Bere Ferrers **church** is off to the left just after the pub. It is earlier than most in the area, dating from the 1200s. The stained glass is some of the earliest in Devon. It has been described as a 'very beautiful, rich and complex church', well worth visiting.

Stage 3 starts at the Olde Plough in the centre of the village (1). Walk up the road then turn left opposite 'The Club', signposted Station, Clamoak and Hole's Hole (2). (Those arriving by bus can start at this junction, which is the village bus stop. If arriving by train either walk into the village centre or pick up the route as it leaves the village near the station.)

Just after the junction the route passes the parish hall. This occupies the former village school, built in 1896.

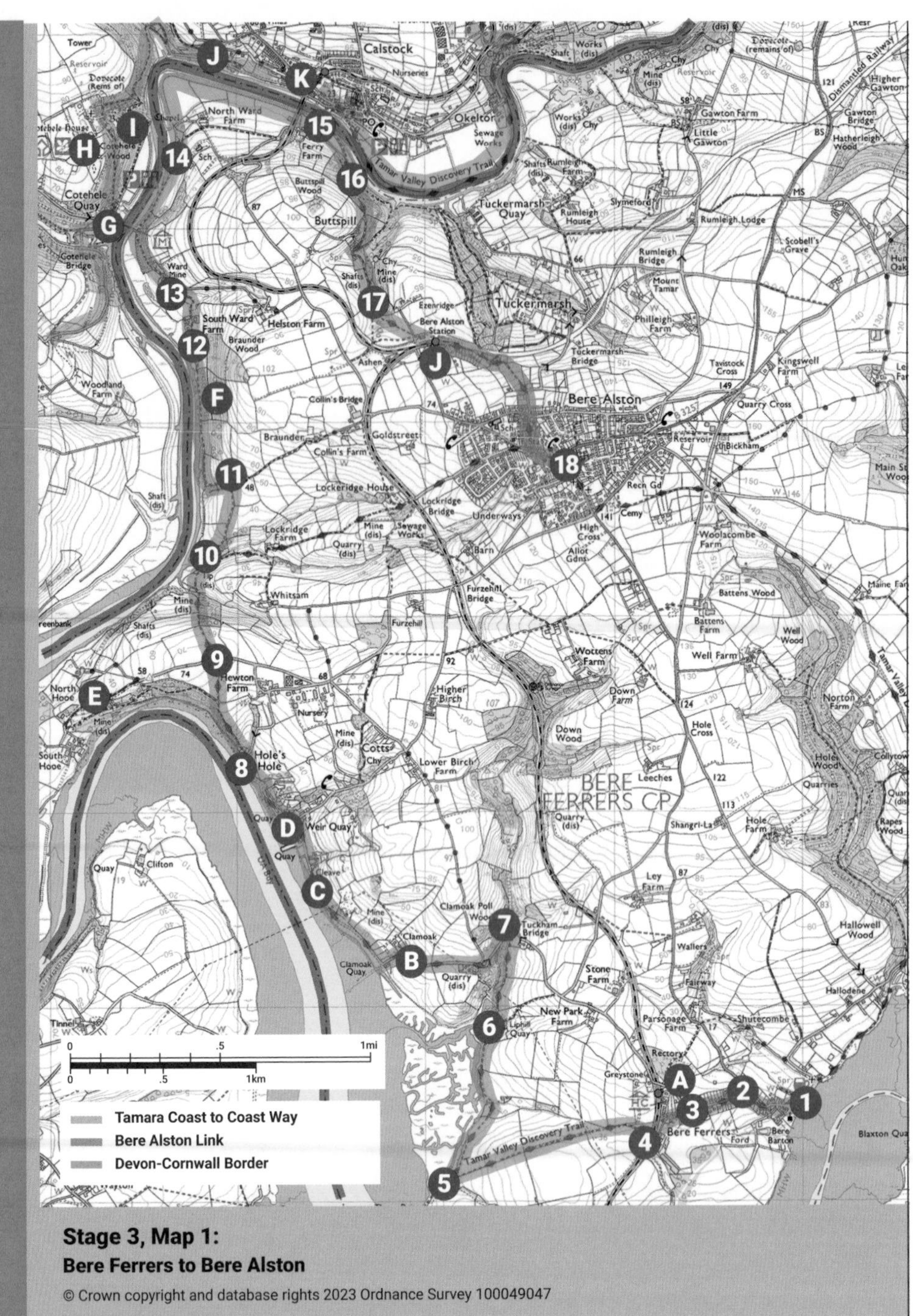

Stage 3, Map 1:
Bere Ferrers to Bere Alston

Bere Ferrers church

Memorial plaque, Bere Ferrers Station

At the top (3) the road bears round to the right, still signposted to the station. Here continue straight ahead, staying on Station Road.

The **station** (A) was opened in 1890 by the Plymouth, Devonport and South Western Junction Railway for the London and South Western Railway's main line between Plymouth and London Waterloo. This main line was closed in the Beeching cuts of the 1960s, but its branch up the Tamar Valley was retained and Bere Ferrers remains as a Tamar Valley branch line station.

In 1917 the station was the site of a tragic accident. During World War I, a troop of 10 soldiers from New Zealand were on their way by train from Plymouth to Salisbury when there was an unscheduled stop at Bere Ferrers. The soldiers, being unfamiliar with English geography, thought they had arrived at Salisbury and alighted from the train. Unfortunately they alighted on the wrong side, on to the other track; by tragic coincidence an express to Plymouth arrived and all the soldiers were killed. There is a memorial railway sleeper at the station as well as a plaque in the church, and in 2001 the names of the soldiers were added to the village's war memorial.

Trains go up the valley to Bere Alston, Calstock and Gunnislake and down the valley to Plymouth.

There has been a Heritage Centre, sleeping car accommodation and refreshments at the 'Tamar Belle' at the station. Check at **07813 360066** or **www.tamarbelle.co.uk** for up-to-date information.

Bere Ferrers Station

If starting this section of the *Tamara Coast to Coast Way* from the station follow the road downhill and turn right and walk along Station Road (3) to pick up the Way.

When you pass underneath the railway bridge (4) continue straight ahead along a farm track over a field to a gate. Continue ahead next to the fence. Go into the next field and carry on alongside the fence, descending towards the Tamar.

The *Tamara Coast to Coast Way* has now crossed the width of the Bere Peninsula and returned to the Tamar. From here there is a superb view ahead over the Tamar to the village of Cargreen on the Cornish side. To the left can be seen the arches of Brunel's Tamar railway bridge.

Upriver is the distinctive dome shape of Kit Hill, surmounted by its chimney. Its prominence makes it something of an icon of the southern half of the Trail (see the Kit Hill Link, page 122).

At the bottom corner of the field (5), turn sharp right and follow the path along the bottom edge.

Over the stile in the corner is an often-wet cul-de-sac path which leads over the marshes to **Thorn Point** on the riverside. (Note if you follow this path you will have to return to this point.) From the 19th century there was a ferry from Thorn Point to Cargreen in Cornwall. Producers of soft fruits and flowers on the Cornish side of the Tamar used the ferry to take their products to the railway at Bere Ferrers for fast dispatch to London or Plymouth, which was quicker than transporting by road to the railway at Saltash. The ferry continued into the early 20th century. The path used by the Way to here from Bere Ferrers follows the same route taken by produce from the ferry.

In 1978 the remains of a boat were discovered on the river bed off Thorn Point. It contained late-19th-century pottery vessels from Bristol and perhaps Honiton. It may have been on its way upriver to Calstock, at that time an important river port.

Walk along the bottom edge of the field, with Tamar marshes to the left, as far as a stile on the left. Cross the stile and continue on the path over a boardwalk.

There used to be a farm settlement here, marked on old maps as 'Egypt'. There is some uncertainty about the origin of this name, although it is popularly believed to derive from the fact that it seemed far and remote.

Continue on a fenced-off path then inland of an area of reeds and rushes. Turn right at the quay, up a track, then left immediately after a wooden gate just after the house (6). Continue along the bottom of another field to a fenced path which then crosses a footbridge to a road (7).

Quiet and relatively remote now, archaeological studies suggest that there may have been a medieval settlement near here, later abandoned and with no obvious evidence remaining.

Turn left at the road (7) and follow this as it rises and then drops back alongside the Tamar at Clamoak.

Passing Clamoak the Way enters the **Cornwall and West Devon Mining Landscape World Heritage Site** (B). (For more information see page 239.) For some way up the valley the Way will be passing old mines and associated buildings, miners' cottages, miners' smallholdings, inclined planes, railways and more.

The route continues on the minor road alongside the Tamar.

The Tamar here is important for its environmental value, because of its habitats and wildlife communities. It is both a Site of Special Scientific Interest and a designated Special Area of Conservation. One notable feature is that in winter the lower Tamar is home to **avocets**, attractive white waders with upturned beaks. These birds are not common in the west – they nest primarily in the east of England though some head west for the winter, most of them to the Exe, but some continue on to the Tamar. The river is nationally important for these birds. Other bird species of importance include black-tailed godwits, whimbrels, greenshanks, spotted redshanks, green sandpipers and golden plovers.

The route soon passes a couple of laybys, the second of which has an information board.

This marks the first of the many historic mine sites passed within the World Heritage Site. Behind this second layby is the site of the **South Tamar Mine** (C), also known as Cleave Mine. Like many of the mines in the Bere Peninsula, this mine dates back to medieval times, worked for silver and lead. In common with other medieval mines, it was worked by the Crown, but this ceased in 1350, when it was leased out. In 1547 it became part of the interests of the Edgcumbe family, and it was profits from the mine that enabled them to build Mount Edgcumbe. This interest in their new house helped preserve the architectural heritage of their earlier property at Cotehele (a little further up the Tamar), as they never modernised it. In the 19th century mining at South Tamar Mine extended under the Tamar and in 1856 the river broke through into the workings. Luckily it happened on a Sunday and there was no loss of life. Attempts were made to reopen the mine, but a few years later it was abandoned.

A large limekiln is then passed, and then **Cleave Farm**. The attractive farmhouse is 18th century in date.

A little beyond is **Weir Quay** (D). This is the site of an 18th-century quay, probably established to serve the local silver mines. Here in the 19th century were the **Tamar Smelting Works**, with workshops, offices and stables. Set up to serve the South Hooe mines slightly upriver, it later processed imported as well as local ore. In the mid-19th century the works were smelting 30 tons of ore a month in 18 furnaces. There was also a limekiln, still standing next to the Way. On closure in the later 19th century the industrial buildings were converted to dwellings, still in use today.

Tamar Estuary, Weir Quay

There is a café in Weir Quay boatyard, open certain days a week only. Check at www.weir-quay.com.

There is an excellent view across the Tamar Estuary, including Pentillie Castle in the woods on the Cornish side. **Pentillie Castle** was named after himself by Sir John Tillie, who acquired the land by marriage in the late 1600s, with the Cornish prefix pen, meaning head or, as in this case, hill. He built the house in 1698, but it was largely rebuilt in 1810. After a period of neglect in the 20th century it was restored in the early 2000s. It is now used as a hotel, a wedding venue and for corporate events. The surrounding gardens were enhanced by the famous garden designer Sir Humphrey Repton in 1810.

The prominent white building on the riverbank, on the Devon side of the large river meander, is South Hooe. Now a private house, it was an important mine site, being extremely productive for silver and lead and, later, fluorspar, during the 19th century. Mining extended under the river. The ore was smelted at Weir Quay.

Follow the road until it bends away from the river.

This location is known as Hole's Hole. In the 19th century the house here was the Tamar Hotel, largely established for the pleasure boating trade from Plymouth. The quay was used to serve some of the local silver mines.

When the road rises and bears right (8), fork off left then go along a narrow path to the left of a wooden gate. The path climbs, and after crossing a stile passes along the field edge ahead to a road.

The view back from here is the last time the Tamar will be seen as a wide estuary.

Cross the road (9) to the public footpath almost opposite (the left-hand gate) and follow the right-hand field edge down. Go through the gate in the bottom right-hand corner.

As the path descends the Tamar is seen again, now very different in character from the estuary recently left behind. This last stretch of the route has cut across a large promontory creating a Tamar meander (E), during which the character of the river has been transformed from a wide estuary to an inland waterway, though it is still tidal.

River Tamar: no longer an estuary

There follows a steep descent to a boardwalk and on to a field. Cross to the gate opposite. Turn left off the next path junction (10) onto another boardwalk over an area of reeds and rushes, then climb into a field. Turn right and follow the field edge.

There is a superb view back down the Tamar from this length, including riverside land enclosed for agriculture in the 19th century. On this stretch, as part of a joint project by the Environment Agency, National Trust and Plymouth University, the tidal Tamar is being allowed to flood the meadows to recreate wildlife habitat. It is also expected to help alleviate flooding along the river, including at the historic Cotehele Quay, seen a little later.

Keep on the path to the metal gate at the end, cross the footbridge then, on emerging at a field (11), turn left alongside the hedge. At the bottom corner follow around to the right, parallel to the Tamar, continuing on to the far corner and a gate into woodland.

The woods here are relatively recent. In the 19th century these slopes were used for the commercial growing of flowers for the Plymouth and London markets, with daffodils a speciality, and in spring flowers can still be seen throughout the woodland (F).

Keep on to the gate at the end, then ahead along the bottom of the fields. Skirt to the right of South Ward Farm (12), then follow the track ahead.

South Ward is a mine of medieval origin, dating originally to the 13th century, one of the royal mines opened for silver and lead. It was reopened in the 18th and 19th centuries, closing around 1880. The engine house was converted to a farmhouse.

At the junction at the top of the track (13), bear left through a gate to Ward Mine Farm, keeping ahead to pass some picnic tables.

This was another of the early mines of medieval origin, opened for silver and lead in the 13th century. It was worked for a while in the 19th century.

Just beyond the picnic tables go through a gate straight ahead and walk down through the woods.

Cotehele Quay (G) is now seen through the trees on the Cornish bank. It has a range of 18th- and 19th-century buildings, including a large three-storey warehouse. It may be possible to spot the *Shamrock*, the last of the Tamar barges, which is often kept in dock here; built at Plymouth in 1899 it was at the time the most advanced ketch-rigged sailing barge in the world.

Cotehele House (H) is usually regarded as the most important Tudor house in Cornwall. It is situated in the woods above the quay but unfortunately cannot be seen from this part of the Way (anybody wishing to visit should follow the *Kylgh Kernow* alternative southward from Calstock ahead). Since 1353 the estate had been owned by the Edgcumbe family (who originated further along the Way, at Milton Abbot), who acquired it by marriage and built the current house in the 1450s. It has remained largely unaltered since then, at least in part because at an early date the Edgcumbes also acquired Mount Edgcumbe at the mouth of the Tamar, and to which they gave priority. In 1947 Cotehele was passed to the National Trust (**www.nationaltrust.org.uk/cotehele**).

Continue on into a field. Keep along the bottom edge and on to a gate at the far end. Follow the path ahead then, when the footpath turns right (14), go left over a stile to follow a permissive path along an embankment.

Just after joining the embankment it is possible to see in the woods on the Cornish side a glimpse of a stone building (I). This is '**The Chapel in the Woods**', built in the 15th century by Cotehele's owner, Sir Richard Edgcumbe, as thanks for his life (see Stage 3K, page 101).

Like other embankments alongside the Tamar, this one was built in the 19th century to create agricultural land by preventing the river spilling onto its flood plain. This process is being reversed in several places. On the river side of the path are reed beds, an important habitat for birds, especially reed and sedge warblers in summer and reed buntings all year round.

As the embankment swings to the right note the very impressive Victorian house on the Cornish side of the river. This is Danescombe Valley House (J). Dating from the 1850s, this is said to have been built as a fishing lodge, but for most of the 20th century it operated as a small hotel, particularly catering for boat visitors coming up the Tamar.

The valley to the left of the house is the valley of **Danescombe** (also spelt Danescoombe). The valley was the site of an early paper mill, at 1788 only the second in Cornwall. There was also a copper and arsenic mine, partly restored. Popular theory has it that Danescombe got its name from the Vikings who fought with the Cornish at the Battle of Hingston Down against King Egbert and the Saxons in AD838 (see Stage 3K, page 101).

Danescombe Valley House

The route is now approaching Calstock, on the Cornish bank. Some of the riverside warehouses built in the 19th century when Calstock was an important river port can be seen.

Dominating the view ahead is **Calstock Viaduct**. This was built 1904–7 to connect the London and South Western Railway's line at Bere Alston on the Devon side with the East Cornwall Mineral Railway, which ran from Callington and terminated at Calstock. The mineral line was converted to passenger use and continues as the Tamar Valley branch line, although since 1966 it has terminated at Gunnislake. The viaduct is 120ft/37m above the river and 870ft/264m long and consists of 11,000 pre-cast concrete blocks, which were constructed on site here on the Devon bank. It is reputed to be the oldest bridge in the country so built.

Calstock Viaduct from the Tamar embankment

Calstock Viaduct before completion, 1907 (Photo courtesy of Kresen Kernow)

Bere Alston Station (Plymouth line left, Gunnislake line right)

After passing under the viaduct, at the junction of paths (15) continue straight ahead along the embankment.

In the 19th century there was a ferry crossing to and from Calstock here. After being discontinued in the 1920s it was briefly revived in the early 2000s. Efforts are currently underway by the Tamara project to reinstate this ferry, initially for a two-to-three-year trial period to see if it can be run as a commercially successful business. This would remove the need for walkers to divert from here to Bere Alston Station to take the train to Calstock. It is hoped the ferry will operate three hours either side of high tide between April/May and September/October. For up-to-date details visit **www.calstockferry.com** and for tide times **www.tidetimes.co.uk**.

On your right is Ferry Farm, getting its name from the old ferry crossing. During the 19th century the farm was a pub serving ferry passengers, known as the Passage Inn.

At the end of the embankment follow the steeply zigzagging path up into the woods. After about 30yd you come to a path junction (16) and the main route continues straight ahead up the hill.

However, if you have time a slightly longer detour is to turn left at the junction and follow the path alongside the river to Tuckermarsh Quay. When you reach the cottage at the quay, take the footpath on the right which will take you up the hill to Bere Alston Station.

The main route climbs through Buttspill Wood. There are no traces seen from the Way now, but the woods once had fluorspar mines as well as lead and silver mines dating back to medieval times.

Climbing through the woods, the path eventually emerges into a field (17). Bear left and cross a stream, then ahead towards a house, where a kissing-gate leads to a road. Turn right and pass under two railway bridges.

The first bridge carries the Tamar Valley branch line to Calstock Viaduct, the second the old main line to and from Plymouth.

Just beyond the bridges turn left to Bere Alston Station.

The **station** (K) was opened in 1890 by the Plymouth, Devonport and South Western Junction Railway for the London and South Western Railway main line between London Waterloo and Plymouth. It became particularly important for the distribution of local market garden produce in the late 19th and early 20th centuries. The fast trains enabled the produce to get to the London markets while still fresh.

In the early 20th century the link between the main line and the old mineral line up the Tamar Valley was built. Looking from the station platform, the main line to Plymouth bears off to the left while the Tamar Valley line forks away to the right. Trains have to reverse from the old main line towards Gunnislake, and vice versa. The line to Okehampton, Exeter and London went to the right, but now ends a few yards from the end of the platform; the Okehampton line was closed in 1968. There have been proposals to reopen the old main line as far as Tavistock in order to use it as a commuter route to Plymouth, so far unsuccessful, but still being pursued.

There is a link route into Bere Alston for those who need its facilities. **See page 92.**

For train times see www.gwr.com.

Stage 3 continues by taking the train across the river to Calstock Station. On alighting from the station (18) go down the main access path and continue downhill, signposted to Village Centre and Quay, and on to the Tamar Inn (19). Turn right here to Calstock Quay.

At this point the *Kylgh Kernow* alternative from Saltash (Stages 2K/3K) joins Stage 3.

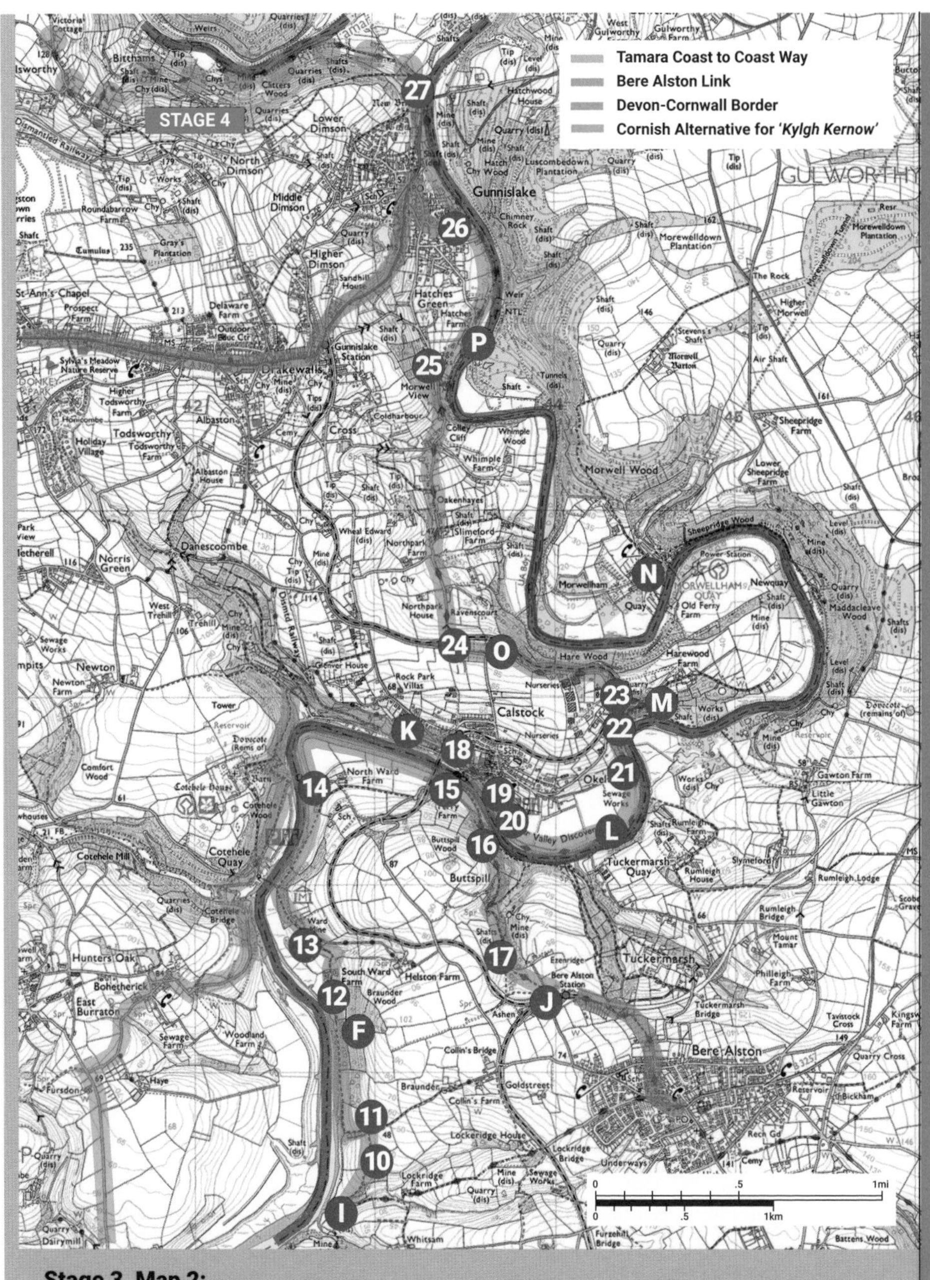

Stage 3, Map 2:
Bere Alston to Gunnislake

Calstock is an old riverside settlement and port. As early as the 14th century craft were being repaired here which were used for transporting mining ores – at that time it would have been silver and perhaps lead. Its importance really grew in the 19th century during the mining boom. This was especially the case after it became the terminus of the East Cornwall Mineral Railway, which served the mines around Gunnislake and Callington, in the 1870s. The railway ended above the town and was connected to the quays by a rope-worked counterbalance inclined plane 0.4 mile/0.6km in length, with a gradient of 1 in 6/17%, which raised and lowered trucks 350ft/106m. The remains of this are clearly visible a little way downstream of the village centre (K), and passed by the *Kylgh Kernow*, Stage 3K (see page 103).

In 1908, after mining had ceased, the mineral line was adapted to standard gauge and linked to the London and South Western Railway main line via the Calstock Viaduct. In 1966 the line beyond Gunnislake to Callington was closed, and then in 1968 the Waterloo main line was also closed. The branch line remained, probably because of the poor north–south road communications, and Gunnislake is now the end of the Tamar Valley branch line to and from Plymouth.

Calstock shipped out copper and lead ore and also granite from Hingston Down. The modern car park was once the Copper Quay, and the lines of the trackways have been retained in the surfacing. In addition, market garden produce and flowers – strawberries, cherries, daffodils and anemones – were all shipped out from the quays at Calstock. In came lime for fertiliser – there were a number of limekilns by the quays – and also offal from the Plymouth slaughterhouses, which was spread on the strawberry beds, and coal.

There were said to be at least 11 pubs in the village in the 19th century, including what is now the Boot Inn in Fore Street (www.thebootinn-calstock.foodndrink.uk), reputed to have been built in 1666, and the Tamar Inn (**www.tamarinn.co.uk**). This began as a customs house, built in the 18th century in Queen Anne style. There were also numerous shops, and several old shop fronts can be seen.

Calstock was popular with Victorian and Edwardian tourists, who came up the Tamar by steamer from Plymouth. Among them in the mid-19th century on one occasion were Queen Victoria and Prince Albert. This boat tourist trade continues into the 21st century.

There are also records of a ferry across the river being established in the 19th century, when there were many active quays on both banks. This continued off and on until the 1920s. It was revived briefly in the early 2000s but proved financially unviable and no longer operates.

Calstock is a pleasant place to wander around. As well as two pubs it has tea rooms/coffee shop ('Lishe' – generally closed Mondays and Tuesdays) and other refreshments can be bought. There is a community shop which operates out of the village hall on the riverside, but only open certain days of the week. Calstock is served by a regular bus service, approximately hourly to and from Callington, Gunnislake and Tavistock (not Sundays). Calstock is on the Tamar Valley railway line, which links to Gunnislake, Bere Alston, Bere Ferrers, Devonport and Plymouth.

It is a further 4.25 miles/6.75km on the Way to Gunnislake.

Street corner in Calstock

Footbridge over the embankment breach

At Calstock Quay (20) climb up to the riverside embankment path and follow this past the car park and football field and on upriver. The path follows a wide bend in the Tamar, a very pleasant section surrounded by river, reeds and birdsong.

This embankment was also built in the 19th century to reclaim the flood plain next to the river for agriculture. Recently the importance of flood plains for their wildlife, and also as a means of flood prevention, has been realised and the Environment Agency has joined forces with a group of local bodies to address this by creating a deliberate breach in the embankment to allow the flood plain to return to its original purpose. A community footbridge has been erected over the breach. The *Tamara Coast to Coast Way* crosses this footbridge, the path now sandwiched between the Tamar and the flood plain (L).

At the end of the embankment the path reaches a kissing-gate (21). Go through to arrive at Okel Tor Quay.

There is a first mention of the quay in 1812, when it had a large warehouse. The shell of the warehouse is still there, into which was inserted a modern house in the 1970s.

The quay also has a fine range of limekilns. Later in the 19th century it became important for taking out ore from Okel Tor Mine, a little way further upstream.

Limekilns, Okel Tor Quay

Okel Tor Mine

Bear right up a track from the quay, signposted as a public bridleway. A little way up the track forks, at an information board (22). The *Tamara Coast to Coast Way* continues uphill ahead but there is an interesting diversion to see the remains of Okel Tor Mine to the right. The diversion is about 0.4 mile/0.6km there and back (M).

Okel Tor Mine is first recorded in the 1840s. It was originally started to mine silver and lead but soon afterwards moved to copper, tin and arsenic. Steam engines were installed to serve the mine itself and also the 'stamps', where the ore was crushed. The mine ceased production in 1887. Several elements of the mine workings remain, including the main engine house, the calciners (which separated out the arsenic) and, especially well preserved, the stamps engine house.

There is a convenient bench giving a nice view over the Tamar. On the opposite bank are the remains of **Rumleigh Brickworks**, although little is seen other than the chimney, which was repaired after being damaged by a lightning strike in the 1990s. The brickworks were in operation between 1879 and 1914.

From the fork continue up the main track, passing above more old mine buildings, including a chimney (all on private land). Keep climbing to a surfaced lane and here turn sharp back left, climbing to an ungated level crossing on the right. Turn right over the level crossing (23).

This is the Tamar Valley branch line again. The unusually sharp bends on the line are evidence of the origins of this length as a narrow-gauge mineral line. If you coincide with a train the squeals of the train wheels as they negotiate the bends will be noticeable. There is a large meander in the River Tamar here and the railway tries to maintain a steady height on the valley side as it swings east and west.

The climb continues over the railway, less steep now, and the route bends to the left.

On the right at this bend is a private drive to **Harewood House** and Ferry Farm. Harewood was traditionally the centre of Duchy of Cornwall land in the area. Research by the Calstock Community Archive has suggested that prior to that it was the location of the centre of the area's Celtic chief. Its prominent position almost surrounded by a meander in the Tamar could well account for its early importance.

The name **Ferry Farm** is a reminder of a ferry established here in the 19th century linking this Cornish side of the river with the important river port of Morwellham on the Devon side. Morwellham has a restored 19th-century village and mine and although it is not on the line of the *Tamara Coast to Coast Way* is well worth a visit at another time (N).

Unfortunately Harewood and Ferry Farm are private and not accessible.

The route begins to level out and passes some nurseries on the left.

The nurseries are a further example of the modern version of the lower valley's traditional flower industry.

Continue on to a road junction, with Calstock church on the right (O).

The church's hilltop site away from the main settlement is typical of an early foundation, but the first mention of a church here is for its consecration in 1290. There are no remains of this building, the earliest parts of the current church being 14th century, with most of it being late 15th century. Unusually, it contains some faded wall paintings, and a fireplace in the porch.

Here is also the site of a **Roman fort**, and there are some details on an information board on the left just after the church, at the cemetery entrance. This was discovered quite recently, in 2007. It used to be thought that the Romans never got further west than Exeter, but Calstock is now one of three forts discovered in Cornwall. It seems to date to around AD50/55, and was occupied for around 30 years. It appears to have been associated with a Roman silver mine, and it may be that the metal was smelted here at that time. It seems likely that the silver was then exported from what is now Calstock via the Tamar.

This location seems to have been important even before Roman times, possibly because of its prominent position, as remains of Bronze Age and Iron Age settlements have also been found here.

There is a toilet in the churchyard to the left of the lychgate.

Continue ahead then turn right at the next junction (24), under the low railway bridge.

This is the branch line again, the bridge architecture typical of its origins as a 19th-century mineral line. The wooded Tamar Valley, lined on the Devon side by steep and high wooded cliffs, is seen on the right as the route descends.

At the junction continue ahead, signposted to Gunnislake.

A short way further on a track on the right is a cul-de-sac public footpath to a Tamar quay, **Slimeford**. It seems to date from the 1860s, developed to serve a nearby manganese mine.

A little beyond is the attractive house 'Oakenhayes', a listed building of 17th-century origin, much extended and altered in each of the subsequent centuries; the main front is 18th century. This is followed by a nursery on the left, the most northerly example of this lower Tamar Valley industry.

Pass along the top of a wooded Tamar-side cliff then, at the 30mph speed sign (25), turn sharp back right along the signed public footpath and descend to the riverside. Turn left here, alongside the Tamar.

Near this path junction is the site of **Netstakes Quay**, where it seems tin smelting was carried on in the 16th century. The name suggests that a fish trap was once sited in the river here. Nearby is a widening of the river which was created so that Victorian and Edwardian pleasure paddle steamers could turn at the limit of navigation.

A little way further on the path crosses a watercourse, then on the right can be seen a lock (P).

In the late 18th century a project to make the Tamar navigable as far as Launceston was proposed. The grand plan was then for a further waterway to link Launceston with the north coast at Bude. This latter plan was nearly achieved by the building of the Bude Canal between the coast and Druxton, north of Launceston (walkers on the Way beyond Launceston will have further experience of this venture).

At this southern end, in 1796 work started on making the Tamar navigable to Gunnislake. Only a short length was completed, just over 500yd/460m bypassing Weir Head. The lock marks the seaward end of this feature. As well as the lock, the lock-keeper's cottage can be seen on the island between the canal and the river.

This length was given the rather unappealing name of the **Tamar Manure Canal** – although at that time 'manure' was applied to any sort of fertiliser. The canal was operational until the 1920s, carrying coal, sand, bricks, lime and granite, as well as the 'manure' that gave it its name.

Lock, Tamar Manure Canal

Lock-keeper's cottage, Tamar Manure Canal

Continue on the path to pass canal workers' cottages. Just beyond, at a parking area, bear right to pass between the canal and some houses, which were old canal warehouses.

There was a major wharf on the canal a little further on, now occupied by a water treatment works. Also along this length were a paper mill, a warehouse (this straddled the towpath, being end-on to the canal) and a limekiln.

Also near the canal was **Bealswood Brickworks**. This was opened in 1850 and became the largest brickworks in Cornwall until it closed in 1914. The clay was dug on Hingston Down, a little to the west, and brought here. Bricks were loaded directly onto barges. As well as bricks, granite was taken down the canal and – in addition to the fertiliser which gave the canal its name – coal was brought in.

The weir on the Tamar bypassed by the canal can soon be seen as the track is followed. This was originally a fish weir built by the monks of Tavistock Abbey. It was rebuilt c. 1800 as part of the canal building works and now also includes fish ladders.

The end of the canal is passed and the track continues next to the Tamar.

The river is now in a relatively deep and wooded valley. The bypassed weir marks the Tamar's tidal limit.

A little way further on the route is joined by another track from the left, and very soon afterwards there is a set of steps on the left (26). While the *Tamara Coast to Coast Way* continues ahead to Gunnislake New Bridge, the steps mark the access into the centre of Gunnislake (climb the steps, follow the path ahead and continue into a residential road – Tamar Way – keep on to the top and at the T-junction turn right and carry on to arrive in the centre of Gunnislake).

Continue on to reach Gunnislake New Bridge (27).

Gunnislake New Bridge marks the formal end of Stage 3, and Gunnislake village is just up the main road to the left (about 0.8 miles/1.25km). However, there is no roadside footway and the road is rather busy, so walkers heading for Gunnislake village centre are strongly advised to take the safe link route from the access noted above.

Gunnislake is a very pleasant large village (or small town perhaps). It is first recorded in 1485, when it appears to refer to a stream rather than a village or town. The first edition OS map of 1809 shows no development here, and it seems largely to be the product of the 19th-century population growth arising from the expansion of mining in the area at that time. The first church was not built until the 1880s – before then, worshippers had to go to Calstock, 1.75 miles/3km away.

Gunnislake prospered in the 19th century, with at one time up to 45 shops. It was often referred to as 'Williamstown', since much of the land around, and most of the mines, were owned by John Williams. From a landed family in Scorrier, near Redruth, he acquired land in this area in the early 19th century. The heritage of that time is commemorated by the surprisingly lifelike statue of 'William the Miner', named after John Williams, on a bench in the centre of Gunnislake, funded by regeneration projects at the start of the 21st century.

As well as a general store, shops, pubs and tea rooms, Gunnislake also has toilets, accommodation and transport links. There is an hourly bus service to and from Callington and Tavistock (not on Sundays). There's also a one-day-a-week service along the Way to Luckett and Horsebridge.

Gunnislake is at the end of the Tamar Valley rail line to and from Plymouth. However, note that the station is 0.75 mile/1.25km from the centre, uphill all the way, a climb of some 330ft/100m.

William the Miner, Gunnislake

Gunnislake is also where the Kit Hill Link leaves or joins the Tamara Coast to Coast Way. Walkers will also pass a later link to Kit Hill from Luckett, providing an option for a circular walk (see Stage 4, page 122).

Stage 3:
Bere Alston Link

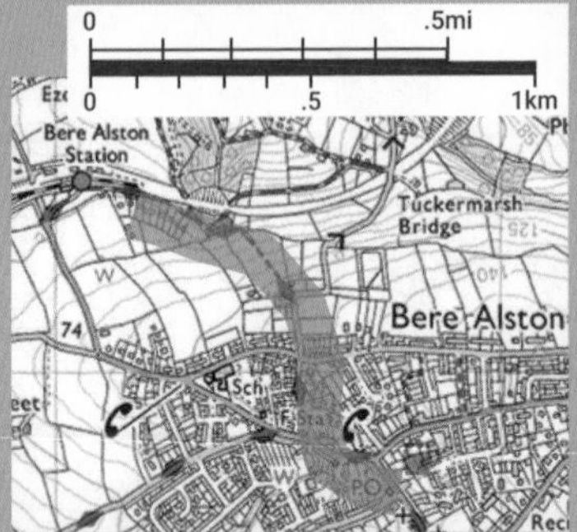

The *Tamara Coast to Coast Way* arrives at Bere Alston Station and then joins the train to cross the river to Calstock. However, for those who wish to visit the settlement of Bere Alston, which has a range of facilities, there is a link route (c. 1 mile/1.6km, about 20 minutes' walk). Alternatively, there is a bus link between Bere Alston and the station.

Map: Bere Alston Link

From the station walk towards the road. Immediately before reaching it turn sharp back left on a concrete track, signed public bridleway. Bear slightly right at a junction of tracks and a little beyond this junction fork right up a narrower path into woodland. This then becomes a fenced grassy path over a field.

Towards the top, looking back there are superb views over Calstock and the Tamar Valley, with the prominent feature of Kit Hill to the left and the heights of Bodmin Moor in the background.

The path leads to a road. Bear right then at the crossroads at Broad Park Road go straight across (Drakes Park). At the end of this road turn left to arrive at the centre of Bere Alston.

Bere Alston has food and general shops, pub, café, bakery, grocer, chemist and toilets. There are buses to and from Bere Ferrers and Tavistock.

Bere Alston grew up in the time of Edward I as a mining settlement. Silver and lead mines were worked in the area from 1290 onwards and Bere Alston became their main

centre. In 1295 a market and fair were established and it became a parliamentary borough from 1584 to 1832, returning two members to Parliament, often with uncontested elections. Mining started earlier in this part of the Tamar Valley than elsewhere and concentrated originally on silver and lead. Silver mines were controlled by the Crown at that time. In the 19th century mining was joined by market gardening and flower growing, which by the latter part of the century had become more important than mining.

Opposite the parish hall is the former smithy (the Old Forge), which worked until the 1960s. The stack still exists. Nearby is 'The Tap', a piped spring in open stone housing, used as a public water supply until the 1950s.

For convenience, the route from Bere Alston to the station is described below:

From the centre of Bere Alston follow Station Road. Pass the war memorial and just after the grocers turn right along a residential road. At the crossroads at Broad Park Road continue straight across. Where this lane swings right continue ahead (initially slightly left) through two gates onto a fenced grassy path across a field.

Follow the path as it then descends through woodland and go ahead at the bottom on a track to a fork. Bear left here and follow on to the end. Bere Alston Station is on the right.

Stage 3K (Cornish Option)
St Mellion to Calstock

From St Mellion the route descends back to the Tamar then continues parallel to, and often close to, the river until it arrives at the historic and scenic National Trust property of Cotehele. A further lovely stretch close to the Tamar is then followed to Calstock, a picturesque old river port. At Calstock, Stage 3K joins the primary route (Stage 3), staying close to the river up to Gunnislake, where the Tamar's tidal limit is reached.

Distance:	6.1 miles /9.8km between St Mellion and Calstock
Total ascent:	740ft/225m
Estimated walking time (without stops):	2hr 50min
Car parks:	Halton Quay (limited), Cotehele (NT), Calstock, Gunnislake (centre – on Stage 3)
Public transport:	St Mellion (bus), Calstock (bus, train), Gunnislake (bus, train – on Stage 3)
Public transport & shorter options:	The start can be reached by bus from Saltash. There is no easy way to shorten this section as there are no buses to Saltash from Calstock – only a train to Plymouth. From Gunnislake on Stage 3 there is a train to Plymouth or a bus (changing at Callington) to St Mellion.

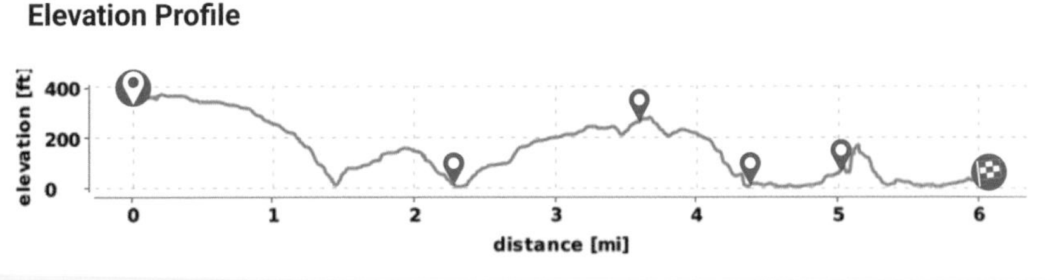

Start / 0m:	**St Mellion**	**5 miles:**	**Cotehele Chapel**
2.3 miles:	**Halton**	**End:**	**Calstock**
3.5 miles:	**Bohetherick**		
4.3 miles:	**Cotehele Quay**		

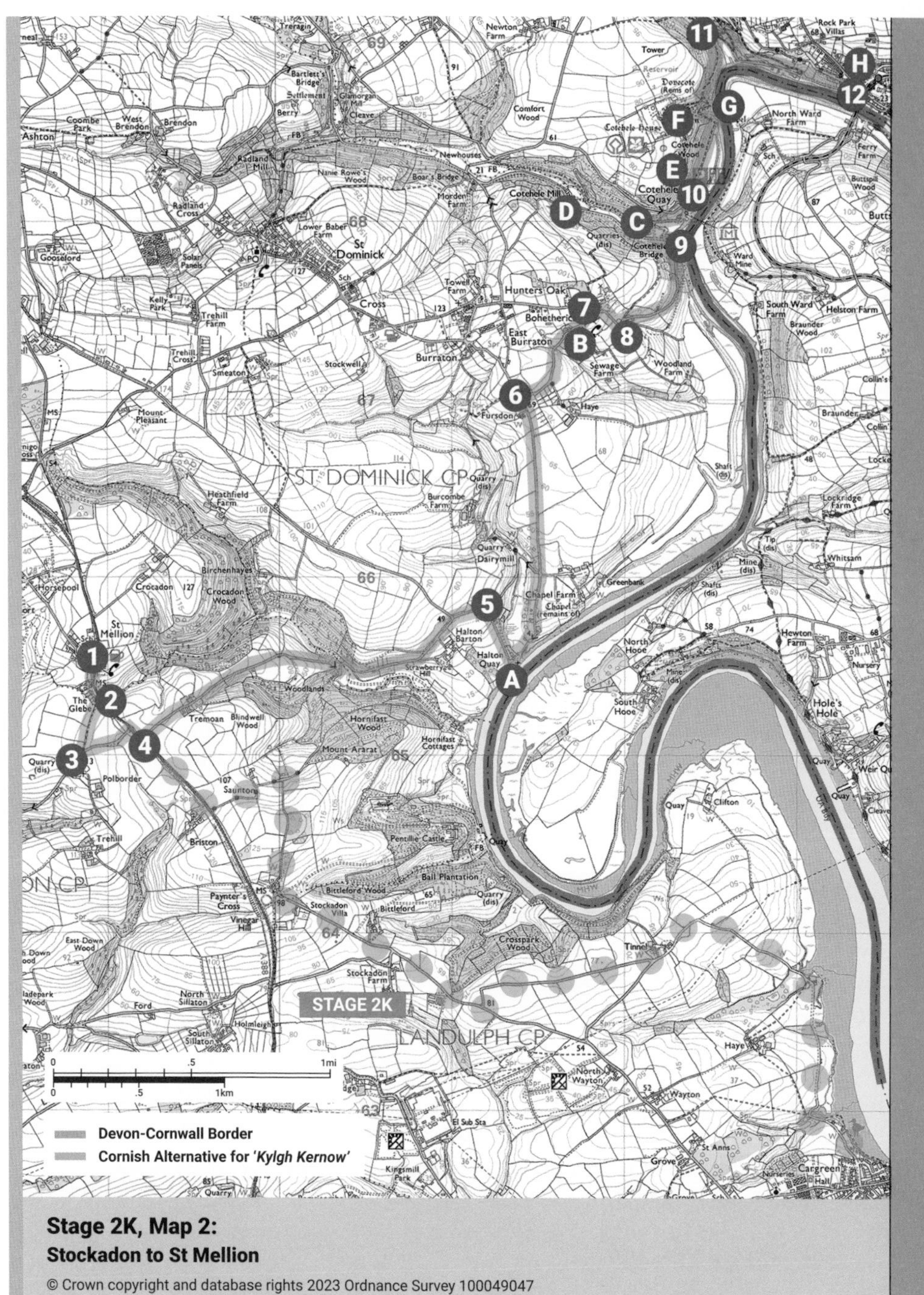

Stage 2K, Map 2:
Stockadon to St Mellion

Stage 3K starts in St Mellion, where the A388 passes through the village.

Using the school (1) as the starting point, walk along the pavement alongside the A388 in the Plymouth direction. After about 200yd, the pavement diverts onto a residential road. After passing the houses take the public footpath at the end (2), next to the A388. Go through a kissing-gate then ahead, next to the hedge on the right. Pass through a gate in the fence on the right onto a track. Keep ahead in the same direction on this sometimes wet track until it arrives at a road. Turn left here (3).

This is where Stage 2K arrives (from the right). Those going straight from Stage 2K to 3K (without visiting St Mellion) follow on from page 68 here.

The route soon arrives at the A388. At the roundabout use the central reservation to cross carefully to the verge on the other side. Turn right then immediately left down the lane signed 'Unsuitable for Long Vehicles' (4).

Walkers from Stage 2K who missed visiting St Mellion continue to follow directions from here.

The road soon begins to descend quite steadily towards the Tamar, joining one of the river's tributary valleys. A little after crossing the tributary stream the route passes a modern Celtic cross on the right. The private track alongside leads to Strawberry Hill, a reminder of the historic local horticultural industry.

When the road reaches a junction (5), bear right and ahead, signposted to Halton Quay. Carry on down to arrive at the Tamar at Halton Quay (A).

This was the traditional landing place in the 7th century of the Irish saint Dominica. She and her brother Indract also landed on what is now the Devon side of the Tamar, at a place recorded as Tamerunta, which may be Tamerton Foliot, now on the northern outskirts of Plymouth. Dominica founded a religious settlement near here at what is still called Chapel Farm (the entrance drive will be passed on the climb away from the quay but it is private). Her centre then moved to where the later church stands, in the nearby village still commemorating her name, **St Dominick**.

Halton Quay was important over the years as a local port. By the 19th century local produce, especially milk, agricultural goods and fruit, were being sent to Plymouth by

Halton Quay, St Indract's Chapel

steamer. There were a number of quay buildings, including the quay office. In 1959 this was consecrated as the chapel of St Indract, reviving the ancient tradition of the religious location. Services are held occasionally in the summer. There are remains of limekilns on the quay. Much of Devon and Cornwall has relatively poor soil, which needs the addition of a fertiliser to make it productive. The earliest use of lime as a fertiliser in this part of the country is uncertain, but kilns are first recorded here in 1411. The high cost of bringing in lime for burning meant a coastal or estuarine location was favoured for the kilns (see Stage 2, page 47).

The kilns here were last used in 1916, burning limestone brought up from Plymouth, or maybe Cremyll, where there was a quarry, for fertiliser for local use. The growing of soft fruit, in particular strawberries and cherries, had become an especially important activity by the 19th century.

The Tamar has now lost its estuarine character. Downstream it is seen to swing to the left, round a large promontory on the Devon side known as 'Hooe' (from the Old English for a high spur of land). Hooe marks the character change from estuary to the middle course of the river.

On the Cornish side can be seen **Pentillie Quay**, the quay for Pentillie Castle in the woods above.

Follow the road away from the quay on a long climb, passing the private entrance track to Chapel Farm on the right. Keep climbing to reach an unsignposted road going off to the right, just after the entrance to Fursdon Farm on the left (6). Turn right here, which then leads to the hamlet of Bohetherick (B).

First recorded as a settlement in 1402, **Bohetherick** ('Hydrek's dwelling' in Old Cornish) became part of the estate of the Edgcumbe family at Cotehele from Tudor times. The houses here were provided for workers on the estate. Bohetherick formerly had a shop and a pub, and also a butchers and associated slaughterhouse. It is now part of the National Trust estate, the Trust having acquired the Cotehele Estate in the 1940s.

Walk on through Bohetherick and at the junction at the far end (7) bear right, descending back towards the Tamar. After a series of bends take the track on the left just before the Gothic-looking Lodge House (8). After about 100yd this takes you along the top edge of a couple of fields with great views down the Tamar. After descending through woodland, at the junction turn right and follow the track downhill.

When you reach the road (9) take the path almost opposite which goes down past some well-preserved limekilns. Turn left after the kilns to return to the road. Take the first right, signposted Cotehele House, and cross Cotehele Bridge (C).

By the junction is a stone indicating 'Private Quay', probably erected by the Cotehele Estate in the 19th century. There is no sign of a quay here now and the stone may refer to Cotehele Quay ahead. **Cotehele Bridge** was built in the early 19th century, but to a 15th-century design. There was no bridge here at the time of the first edition of the OS map in 1809. It may be the old design was part of the Edgcumbes' deliberate policy of using early styles to accentuate their own old roots. Crossing Cotehele Bridge the route enters the **Cornwall and West Devon Mining Landscape World Heritage Site** (for more information see page 239). From here for some way up the valley the *Kylgh Kernow* option passes a range of mining heritage features, including old mines and associated buildings, miners' cottages and miners' smallholdings, inclined planes, railways and more.

On the far side of the bridge, to continue on the *Kylgh Kernow* option turn right. However, it is well worth considering visiting Cotehele Mill. To do this turn left on the path through the woods then fork left and over the footbridge across the stream. It is about 0.3 mile/0.5km from Cotehele Bridge to Cotehele Mill, and takes about 10 minutes to walk. (For opening times see www.nationaltrust.org.uk/cotehele).

Cotehele Mill (D) consists of an attractive range of 18th- and 19th-century buildings. Here there are craft workshops, a working mill with waterwheel and a small shop.

Return to Cotehele Bridge and follow the road to arrive at Cotehele Quay (E).

Cotehele Quay has a range of 18th- and 19th-century quay buildings, including a large three-storey warehouse and limekilns. There are barge docks, some with cranes, and a large boathouse. One barge dock has granite edgings and here is usually kept the *Shamrock*, the last of the Tamar barges, built in 1899 at Plymouth and at the time the most advanced ketch-rigged sailing barge in the world. Here also, unusually for this part of the world, may be found the maidenhair fern, generally found on limestone cliffs but which has found a suitable environment in the neighbourhood of the kilns.

Cotehele Quay has refreshments and toilets.

There are information boards around the quay and also the Discovery Centre. The centre contains fascinating models of the quay and the surroundings of Cotehele as they were in the 19th century, old maps and a history of the area, its trade and also information about the limekilns. It is well worth visiting, helping to explain the importance of the quay to Cotehele House and the general area in the 18th and 19th centuries.

There are several paths leading to Cotehele House from the *Kylgh Kernow* route, but for the original access drive, follow the road away from the quay then turn sharp right and back uphill past The Lodge. The diversion to Cotehele House (F) is about 0.3 mile/0.5km and will take about 10 minutes: it's all uphill, but well worth it.

Cotehele is usually regarded as the most important Tudor house in Cornwall. Picturesque both in its setting and its architecture, it came into the Edgcumbe family by marriage in 1353. (The Edgcumbes originated near Milton Abbot, on the primary route on the Devon side of the river further up the *Tamara Coast to Coast Way*.) It was retained in the same family until 1947 when it was passed to the National Trust. The present house largely dates from the 1450s and is relatively unaltered, because at an early date the Edgcumbes also acquired Mount Edgcumbe (which took its name from the family) at the mouth of the Tamar, and shifted their prime interest there. They also deliberately retained or copied old features here in order to demonstrate their own deep roots in the past. It is well worth spending some time here – some of its exterior highlights are the Gatehouse, Hall Court, the Great Hall, the Chapel and the North Gate, as well as a range of interiors. And all this in the setting of extensive gardens and parkland, including laid-out walks; there is also a restaurant.

Above the house is the **Prospect Tower**, a folly built in the late 1700s. One suggestion is that it was built to commemorate a visit by King George III in 1789, but this is not certain. There is a staircase inside the three-sided tower which is usually open to the public.

Cotehele House

It would be easy to spend the best part of a day at Cotehele, with its range of facilities and attractions – historic house, old quay, working mill, gardens and range of walks, plus shops, refreshments and restaurant, all in a superbly picturesque environment. *Kylgh Kernow* walkers might consider factoring in a stay in the area to do so (**www.nationaltrust.org.uk/cotehele**).

Back at the bottom, at the entrance to the car park (10), fork left up the footpath and then bear right onto the wide track.

It will be noticed that on the field on the right, between the track and the river, a breach has been created in the mid-19th-century embankment to allow controlled flooding. This improves the local wildlife habitats and should also help to alleviate flooding where it is not wanted, such as at Cotehele Quay and car park. The breach can be seen from a little way along the path. There are information boards alongside the track explaining this work, undertaken by the National Trust, Environment Agency and Natural England.

The path then climbs to arrive at the 'Chapel in the Woods' (G).

This was built in the 15th century by Cotehele's owner, Sir Richard Edgcumbe, as thanks for his life. During the Wars of the Roses as a Tudor supporter he was pursued through the woods by followers of Richard III. At this wooded headland overlooking the Tamar he threw a stone with his cap into the water. Hearing the splash and seeing the cap his pursuers assumed he had drowned and gave up the chase. The **chapel** was built as a thanksgiving at the headland after Richard had been defeated at the Battle of Bosworth.

Chapel in the Woods, Cotehele

Calstock from Cotehele viewpoint

The climb continues to a junction, with a track to Cotehele House going to the left. At the junction continue ahead, signposted to Calstock, keeping right at the fork immediately after. The path descends to a junction. Turn right here (11).

The valley to the left here is **Danescombe** (also spelt Danescoombe). The valley was the site of an early paper mill, at 1788 only the second in Cornwall. There was also a copper and arsenic mine, partly restored.

Popular theory has it that Danescombe got its name from the Vikings who fought with the Cornish at the Battle of Hingston Down against King Egbert and the Saxons in AD838. The Saxons won. The Vikings would have arrived and left via the Tamar and the valley of Danescombe is the obvious easy way to get to and from Hingston Down. Less romantically, it has been suggested that the first part of the name is from the Old English *denu*, meaning a valley. There is a mixture of English and Cornish names around here, so it is possible. A further suggestion is that its origin is *duna cumb* – valley in the downs. Take your pick – the Viking origin option is obviously the most romantic, but unfortunately not proven.

A little after turning right here the path becomes a surfaced lane.

Shortly on the left the lane passes **Danescombe Valley House**, an elegant building dating from the 1850s. Said to have been built as a fishing lodge, for most of the 20th century it operated as a small hotel, particularly catering for boat visitors coming up the Tamar from Plymouth. This was a popular excursion in Victorian and Edwardian times and, indeed, continues to the present day.

After Danescombe, Calstock is seen ahead, the railway viaduct prominent.

Calstock from Danescombe

As **Calstock** is neared the most prominent feature is the railway viaduct across the river (H). This was built 1904–7 to connect the London and South Western Railway's line at Bere Alston on the Devon side with the East Cornwall Mineral Railway, which ran from Callington and terminated at Calstock. The mineral line was converted to passenger use and continues today as the Tamar Valley branch line, although since

1966 it has terminated at Gunnislake. The viaduct is 120ft/37m above the river and 870ft/264m long and consists of 11,000 pre-cast concrete blocks, which were constructed on site on the Devon bank. It is reputed to be the oldest bridge in the country so built. For a while there was a vertical wagon lift on the side of the viaduct connecting to the quay.

A little further on the route passes a large limekiln and then goes underneath a bridge. The kiln burnt lime brought up the Tamar from Plymouth – there were limestone quarries on the edge of the city and also at Cremyll. The burnt lime was then distributed around the area by river and by the mineral railway connected to the river by the overbridge nearby. It was used until the early 20th century.

The overbridge carried an inclined plane which linked the original mineral railway, which ended above the town, to the riverside quays. This was a rope-worked inclined plane, the wagons counter-balancing each other as they were raised or lowered. The plane was 0.4 mile/0.6km in length with a gradient of 1 in 6/17% which raised and lowered trucks 350ft/106m. The inclined plane was superseded by the viaduct which stayed at high level and linked the old mineral line to the London and South Western Railway line at Bere Alston.

Inclined plane bridge, Calstock

Like much of the Tamar's banks in this part of the valley this area would originally have been wooded. The name of the lane, **Lower Kelly**, reflects this, 'Kelly' being the Cornish word for a wood. Over the years many boatyards were established along the riverside here, especially when the mineral railway was being used, and several still remain.

Continue ahead and after passing beneath the viaduct go forward, signposted to Village Centre and Quay, to the Tamar Inn. Turn right here to Calstock Quay (12).

At this point the *Kylgh Kernow* Stage 3K joins the primary route's Stage 3, which arrives here from Calstock Station. To continue north on the *Tamara Coast to Coast Way* see the Stage 3 description on page 83.

Stage 4
Gunnislake to Lifton

The first part of this stage stays close to the Tamar on the Cornish side, much of it through woodland. After crossing into Devon at Horsebridge there are superb views west over the Tamar Valley as far as Bodmin Moor, until Milton Abbot is passed. The final stretch passes through quiet, attractive and remote pastoral countryside, though often with relatively little sense of following the Tamar. Lifton is the end of the Tamar Valley Discovery Trail, so heading northwards the waymarking reverts to the Tamara Coast to Coast Way discs.

Distance: 13.5 miles/21.8 km between Gunnislake and Lifton.
Total ascent: 2,100 feet / 640 metres.
Estimated walking time (without stops): 6hrs 35min.
Car parks: Gunnislake centre, Luckett.

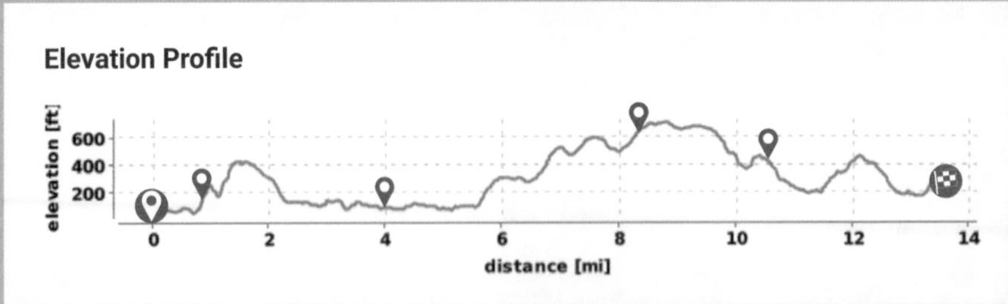

	Start / 0m:	**Gunnislake (New Bridge)**
	1.5 miles:	**Chillsworthy**
	4 miles:	**Luckett**
	8.5 miles:	**Milton Abbot**
	10.5miles:	**Kelly**
	End:	**Lifton**

Public transport & shorter options: Gunnislake is at the end of the Tamar Valley rail line to and from Plymouth: the station is 0.75 mile/1.25km uphill from the centre, a climb of some 330ft/100m. There is an hourly bus service to and from Callington and Tavistock (not Sundays). There is no public transport along the valley between Gunnislake and Launceston.

If you choose to join the Way from Tavistock there are buses once or twice a week to Luckett, Horsebridge, Milton Abbot and Lifton; walk south to Gunnislake to catch the bus back to Tavistock.

Link routes: Kit Hill Link to/from Luckett; loops north and south of Greystone Bridge (*Kylgh Kernow* Stage 4K and Greystone Link; Launceston Link to/from Lifton).

The T*amara Coast to Coast Way* bypasses Gunnislake. Stage 4 (and Stage 4K) starts at Gunnislake New Bridge, where the A390 crosses between Devon and Cornwall. Those walkers who have visited or arrived in Gunnislake should not walk down the main road to the bridge. Instead, from the centre of Gunnislake head along Under Road, which leaves the main road almost opposite the Buccaneer Inn, by the traffic lights. Take the second turning on the left (Tamar Way). Carry on to the end then onto a footpath ahead which descends to the riverside and the *Tamara Coast to Coast Way*. Turn left for Gunnislake New Bridge.

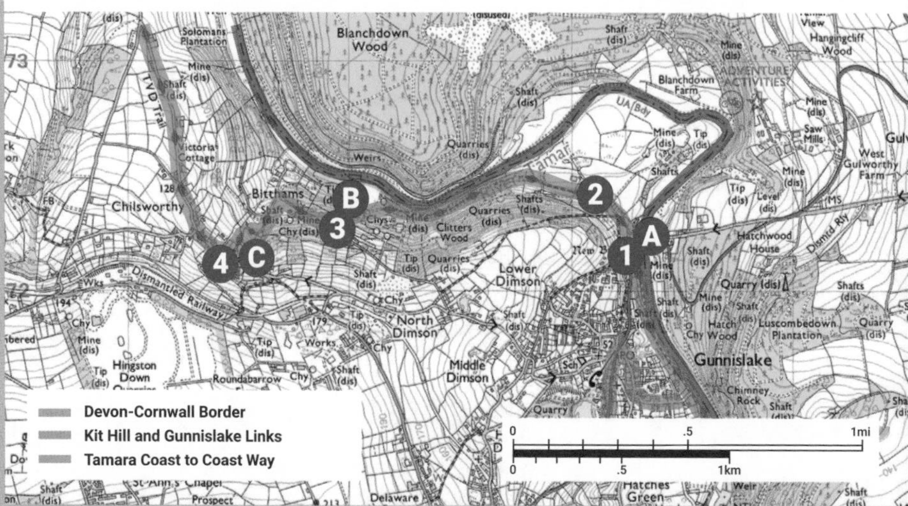

Stage 4, Map 1:
Gunnislake to Chilsworthy

Despite its name, **Gunnislake New Bridge** (A) is an old structure, and was built in 1520 by Sir Piers Edgcumbe of Cotehele House. It immediately became one of the principal routes into Cornwall and was the lowest bridging point of the Tamar until Brunel's railway bridge was built at Saltash in 1859. It remained the lowest road bridge until the current A38 Tamar Bridge was completed in 1962. It has often been regarded as the site of J.M.W. Turner's famous painting Crossing the Brook, painted in 1815 during a visit to Devon and Cornwall, although doubts about the exact location have been raised.

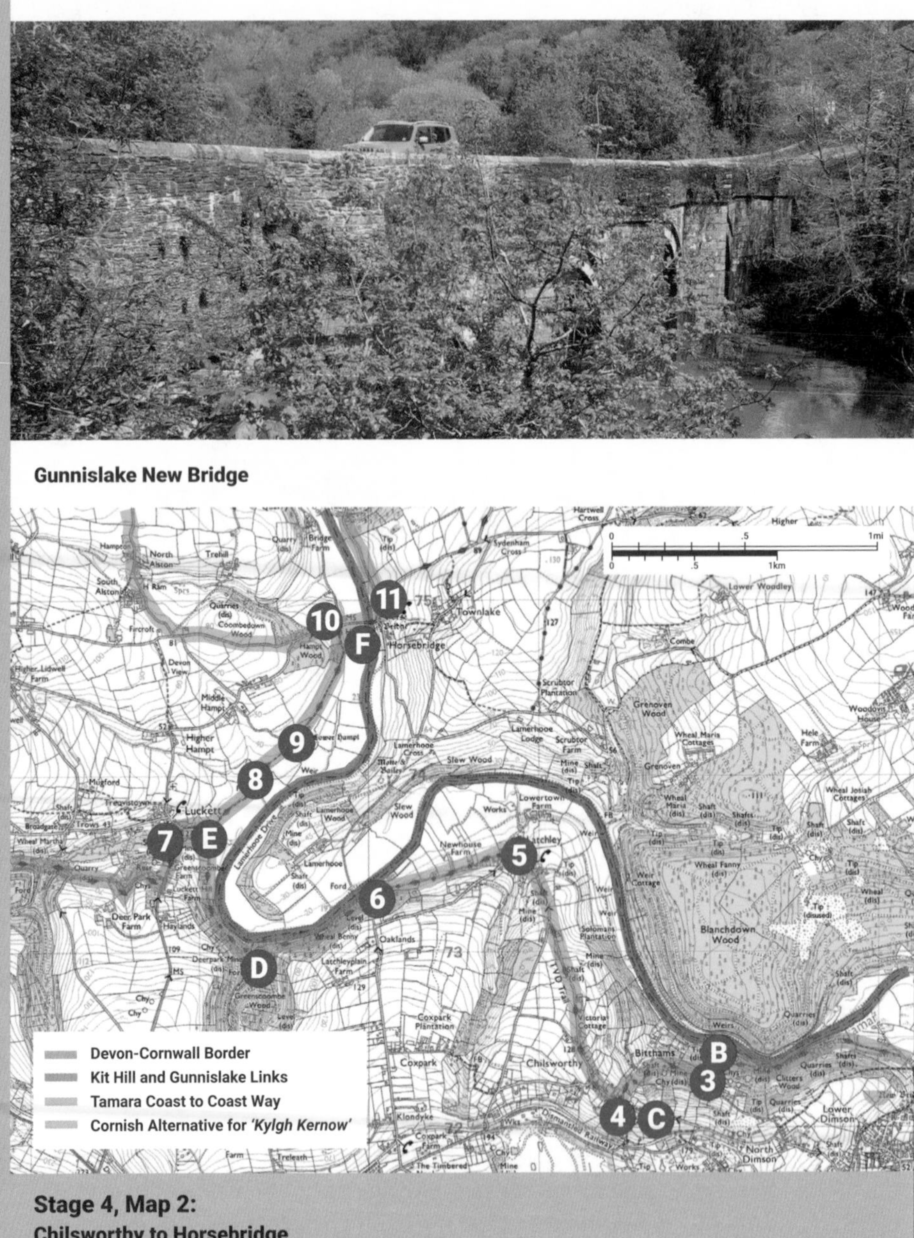

Gunnislake New Bridge

Stage 4, Map 2:
Chilsworthy to Horsebridge

The *Tamara Coast to Coast Way* heads north from the bridge (1) along the broad track with the river on the right. The track climbs to a junction of paths. Keep straight ahead here, then at the next junction (2) take the middle option, to the left of a shed. The path then runs alongside the Tamar, through an area of woodland.

This path is the line of a track which was used to take ore from Gunnislake Clitters Mine to the navigable waterway of the Tamar Navigation Canal, passed towards the end of Stage 3.

The path climbs through the woodland of Gunnislake Clitters.

These woods are the site of **Gunnislake Clitters Mine** (B). Mining took place between 1820 and 1827 and then between 1858 and 1909, with copper, arsenic and tungsten being extracted. The mine briefly reopened during World War I for the production of tungsten, and finally closed in 1920.

Remains of the mine can be seen through the trees, especially a chimney and a riverside pumping engine house. It is not recommended to leave the path to investigate because of the danger of old mine shafts, unstable buildings and contaminated spoil.

The path climbs steadily to reach a surfaced lane (3). Turn right, passing the entrance to Wheal Bramble.

This was one of the 19th-century mines in the area. The 'wheal' in its name comes from the Cornish word for a working but it was at one time, confusingly, called South Devon Mine.

Continue along the lane and at a junction go left, uphill, still on the tarmac lane, before continuing uphill past the 'Unsuitable for Motors' sign. This then becomes a steep and rocky path.

Old mine building, Gunnislake Clitters

Although in the 19th century this track gave access to a number of local mines, it is much older in origin, probably a medieval 'holloway' giving access to the Tamar and preceding the mining by several centuries.

Near the top the path joins a lane (4) which then climbs to the village of Chilsworthy.

This scattered village is first recorded in 1337 but grew substantially during the 19th century as mining became important in the area. Old mine chimneys can be seen above left as the *Tamara Coast to Coast Way* leaves the village.

Of particular interest to walkers on the Way will be the village's pub, the White Hart Inn (C) (www.whitehartchilsworthy.com). To reach it turn left for a couple of hundred metres; to continue on the Way return to the track/road junction and keep straight on.

The **White Hart** is first mentioned in the census of 1841 – it seems possible that it was established to serve the mining community. The building itself is probably older.

The White Hart Inn, Chilsworthy

Latchley

To continue on the *Tamara Coast to Coast Way* turn right at the road. Follow the road as it descends, increasingly steeply, to arrive at the little settlement of Latchley (5).

A church was built in this small settlement, and opened in 1883 by the Bishop of Truro. **Latchley** is within the large parish of Calstock, and the church is several miles away, so a local church was regarded as essential, especially as the population grew during the later 19th century. It could no longer be maintained by the mid-20th century, largely because of woodworm, and became disused in 1968. It was redeveloped as a private dwelling in 1985.

During the first half of the 20th century Latchley had its own station on the railway line between Plymouth and Callington, but as the station was about a mile away up a steep hill it was never very convenient. This part of the line closed in 1966.

There are no facilities for walkers in Latchley.

Go through the village then, where the road bears left, uphill, continue straight ahead on the lane next to Kearton Bank. Keep ahead at the next crossroads on the 'No Through Road'. This lane becomes a track into woodland and arrives at a junction (6). Fork left here.

The fork on the right leads to an old ford over the Tamar, referred to as **Lamerhooe** or **Latchley Ford**. Although consistently marked on old maps it is now only rarely usable, and attempting to cross the river here is strongly discouraged. It seems never to have been a major crossing, but remains have been found on the Devon side which are presumed to be of a small watch tower constructed during Norman times as a defensive site on the Devon–Cornwall border.

Site of Lamerhooe/Latchley Ford

From the left fork the path passes through the Duchy of Cornwall's Greenscoombe Wood, parallel to and above the Tamar.

Greenscoombe Wood (D) is a Site of Special Scientific Interest. It comprises broad-leaved woodland, including some which is semi-natural, with areas of dry heath, all on the flanks of the River Tamar.

It is especially notable for its butterflies, with over 20 species being noted, including the very rare heath fritillary – one of only four UK sites where this has been recorded. Birdlife includes woodpeckers, willow warblers, nuthatches and long-tailed tits, and there are several species of orchid. Part of the area was once used as a market garden and old cultivated strawberry plants also occur.

Keep on the track to a fork; bear right here, downhill, then keep ahead to cross two Tamar tributaries, the first at a stone bench. The track then leaves Greenscoombe Wood and becomes a lane which leads to the picturesque little village of Luckett.

Luckett (E) is not recorded by name until 1557 but it is known to be an ancient possession of the Duchy of Cornwall. Mining began here in the mid-1700s at what was known at various times as New Consols Mine and Great Wheal Martha. Tin and arsenic were worked and in 1876 the village was described as 'seen to be filled with buildings, tramways and inclines', a far cry from the quiet and pleasant rural retreat of today. Mining finally ended in 1952.

There are no facilities for walkers at Luckett other than a bench and a car park, which might be useful if planning short walks or a circuit. There's still over 9 miles/14.5km to Lifton (or Launceston), but if tempted by a bus from Luckett (to Horsebridge, Tavistock and Gunnislake) careful planning is needed, as buses only serve the village one day a week (Friday), and only twice on that day.

Former miners' cottages, Luckett

At Luckett the Kit Hill Link leaves or joins the *Tamara Coast to Coast Way*. An earlier link to Kit Hill (from Gunnislake) was passed at the end of Stage 3 (page 91), and the two links provide an option for a long circular walk. For details of the link between Luckett and Kit Hill see page 131.

Arriving in Luckett (7) turn right, over the bridge, then right again along the track immediately afterwards. Go into the field at the end and continue alongside the fence.

On leaving Luckett the *Tamara Coast to Coast Way* also leaves the Cornwall and West Devon Mining Landscape World Heritage Site (see page 239). The designation covers ten distinct areas, one of which is the Tamar Valley, which walkers on the Way entered at Weir Quay (primary route) or Cotehele (*Kylgh Kernow* route.) From here on visible evidence of the area's mining heritage all but disappears.

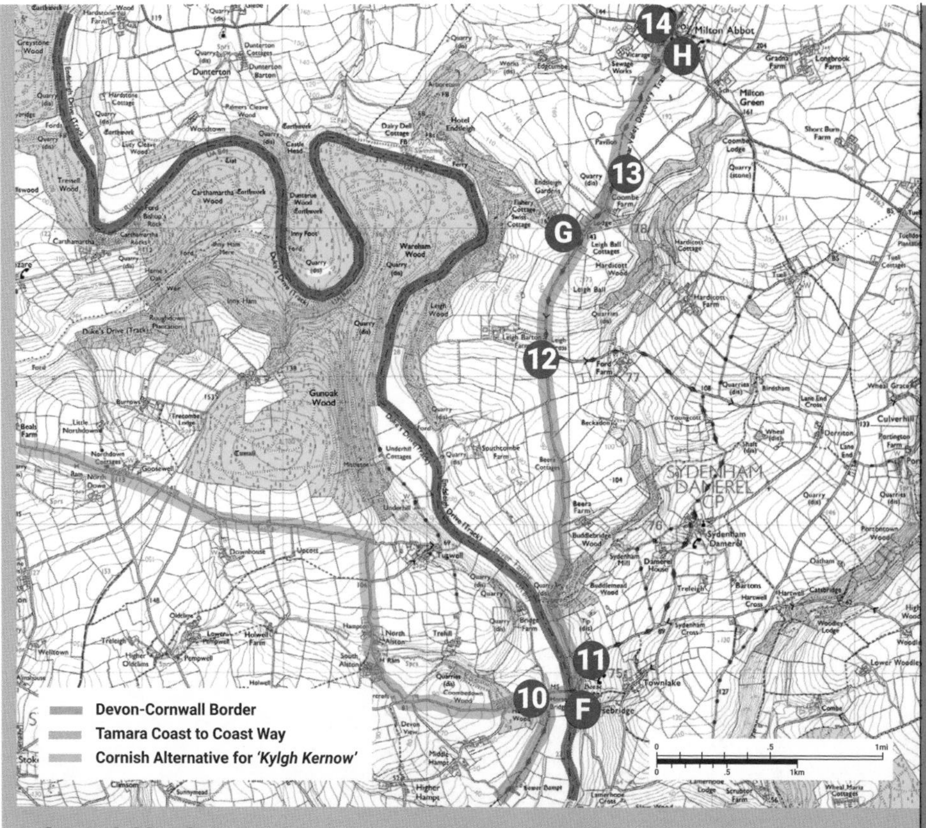

Stage 4, Map 3:
Luckett to Milton Abbot

Cross the stile at the end of the field (8) and follow the at times wet footpath round to the right and then on, next to a hedge on the right to a surfaced track (9). Bear right then ahead, passing the farmstead at Lower Hampt.

Little is visible of this farmstead from the Way, and it is on private land so cannot be visited, but it is of considerable historic interest, being 16th century in origin and based on a long hall.

Continue on the track, parallel to the Tamar, to arrive at a kissing-gate onto a road. For the primary route (Stage 4) turn right here (10).

The *Kylgh Kernow* alternative to Launceston (Stage 4K) leaves the primary *Tamara Coast to Coast Way* here (see page 136).

Cross the Tamar into Devon at Horsebridge.

A little way before the bridge note the granite stone on the right, carved with a faint letter 'C'. From the 16th century certain bridges were deemed to be of such importance that their maintenance was governed by the county court. Usually the county also took over responsibility for a length of the approach roads to such a bridge, normally 100yd/95m. In the 19th century stones were erected at these limits marked with a 'C', for 'county', and then maintained by the county council. Most of these stones have now been lost but some, as here at Horsebridge, survive.

County bridge stone, Horsebridge

River Tamar, Horsebridge

Cross the river and turn left, past the Royal Inn.

Horse Bridge (F) is the oldest bridge across the Tamar. It was built in 1437 with contributions from Tavistock Abbey, who owned large areas of land in the area. It was an 'indulgence bridge', the Abbot granting indulgences to penitents who contributed to the cost. This meant they would spend less time in purgatory following death (a considerable attraction to the medieval sinner). It is almost

Horse Bridge

identical in design to Greystone Bridge a little upriver; it was built just two years earlier, probably by the same builder. It is first documented under the name *Hautesbrygge*, so may have no connection with horses but rather derive from a medieval personal name – one of the sinners, perhaps? There are notches cut into the underside which may be part of a salmon weir connected with Tavistock Abbey's fishery. (Strictly speaking Horse Bridge is the bridge itself and Horsebridge the settlement, but the one-word version tends to be used for the structure as well.)

The **Royal Inn** was built in the early 19th century presumably because of its position next to the Tamar crossing point (www.royalinn.co.uk). On the opposite side of the road is a stone and brick shelter housing a cast-iron hand pump and granite trough, probably also 19th century.

Horsebridge has a pub and very occasional buses, Fridays only, linking to Gunnislake, Luckett and Tavistock.

Immediately after passing the Royal Inn (11) bear left, signposted to Beera and Leigh. There follows a steady climb away from the Tamar while, initially, staying parallel to it. Pass Beera Cottages and keep ahead at the junction at Leigh Cross (12). A stiff climb follows.

Looking back, Kit Hill and its attendant Hingston Down (see Stage 3K, page 101) is very prominent on the skyline.

To the left the extensively wooded sides of the Tamar Valley can be seen. Although the river is not in sight, the Tamar here undertakes a series of meanders in a deep-sided valley with, on both sides, early earthworks. It has been suggested that these may indicate the Tamar was a very early boundary, at least in this stretch. However, it is more likely they were there to defend against invaders coming up the Tamar. The Roman geographer Ptolemy's work *Geographica* is a description of the Roman Empire c. AD140 and includes a section on Britain. The southwest is indicated as being inhabited by the *Dumnonii*, one of whose 'cities' is Tamara, which as it is mapped as being inland could well be one of these Tamar forts. That on the Cornish side is called Carthamartha, which has been explained as being derived from the Cornish Ker Tamar, the fort on the Tamar.

A little further on the route passes Leigh Ball Cottages on the right and Endsleigh Lodge on the left.

The *Tamara Coast to Coast Way* now passes the grounds of **Endsleigh** (G). In 1810 the 6th Duke of Bedford built a 'cottage' to use as a base for the family when they were visiting their extensive lands in Devon and Cornwall. These were obtained when they acquired Tavistock Abbey lands following Henry VIII's dissolution of the monasteries and subsequent sell-off. A rather grander house than the name 'cottage' implies, Endsleigh was designed by the eminent 19th-century architect Jeffry Wyatt, later knighted as Sir Jeffry Wyatville. The gardens were laid out by the eminent garden designer Humphrey Repton and are listed in the English Heritage Register of Historic Gardens. The house is not visible from the Way but the gardens are open to the public at certain times (www.hotelendsleigh.com/garden). Alongside the road are various lodges for the Endsleigh grounds, some early 19th century and some early 20th century. Leigh Ball Cottages are estate cottages built in 1910.

At the top of another climb, by a right-hand bend (13), go through the right-hand of two gates on the left and cross the field diagonally to a wooden gate in the far hedge (to the left of the larger and more obvious metal gate). Go through and ahead alongside the hedge on the left, towards the village of Milton Abbot.

On the southern edge of **Milton Abbot** the Way leaves the Tamar Valley AONB, which it entered on leaving Plymouth. The *Tamara Coast to Coast Way's* landscape continues to be extremely attractive from here onward, although without national recognition, until it reaches the hinterland of the north coast where it enters the Cornwall and North Devon AONBs.

Approaching Milton Abbot from the south

Old Vicarage, Milton Abbot

Go through the gate in the bottom corner and follow the hedged path to arrive at a lane, then continue ahead uphill. At the Old Vicarage on the left either continue straight ahead or fork left – both routes lead to the B3362 Tavistock–Launceston road through Milton Abbot (14).

The 'Abbot' part of the village's name derives from the fact that the manor was part of the original endowment to Tavistock Abbey in Saxon times, c. AD974. At Henry VIII's dissolution the abbey estates were granted to the Russell family, later Dukes of Bedford.

Milton Abbot (H) is very unusual in Devon and Cornwall in being a village whose centre was comprehensively planned and rebuilt. In 1909 the 7th Duke of Bedford commissioned designs by the renowned architect Sir Edwin Lutyens. Today, many houses and cottages, and even the public shelter, are the work of Lutyens in his 'arts and crafts' style. It is remarkable that a small village near the Devon–Cornwall border is endowed with so much work by the architect responsible for the design of New Delhi, for the Cenotaph in Whitehall, for Lindisfarne Castle and, on the edge of Dartmoor, Castle Drogo. Lutyens' buildings are found in both the roads on either side of the church, Venn Hill (straight ahead) and The Parade (to the left), and also on the B3362 road (Fore Street).

However, the first major building encountered, the **Old Vicarage**, was not designed by Lutyens but is rather older. It has a datestone of 1837 and was designed by Edward Blore, a Victorian architect and architectural artist and draughtsman. He was involved in work at Buckingham Palace and St James's Palace. He was especially interested in Scottish baronial architecture, which may have influenced his design of the Vicarage, although it is said that his designs were supervised and modified by the Duke of Bedford.

Because of the Lutyens connection, unusually the church is perhaps not the main item of architectural interest. Milton Abbot church is mainly 15th century, as are many local churches, but much restored in the 19th century. It has an inner doorway which probably dates back to the 14th century. It also includes several family memorials to the Edgcumbes. This family originated at the farmstead of Edgcumbe nearby, but prospered and became major landowners in the lower part of the Tamar Valley (Mount Edgcumbe and Cotehele).

Milton Abbot has a pub – the Edgecumbe Arms (mirroring the name of the pub at the start of the Way at Cremyll) – phone (01822) 870603. There is no village shop. There are occasional buses to and from Launceston, Tavistock and Lifton; check carefully beforehand as buses run on certain days of the week only.

Lutyens buildings, Fore Street, Milton Abbot

Cross the main road (14) and follow the public footpath alongside the Edgcumbe Arms, up the track and then next to the field. At the top go ahead in the next field to the gate in the top right-hand corner, then go diagonally left over the following field to stiles in the top left-hand corner. Then turn left alongside the hedge, through a gateway and on to reach a road (15). Turn left here, passing an unusual 'corrugated' house.

Just after this house, off the Way to the right but just visible, is Kelly Lodge. Built in the 19th century, this was a lodge at one of the entrances to the Kelly estate, which will be passed a little further on.

Keep ahead on the lane, heading now for the prominent clump of trees.

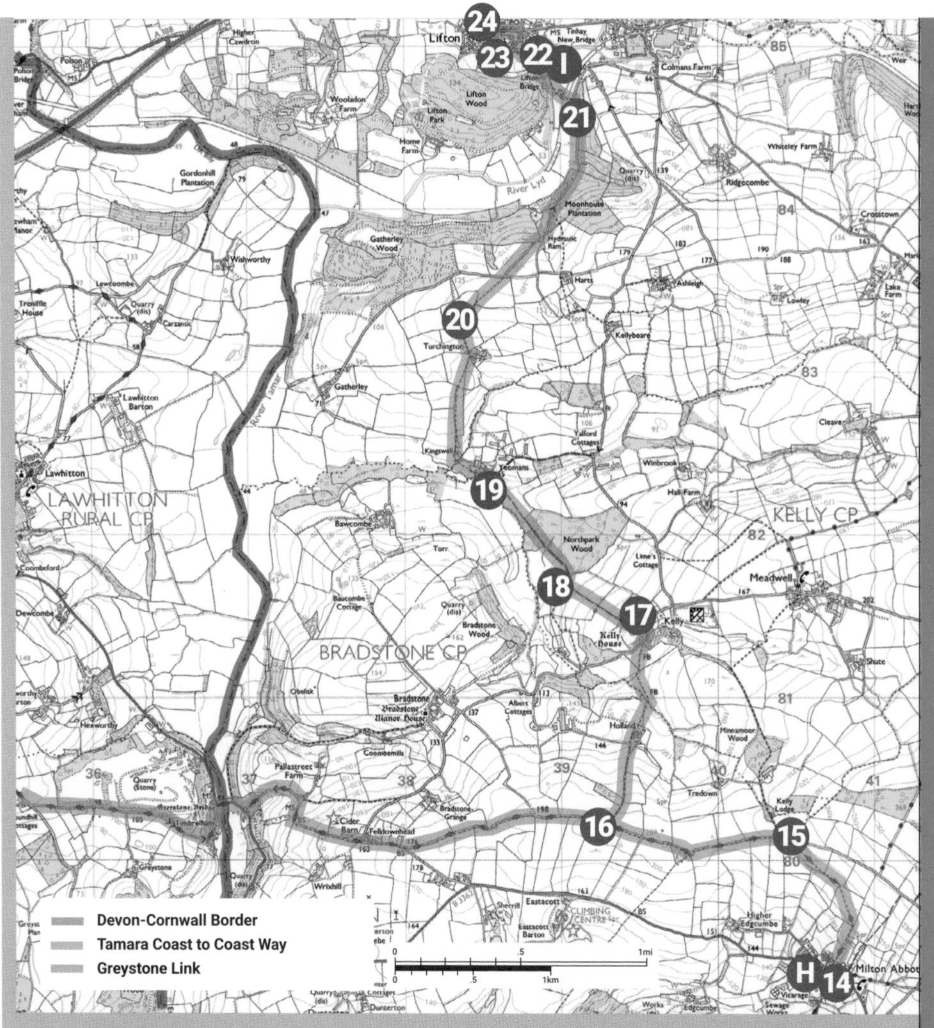

Stage 4, Map 4:
Milton Abbot to Lifton

Along here there are more distant views back to Kit Hill and the Tamar's wooded slopes. There are also excellent views to the eastern side of Bodmin Moor, including Caradon Hill with its mast and the high points of Brown Willy (the highest point in Cornwall) and Rough Tor.

Continue along the road, passing the clump of trees, then after about 0.25 mile/0.4km look out for the public footpath on the right on the drive to Holland (16).

From here the Greystone Link, between the primary *Tamara Coast to Coast Way* and the parallel *Kylgh Kernow* alternative on the Cornish side of the river, creates the possibility of circular loops (see page 132).

The Greystone Link leaves or joins the primary *Tamara Coast to Coast Way* here, via the road ahead.

To continue on the *Tamara Coast to Coast Way*, turn right and go down the track, keeping straight ahead where it forks.

The track bypasses the farmstead of **Holland** which is on the right. Holland is an old settlement, recorded as early as 1281, with an Old English name meaning 'the farm in the hollow'. The current farmhouse dates from the late 16th century, with more recent additions. Ahead can be seen the church and buildings at Kelly.

At the bottom go ahead to a metal kissing-gate, then right on a track and through the smaller metal gate on the left at the end. Follow the fence down to a footbridge over a Tamar tributary stream. Cross and go left in the next field parallel to the stream, bearing away slightly right to a stile. Follow the stream to the right to yet another stile, then bear left over the field to a gap and up to a stile onto a road. Turn right here to arrive at Kelly.

Unusually, **Kelly** is a name of Celtic or Cornish origin on the east side of the Tamar, where most names are Saxon, meaning 'wood' or 'grove'.

On the left of the road here is a range of interesting and historic buildings. First is the church, built c. 1250 by the Kelly family of the adjacent manor house; the church was much added to in the 15th century and restored in 1760. Although a parish church it is regarded as a 'manor church', there being no village here.

Next to the church is Kelly House. The current house is Tudor in origin, although much remodelled in the 18th century. The family, descended from the Norman Motbert who is recorded as owning the estate at the time of the Domesday Book in 1086, took on the name of Kelly from the location at the time of Henry II, and remains here today.

Kelly House

Kelly House, stables

A little beyond Kelly House and the stables is a granary and dovecote mounted on staddle stones. Both the stables and the granary date from the 18th century, at the time of the rebuilding of the house. The whole location is very atmospheric, and has been described as 'having escaped the passage of time'.

Leave the road on the left immediately after the granary and 'Kelly House' sign on a signed public bridleway (17), following the track until it ends at a fork. Bear right, through the gate and downhill next to the hedge.

Launceston can now be seen on the far hillside ahead.

After passing through the second gate (18) turn right – not through the other gate, but keeping alongside the hedge on the right. Follow this path through a gate round to the left and on a path, sometimes muddy in places, first alongside then through woodland. Do not divert off into either the fields or the main body of woodland.

Go through the gate at the end alongside the fence and then straight across the field to a gate (19). Cross the stream then, just before the track climbs to a farmyard, go left on a narrow path through scrub on a signed public footpath. Bear left through an orchard to a stile at the far end then diagonally right across the field to a gate almost hidden in the corner. Go through and follow the fence up to the right.

The ruined building on the right here is **Kingswell**. Lifton was a royal estate in Saxon times and this name may well date from then. The stream here, a minor tributary of the Tamar, is the Lifton parish boundary, probably the edge of the royal estate.

Arriving at two gates go through the one on the right and follow the hedge up on the left through a metal gate. At the top bear diagonally right ahead to the fence line and through the gate ahead onto a concrete track.

At the top of the first field go through the gate on the right (20). Cross the field diagonally to a stile in the opposite hedge, then diagonally over the next field to a gate to a road near the far corner. At the road go straight ahead and descend into the valley of the River Lyd.

Launceston is visible to the left on the descent, the distinctive shape of its castle on the skyline to the right of the town very clear.

The **River Lyd** rises on the northwest side of Dartmoor. After being joined by another Dartmoor river, the Lew, it arrives at Lifton to be further joined by two more rivers flowing from the western edge of Dartmoor, the Wolf and the Thrushel. The combined river is one of the largest of the Tamar's Devon tributaries.

Reaching the valley floor, turn left along the public footpath at Leat Mill and Penleat House (21).

Immediately after starting on the drive it crosses the line of an old railway, now only evidenced by a bridge which carried a road over the railway away to the right. The railway was the GWR line between Plymouth and Launceston, which opened in 1865 and closed in 1962.

The existence of the railway was important in establishing the Ambrosia dairy in Lifton in 1917. Drawing on local dairy farms and using the railway for speedy transport it became, and remains, an important part of the local economy by the old station site a little to the east of the village.

Continue along the drive and then alongside the River Lyd to the road at Lifton Bridge.

Lifton Bridge (I) is probably 17th century, but built on earlier origins. It was rebuilt in the 19th century and carried traffic on what was once the important road between Tavistock and Lifton, and thence to Launceston.

Lifton Bridge

Turn left over the bridge.

On the left just immediately after the bridge is the entrance to **Lifton Park**. A mansion was built here in 1815 for William Arundel, a local landowner, but this was largely destroyed in World War II. Next to the entrance is one of the Victorian lodges.

Continue up the road and a little way up the hill a flight of steps on the left leads to a public footpath (22). Follow this and when you reach the road, continue straight ahead and after about 50yd turn right into the grounds of the church of St Mary (23).

The church, mainly 15th century, is the largest in this part of Devon and its tower is very prominent. Inside, there is a Norman font, some 16th-century bench ends and monuments to local worthies of the 16th and 17th centuries. The bench by the lychgate may be welcome at this point.

Leave by the lychgate on the far side and descend to arrive at the main road through Lifton.

The lane passes the end of Broad Street – not very broad by modern standards, but once an important and prestigious thoroughfare.

Lifton (24) was an early Saxon settlement, regarded as of military importance because of its proximity to the Tamar and potentially unreliable Cornwall, and, even at that early date, on the main road to Cornwall. King Athelstan held his court here in AD931 – an important occasion attended not only by West Saxon nobles but also leaders of the Danes of eastern England and the kings of South Wales and Gwynedd, and probably Cornish leaders. Probably because of its strategic location Lifton was an important royal estate; it is mentioned in King Alfred's will of the late 9th century, where it was bequeathed to Aethelweard, his youngest son. Its royal ownership lasted until it was disposed of by Elizabeth I.

Today the most notable buildings are the church and the Arundell Arms Hotel, a former coaching inn around 250–300 years old. The Courthouse Bar was Lifton's magistrates court until 1900, and behind the hotel is a cockpit.

Into the 20th century the road through Lifton remained the main road into Cornwall, becoming the A30. It reverted to local use when the modern A30 was built in the 1970s.

Lifton has a post office and shop as well as the Arundell Arms Hotel (www.thearundell.com) and the Lifton Hall Hotel (www.liftonhall.co.uk). A little further on the Way (Stage 5) is Strawberry Fields Farm Shop and Restaurant (www.strawberryfieldslifton.co.uk). Lifton has a bus service to Launceston and Okehampton and thence on to Exeter.

Accommodation and other facilities are much more plentiful in Launceston than Lifton, and walkers may consider continuing for a little way on Stage 5 before taking the Launceston Link and returning here to the primary route the following day (see pages 152 and 153). From Lifton to Launceston is a further 5 miles/8km. A bus service links Lifton and Launceston.

Kit Hill Link

The Kit Hill Link (*Kevren bys Bre Skowl*) is a worthwhile detour from the main route to the amazing viewpoint on the summit, seen from much of the southern half of the *Tamara Coast to Coast Way*. This can be done either as a there-and-back route from Gunnislake (described below), or from Luckett (see page 131), or (as also described below) by leaving the main route at Gunnislake and re-joining it at Luckett. The final option is to combine both routes into a 13.1 miles/21.1km circular walk.

Distance:	8.7 miles/14km between Gunnislake and Luckett (c. 5 miles/8km Gunnislake to Kit Hill; c. 4 miles Kit Hill to Luckett)
Total ascent:	1330ft/405m
Estimated walking time (without stops):	4hr 10min

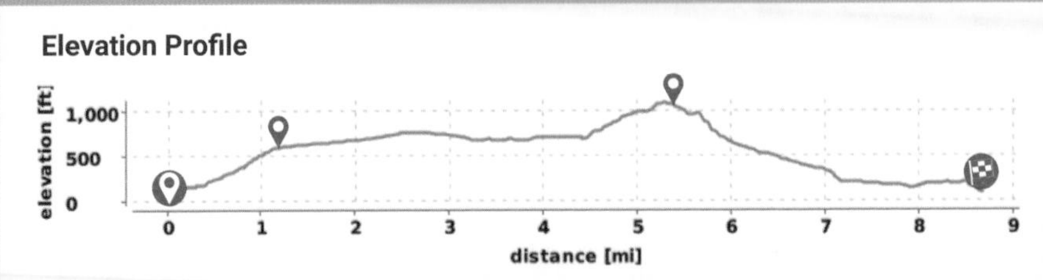

Start / 0m:	**Gunnislake**
1.2 miles:	**Gunnislake Station**
5.5 miles:	**Kit Hill**
End:	**Luckett**

The route starts in the centre of Gunnislake. (For access to the village from the *Tamara Coast to Coast Way* see the end of Stage 3, page 90).

Follow the main A390 road uphill out of Gunnislake (1). Keep on the right-hand side of the road.

A little way up the hill from the village centre there is a **toll house** on the left (A), featuring windows with a view up and down the road so that the keepers could see all coming traffic.

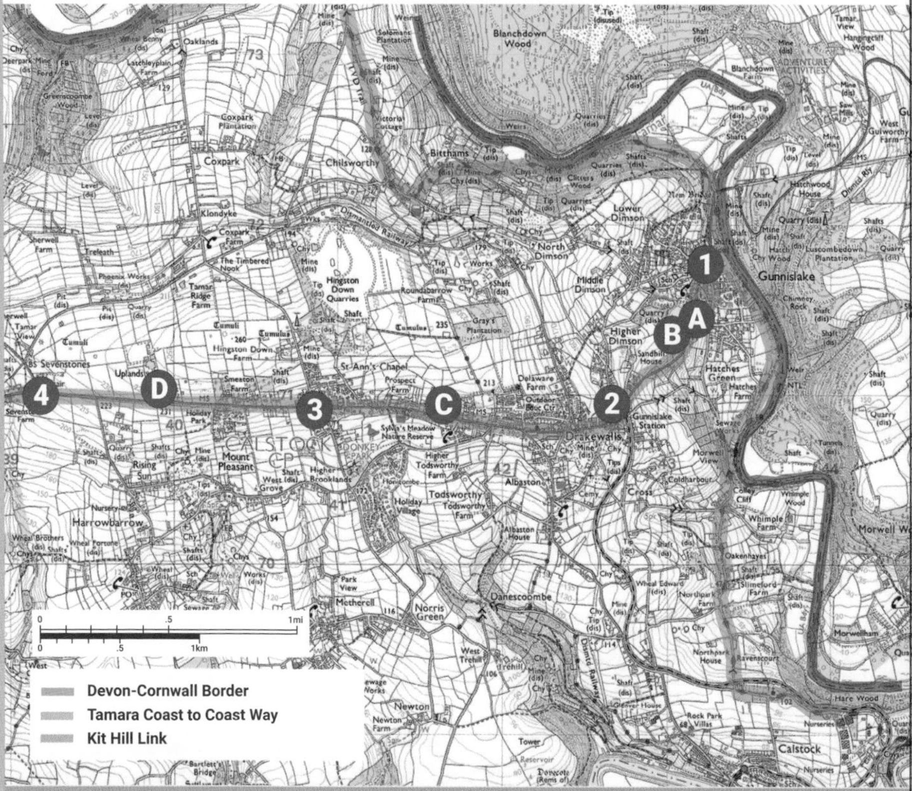

Gunnislake Toll House

Devon-Cornwall Border
Tamara Coast to Coast Way
Kit Hill Link

Kit Hill Link, Map 1:
Gunnislake to Sevenstones

The toll house was erected by the Callington Turnpike Trust, set up in 1764 to maintain the main roads to that town and provide signing. As now, this was the main road between Callington and Tavistock. The house dates from the late 18th or early 19th century.

On the way up the hill, opposite Kingswood House, there is a **milestone** erected by the Callington Turnpike Trust (B). It reads C4 T7½, meaning 4 miles to Callington and 7½ to Tavistock.

There follows a steady climb. Towards the top of perhaps the steepest part of the hill, Gunnislake railway station (2) is passed on the left.

This railway began its existence as the **East Cornwall Mineral Railway**, built in the 19th century between Calstock and Callington, passing through Gunnislake on the way. This brought in coal for the mine steam engines and took out ore via the quay at Calstock. In 1908, after mining had ceased, it was adapted to standard gauge and linked to the London and South Western main line between London Waterloo and Plymouth beyond Calstock.

In 1966 the line beyond Gunnislake to Callington was closed. In 1966 the main line to Waterloo was also closed but the branch line between Gunnislake and Plymouth was retained, probably because of the poor north–south road communications in the Tamar Valley.

Near the station, on the left-hand side of the road, is another milestone. This one reads Liskeard 13 and Bodmin 26. It is much later than the Turnpike Trust milestone seen earlier, erected after the county council had taken over responsibility for the main roads in the later 19th century.

Continue alongside the A390, to pass through the settlement of St Ann's Chapel.

Approaching St Ann's Chapel (and also after leaving it, later), see the excellent views to the left down the Tamar Estuary.

St Ann's Chapel (C) is a relatively new settlement, there being nothing here until the mining boom of the 19th century. On the way through, the route passes a housing development given the name 'Turnpike', a reference to its location on the historic road route.

A little way further on the route passes a pub, the **Rifle Volunteer** (**www.riflevolunteer.com**). This is said to have originally been a mine captain's house, converted to a coaching inn on the turnpike during the 19th century.

At the far end of St Ann's Chapel (3) cross to the footway on the left-hand side of the road, crossing back to the right-hand side at the holiday park to the footway and cycleway.

Almost immediately after crossing the road there is another Turnpike Trust milestone on the verge, this one C3 T6½ (Callington 3 miles, Tavistock 6½).

On the right a little further on is the '**Pleasure Piece**' (D), one of the last remnants of the open heathland of Hingston Down, which once stretched all the way between Gunnislake and Kit Hill. It has been used since Victorian times for picnics and outings, especially in the 19th century by the local mining community. It is still valued locally, with a circular walk maintained around it.

A little further on, also on the right, is a series of rectangular fields. In the 19th century these were miners' smallholdings, taken out of the heathland of Hingston Down.

It is areas such as the picnic site and the smallholdings that are regarded as important as part of the Mining World Heritage Site as well as the more obvious and impressive building remains.

Cross the B3257 Launceston road (4) and continue along the cycleway.

To the right just after the junction is the site of **East Kit Hill Mine**. This operated for a relatively short time in the mid-19th century producing tin, arsenic and copper. Further along here, on the verge between the cycle track and the road, is yet another milestone, reading C2 T7½ – 2 miles to Callington, 7½ to Tavistock.

At the next junction (5) leave the footpath and cycleway and turn right, signposted to Kit Hill.

On the right is an unusual **direction stone**, to Tavistock and Horsebridge. The

Turnpike Trust maintained the road to and from Horsebridge to ensure Devon traffic crossing the Tamar at what was then an important crossing point came into Callington.

Direction stone, A390 junction

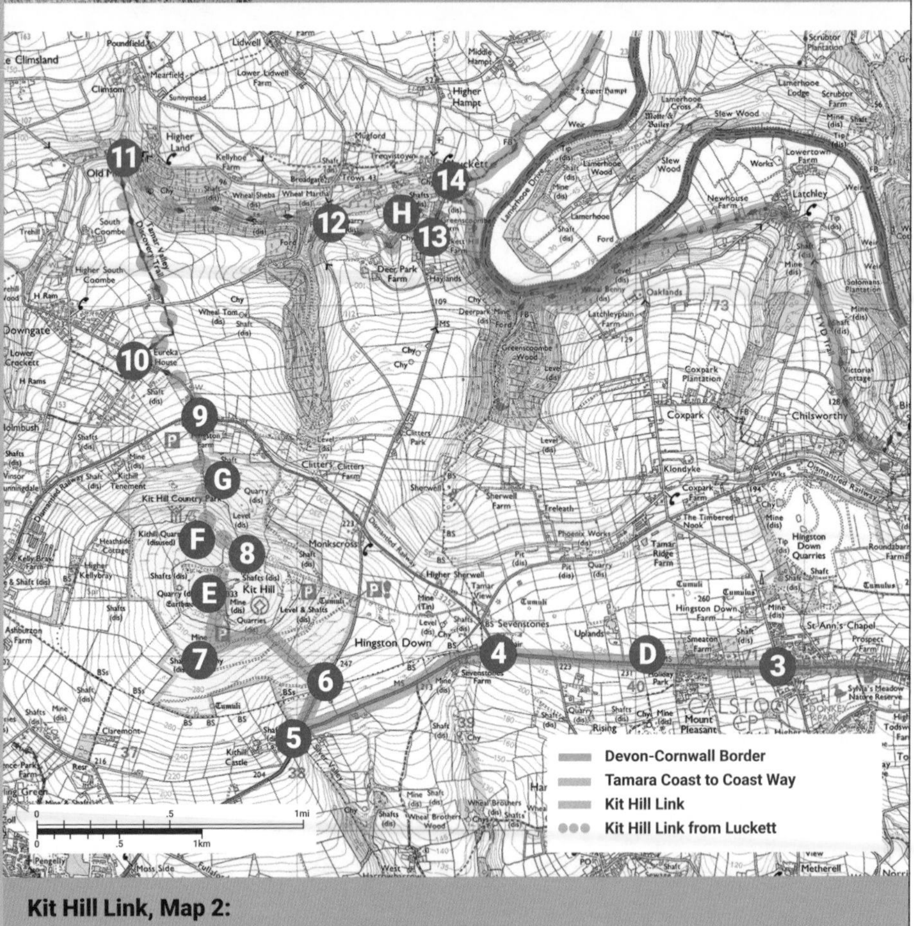

- Devon-Cornwall Border
- Tamara Coast to Coast Way
- Kit Hill Link
- Kit Hill Link from Luckett

Kit Hill Link, Map 2:
St Ann's Chapel to Kit Hill (and on to Luckett)

Be aware of local traffic on this more minor road. A little way up is Louis Tea Rooms and farm shop (www.louistearooms.co.uk) (6). Go through the gate on the left opposite and walk up the grassy path half-right ahead, aiming for the chimney on the summit. Keep climbing, crossing a track at a crossing of paths. Just beyond, reach another cross track with a gate opposite to a bench. Turn left on this track, at a granite waymark stone with a depiction of the chimney.

Follow this track as it climbs gently. As the track begins to descend turn off, sharp back right by another granite waymark stone (7) and climb the path heading for the chimney on the summit. Go through a gate and continue climbing to the top (E).

This is all part of **Kit Hill Country Park**, given to the people of Cornwall by the then Prince Charles, Duke of Cornwall, to celebrate the birth of Prince William in 1982. The climb from the road has been across Hingston Down, the almost whale-back shaped hill which culminates in Kit Hill. Hingston Down is usually regarded as the site of a battle in AD838 recorded at *Hengestdun*, where King Egbert of Wessex defeated a combined force of Cornish and Vikings, although the exact location has never been discovered.

Kit Hill (E) has always been important, for a variety of reasons. Its height and prominence seem to have given it a significance in prehistoric times, with a Neolithic long barrow of c. 3000BC and Bronze Age round barrows (c. 2000–1500BC). Traces of early field systems have been noted.

In the 18th century Sir John Call of Whiteford near Stoke Climsland built a folly on the summit in the form of a five-sided enclosure in the style of a Saxon or Danish fort. He is said to have been inspired by the battle site between Saxons and Cornish and Danes on Hingston Down. The remains of the folly form the embankments around the grassed area on the hill top. The most prominent feature, the chimney, dates from 1858 and was part of the pumping arrangements for mines on the hill. Mining ceased in the 1880s apart from a brief revival during World War I. The chimney, however, remains as an iconic landmark in the Devon–Cornwall border area.

This location is seen from some distance along the *Tamara Coast to Coast Way* and arriving here it is easy to see why. The views in all directions are superb and there are toposcopes to help with recognition of the features seen. These stretch in the west over Callington and on to Bodmin Moor, in the east to Dartmoor, in the south to the Tamar Estuary and Plymouth and in the north up the Tamar Valley – in perfect conditions it is just possible to see the north coast near Bude.

Kit Hill to Gunnislake

A description of the link route in the opposite direction is set out below.

Either retrace your outward steps, or – to shorten the walk – catch a bus from outside the Rising Sun pub in Harrowbeer. For the bus stop, first retrace steps off Kit Hill by following the path from the summit car park between the trig point (left) and the embankment (right). Go downhill through a gate to a junction with a track and turn left here. At a gate on the left just after a granite waymark stone turn right down a grassy path, cross a junction and continue downhill to a road. Turn right here, at Louis Tea Room and farm shop, then left on the cycleway alongside the A390 at the stone signpost.

Cross the B3257 Launceston road, then 0.2 mile/0.3km further on cross the A390 to turn right down the road signed to Rising Sun and Harrowbarrow. Continue down this road for 0.4 mile/0.6km to a junction; here on the left is the bus stop to Gunnnislake.

View north from Kit Hill

View south from Kit Hill

Kit Hill to Luckett

To continue onwards to re-join the *Tamara Coast to Coast Way* at Luckett, from the car park by the chimney walk down the main access road. After about 330yd/300m turn sharp back left (8) along a partly cobbled track going downhill (it's the third access on the left from the top and is by a litter bin – there is a 'no parking' bollard in the middle of the track). Follow the track until it arrives at Kit Hill Quarry on the left.

If you look carefully, it is possible to see a few granite 'setts' on the track near the end. These were used to hold tramway rails in place.

This **granite quarry** (F) was opened in the 1880s and continued in use until 1955. Granite from Kit Hill was used for sea defences in a variety of locations, including Plymouth, Gibraltar and Singapore. It is also found in six of London's bridges, the Thames Embankment, docks at Tilbury and London and the Bishop Rock lighthouse off the Isles of Scilly.

At the quarry turn right to arrive at the top of the inclined plane.

This long straight descent is the site of the **Kit Hill Incline** (or inclined plane). It was used to take granite down from the quarry to a railway at the bottom.

The inclined plane (G) worked on a balance system whereby the weight of descending loaded wagons pulled empty trucks back up. At the top and bottom the incline had three rails, the middle one being common to both uphill and downhill tracks. In the middle there were two full sets of rails where the descending and rising wagons passed.

Descend the inclined plane, losing some 1000ft/300m of height in a single straight line.

At the bottom is a car park, the site of sidings where the granite was transferred from the incline trucks to normal railway trucks on the adjacent railway. The embankment which is passed through leaving the car park for the road marks the line of the former railway. This was originally a narrow gauge line, the East Cornwall Mineral Railway, built in the 19th century between Callington and Calstock on the Tamar (see above).

Leave Kit Hill Country Park and turn left at the road and then immediately right (9), signposted to Downgate and Stoke Climsland. Be aware of local traffic on this road.

A little way down this road there is a house called **Deer Park Cottage**. Although it became used for mining later, the whole area passed through to Luckett was part of a large early deer park. It is first documented as such in 1215, owned by the Earl of Cornwall and used exclusively for hunting. It was 'disparked' by Henry VIII in 1542. The land is still owned by the Duchy of Cornwall.

At Higher Downgate (10) turn right along the signed public bridleway opposite the narrow side road. Follow the track then cross a road to the track opposite, another public bridleway, which eventually becomes quite rocky as it descends to reach a road at the picturesque hamlet of Old Mill (11).

Turn right then immediately right again, before the bridge, onto a permissive path.

After it lost its deer park status, in the 19th century this area was extensively mined. It's difficult to envisage now, but this pleasant wooded valley would have been busy with mining activity and the path an important access route. A little way along on the left are the remains of tanks used for settling out the ore and further on the path passes one of the mine chimneys.

Arriving at a road cross at the ford then bear right uphill. Where the road turns right continue straight ahead on another permissive path (12). Reaching a junction go through the gate ahead then bear right along a path next to a fence.

The path now passes through the area of Luckett's **New Consols Mine** (H). It is thought some small-scale streaming for tin might have occurred here as early as the 16th century but mining really started in the 19th century, when copper, lead, silver, arsenic and tin were all produced. Mining ceased in 1877 until World War I when some of the waste dumps were worked. The mine was reopened between 1946 and 1953, producing tin and tungsten. Just to the left of the path, and parallel, is one of the mine leats, dry now.

The path crosses a stream that was used to feed the leats. At the next gate, straight ahead is the site of the Luckett Down Miners' Cottages. To continue on the link go right here to arrive at a road (13) then turn left, downhill, into Luckett (14).

To continue north to Horsebridge and beyond on the *Tamara Coast to Coast Way* continue ahead over the bridge. To follow the Way south, back to Gunnislake, turn right along the lane immediately before the car park.

Luckett to Kit Hill

A description of the link route in the opposite direction is set out below.

Arriving at Luckett from the Gunnislake direction, turn left and climb the hill, passing Luckett's former school on the right.

Keep climbing and immediately after the 'Steep Hill 15%' and 'road narrows' signs turn right onto a permissive path. Go left at a junction of paths and pass a chimney for one of Luckett's former mines.

The path crosses a stream that fed the mine leat then goes through a gate onto a track which in turn leads to a lane. Continue ahead here then at the road junction go ahead at the ford and bear right on a track to a gate to another permissive path.

Follow the main path parallel to the stream. Pass another old chimney and other mining remains then after a gate the route arrives at a narrow lane. Turn left here. Almost immediately turn left again, up a signed public bridleway just after a stone house. The rocky track climbs quite steeply before easing somewhat to arrive at a road. Go straight across on the signed public bridleway opposite, still climbing, to reach another road at a junction. Turn left here.

Climb to reach the B3257 Tavistock–Launceston road. Go left for a short way then almost immediately right up the signed Kit Hill Incline. Go into the car park and turn left up the broad track to a kissing-gate. Go through and on up ahead (the inclined plane).

At the top of the inclined plane bear left on the track before the quarry. Follow this until it arrives at a tarmac road then turn sharp right to the car park at the top and the Kit Hill chimney.

Greystone Link

The Greystone Link (Kevren bys Greston) connects the primary *Tamara Coast to Coast Way* on the Devon side of the Tamar with the Cornish *Kylgh Kernow* alternative (Stage 4 to Stage 4K). The link provides a possible route to switch from one alternative to the other, and two circular routes: a north circuit via Launceston and a south circuit via Horsebridge.

Distance:	2.6 miles/4.2km between the primary route north of Milton Abbot near Holland Farm and the *Kylgh Kernow* route south of Lawhitton
Total ascent:	220ft/80m
Estimated walking time (without stops):	1hr 10min

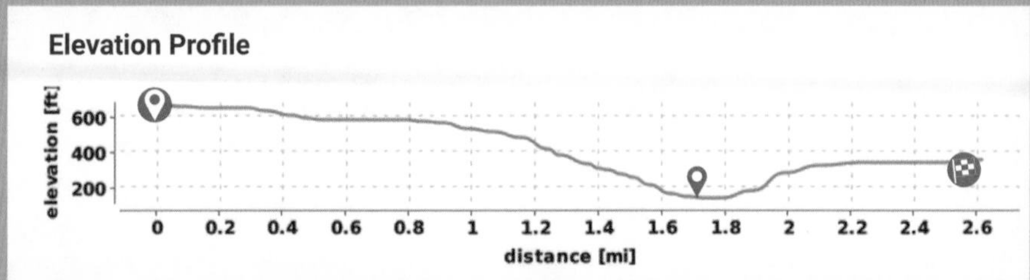

Start / 0m:	**Holland**
1.7 miles:	**Horse Bridge**
End:	**Roundhill Cottages**

Directions from east to west

Arriving at the farm drive to Holland (1) continue straight ahead where the primary *Tamara Coast to Coast Way* turns right.

There are some splendid views ahead over the Tamar Valley to the eastern side of Bodmin Moor, including Caradon Hill and its mast and the high points of Brown Willy and Rough Tor, the former the highest point in Cornwall.

A little further on a gateway on the right gives a nice view of **Bradstone church** and its manor buildings. Although located in Devon the church has a Celtic dedication, to St Nonna, and the manor has an impressive gatehouse of early 17th-century date.

Keep ahead at the two junctions, descending now into the Tamar Valley.

At the first junction, between the two roads, is a parish boundary stone (A). The granite stone is probably 18th century and the lettering is worn and difficult to read, but has Brad/stone and Dunter/ton on the two main faces.

Ahead now can be seen the very substantial **Greystone Quarry**, on the far side of the Tamar. Originally a 19th-century lead mine, the quarry was then established primarily for roadstone, still its main use.

As the road descends, there is a private drive on the right at a sharp bend to the left. This leads to **Pallastreet**, which has an interesting name, first recorded in 1281 as *Pillestrete*. In Old English 'street' implies a paved road, often a Roman one, and it has been speculated that this coincides with a Roman road which ran west from the known Roman settlement at North Tawton, on the northeast side of Dartmoor, to a crossing of the Tamar at what is now Greystone Bridge. If so, it would be interesting to know where this road went on the Cornish side.

Continue down the hill, quite steeply now, to arrive at the B3362 Tavistock–Launceston road (2). Turn right here, taking care especially with children and dogs on what can be a busy road.

At the road junction on the right is Angars Ball Cottage. This is probably the former **toll house** from Turnpike Trust days, with its angled end and window facing the road to and from Greystone Bridge. On the left of the road is a small stone building and drinking trough, dated 1894 and inscribed 'Rest and Be Thankful'.

Continue on to Greystone Bridge over the Tamar.

Greystone Bridge (B) is the second oldest existing crossing of the Tamar. It was built

c. 1438, just after Horsebridge a little downstream, and like that bridge partly paid for by Tavistock Abbey, which held many lands around here and therefore needed good access. It takes its name from the manor of Greystone, or Greston, on the Cornish side, a name interpreted as 'badger stone', and not from the appearance of the bridge.

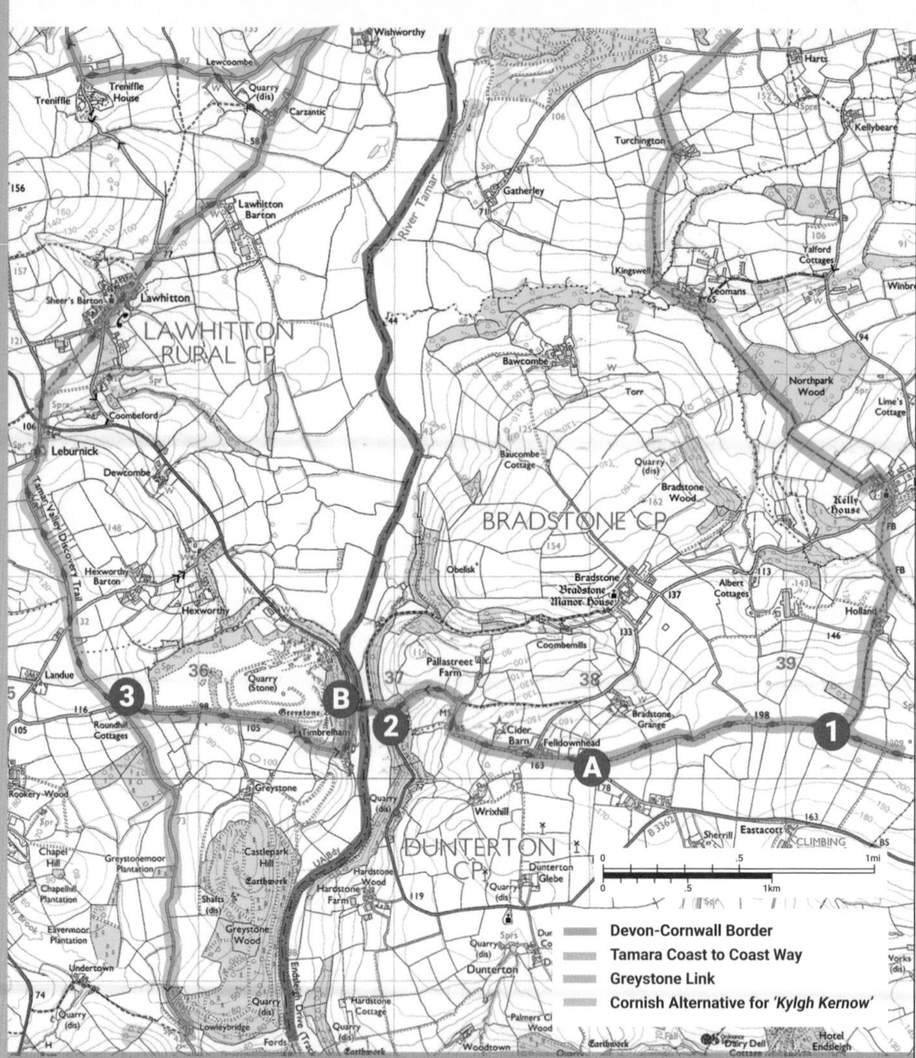

Greystone Link

It was what was called an 'indulgence bridge'. Wealthy residents put money towards the building of the bridge and in return received an 'indulgence' from the Abbot of Tavistock whereby on their death they were granted a shorter period in purgatory before being admitted into Heaven.

The road approaches were originally steeper, the gradients and alignments altered for stagecoach traffic in the 19th century by the Turnpike Trusts, Okehampton on the Devon side and Launceston on the Cornish. On the Devon side the steep hill descended by the link route was originally the main road to and from the bridge, still known as Old Greystone Hill.

Greystone Bridge

Cross the bridge into Cornwall and turn left immediately afterwards on the road signed as 'Unsuitable for HGVs'. The road climbs, steeply for a while, out of the Tamar Valley, passing the now unseen Greystone Quarry on the right. It then reaches a road junction and Stage 4K of the *Kylgh Kernow* route (3). Turn sharp back left for Horsebridge, bear right for Launceston.

Directions from west to east

At the junction on the *Kylgh Kernow* route (3) turn sharp back to the right. The route descends, gently at first and then more steeply, into the Tamar Valley, passing on the left the largely unseen workings of Greystone Quarry. (For a panoramic view of the quarry, look back when climbing out of the valley on the Devon side.) The route arrives at the B3362 Launceston–Tavistock road at Greystone Bridge. Take care with children and dogs as traffic can be busy here. Cross Greystone Bridge (B) and climb the hill on the Devon side. Take the first turning on the left, next to Angars Ball Cottage (2).Keep on the road as it climbs right then left, out of the Tamar Valley. Keep ahead at the first junction and fork left at the second (A).

About 1.8 miles/3km after leaving Greystone Bridge look out for a farm track on the left for Holland, also signed as a public footpath. This marks the meeting with Stage 4 of the primary *Tamara Coast to Coast Way* on the Devon side of the Tamar (1). Turn left for Lifton and right for Horsebridge.

Stage 4K (Cornish Option)
Gunnislake to Launceston

Stage 4 of the primary route of the *Tamara Coast to Coast Way* follows the Cornwall side of the Tamar from Gunnislake to Horsebridge, then continues on the Devon side to Lifton. The primary route then continues, still in Devon, on Stage 5 to Heale Bridge, north of Lifton.

For those wishing to complete *Kylgh Kernow* – a circuit of Cornwall – an alternative option is offered: to follow Stage 4 from Gunnislake to Horsebridge, then the alternative Stage 4K from Horsebridge to Launceston. Continuing north the *Kylgh Kernow* option then follows the Launceston Link (p147) on to Heale Bridge to re-join the primary route (see Stage 5, page 156).

The disadvantage of Stage 4K is that it mostly follows roads, albeit quiet and minor ones, and offers fewer views, whereas Stage 4 on the Devon side is largely off-road and probably has better views.

Distance: 15.9 miles/25.6km between Gunnislake and Launceston

Total ascent: 2230ft/68m

Estimated walking time (without stops): 7hr 35min

Car parks: Gunnislake (centre), Luckett, Launceston

Public transport & shorter options: There are few options for public transport or to shorten this section. Combined with Stage 4 and the Greystone Link it can be split into two loops, north and south of Greystone Bridge. Buses go from Gunnislake to Luckett and Horsebridge once a week. A diversion off the route at Rezare into Treburley on the A368 gives access to regular buses to Launceston.

Link route: Greystone Link between the Kylgh Kernow route south of Lawhitton and the primary route near Holland Farm, north of Milton Abbot

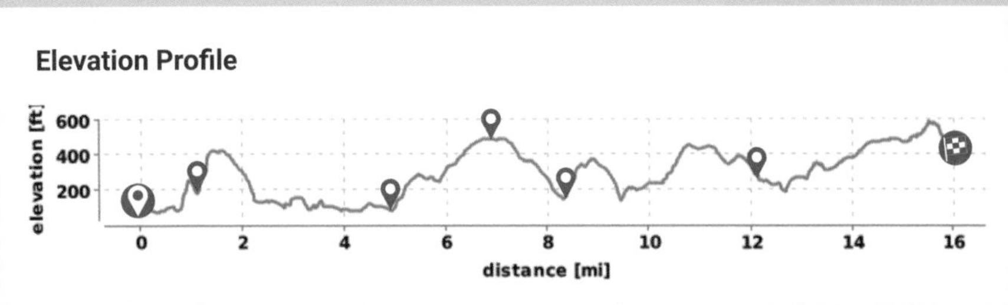

Start / 0m:	**Gunnislake (New Bridge)**	**7 miles:**	**Downhouse**
1.5 miles:	**Chilsworthy**	**8.5 miles:**	**Bealsmill**
5 miles:	**Horsebridge**	**12 miles:**	**Lawhitton**
		End:	**Launceston**

Stage 4K initially follows the same route as Stage 4, from Gunnislake to Horsebridge (see pages 105-112). If you decide to visit **Horsebridge** (and perhaps call in at the Royal Inn), a little way before the bridge note the granite stone on the right (A), carved with a faint letter 'C': a county bridge stone dating from the 19th century (for more information see Stage 4, page 112).

Just over the bridge is a pub, the Royal Inn (www.royalinn.co.uk); there are occasional buses from Horsebridge to Gunnislake, Luckett and Tavistock, but generally only on Fridays.

If Horsebridge has been visited, return to the kissing-gate (1) and continue on the road, up the hill (if Horsebridge is bypassed, turn left up the hill from the kissing-gate). At the junction bear right, signposted to Stoke Climsland and Launceston, the road climbing away from the Tamar.

Keep ahead at the next junction, then go right at the one immediately following, signposted to Alston and Tutwell (2). Keep climbing ahead, with intermittent views to Dartmoor on the right, until reaching a T-junction (3). Turn left here, signposted to Bealsmill and Launceston.

Although now heading west, the *Kylgh Kernow* route is still shadowing the Tamar, which itself turns west via a couple of large meanders through a deep-sided section of the valley. The southern edge of the woodland which clothes the deep valley sides is seen off to the right. On the left there are excellent views of Kit Hill and its attendant Hingston Down, bypassed earlier on the *Tamara Coast to Coast Way* (see Stage 3K, page 101).

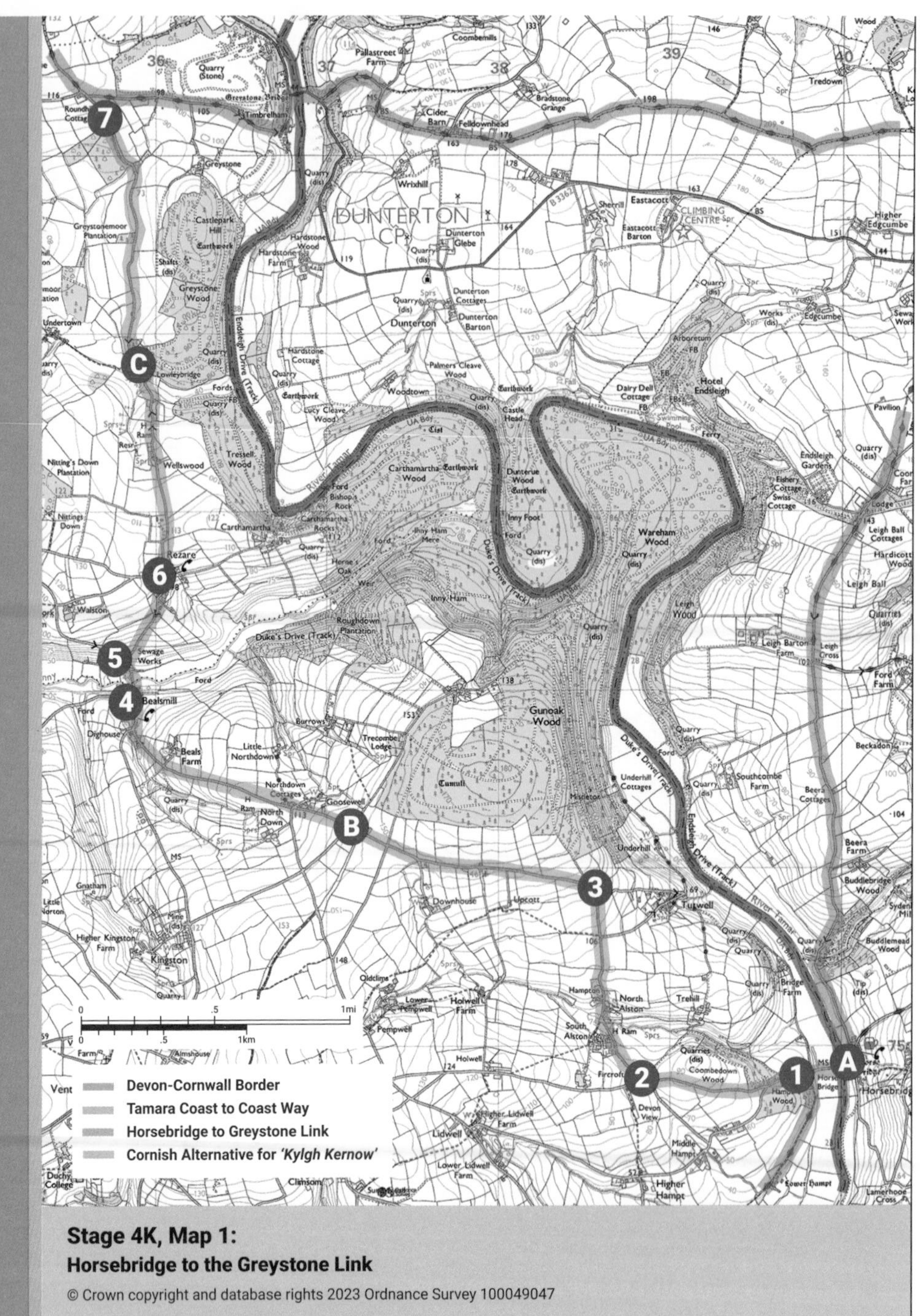

Stage 4K, Map 1:

Horsebridge to the Greystone Link

Continue ahead at the next junction and also at the following one, at the 'finger' direction stone pointing to 'Lanson' (B).

The date of this distinctive **direction stone** is not certain. However, similar stones with hand or finger pointers in Penwith in West Cornwall have been dated to the early 19th century. Note the phonetic spelling of Launceston.

The road descends steadily and at the next junction meets the edge of the Tamar Valley AONB, the road now marking the boundary. Everything on the right is within the AONB, surrounding the Tamar and its valley, while the land on the left is outside.

'Finger' direction stone

The route descends to Bealsmill (4). Turn right at the T-junction, signposted to Launceston.

A little way along on the left is a stone marked with a slightly faint 'B'. This marks the **Bealsmill** boundary of the responsibility of the Callington Turnpike Trust. This was set up in 1764 to improve and maintain the principal routes to and from Callington. The Callington Turnpike met that of Launceston here.

Go through Bealsmill, crossing the River Inny.

The name of this location goes back to medieval times, when in 1388 John Bile is recorded as keeping the mill at Biles-Brigge. None of the present buildings date back that far. It may have had an earlier name, as described a little later.

The **River Inny**, crossed here, is about 20 miles/32km long, flowing east from its source on the northeastern edge of Bodmin Moor. Its name is Old Cornish for 'ash-tree river'. It is one of the larger Cornish tributaries of the Tamar.

At the junction a little way up the hill (5) turn right, signposted to Rezare.

It has been 5.5 miles/9km from Gunnislake, and is a further 9.5 miles/15km to Launceston. There is an 'escape route' from here: continue ahead at this junction (5), signposted to Treburley and Launceston, which in 0.75 mile/1.25km reaches the A388 at Treburley. Here it is possible to catch a bus to Launceston or Callington, or on to Plymouth.

Turning right at this junction, *Kylgh Kernow* now heads north, still shadowing the Tamar which is over to the right here in a series of deep-sided, wooded meanders, where it is joined by the River Inny.

Among these Tamar meanders are the remains of prehistoric earthworks. It has been suggested that they indicate the Tamar may have been a very early boundary, at least in this stretch. Far more likely is that they were there to defend against invaders coming up the Tamar. The Roman geographer Ptolemy's work *Geographica* is a description of the Roman Empire c. AD140 and includes a section on Britain. In this, the southwest is indicated as being inhabited by the *Dumnonii*, one of whose 'cities' is Tamara which, being mapped inland ,could well be one of these Tamar forts. The name of one of these earthworks, Carthamartha, has been explained as derived from Ker Tamar, meaning the 'fort on the Tamar' in Cornish.

A stiff climb leads to the hamlet of Rezare, picturesque but with no facilities other than a welcome bench on the little green (6).

The name of this little settlement appears to mean 'ford by the fort' (*ris-ker* in Cornish). This would be partly appropriate as it is close to the ancient earthwork of Carthamartha, which overlooks the Tamar, although there is no river, stream or ford at Rezare. It is, however, not far from Bealsmill, where the road crosses the River Inny, and it is thought the name could have originally applied to that place.

On the edge of the green, opposite the bench, is a **holy well**. This is a medieval small stone building over a well basin with a steeply pitched granite roof with modern Latin crosses at each end.

There is another 'escape route' to Treburley from here – turn left along the road signed to Treburley and Launceston for about 0.75 mile/ 1.25km to the A388.

Rezare, Holy Well

Continue ahead on the road through Rezare. There follows a partly steep descent to cross a minor tributary of the Tamar, Lowley Brook, at Lowley Bridge (C).

Since leaving Bealsmill the route has been following a minor road which was once the main route between Callington and Launceston. However, when the Launceston Turnpike Trust took over responsibility for the main roads to and from the town in the late 18th century, it established a new route to the west, now partly the route of the A388. This was in order to avoid these steep slopes either side of **Lowley Bridge**, which proved difficult for stagecoaches to negotiate (C).

Keep on the generally pleasant, very quiet road to arrive at a junction 2 miles/3.25km after leaving Rezare, where the *Kylgh Kernow* is met by the Greystone Link (7).

The **Greystone link** runs between here and across to the primary *Tamara Coast to Coast Way* on the Devon side of the river. For details of the link see page 132.

To continue on the *Kylgh Kernow* to Launceston continue straight ahead.

At this point the *Kylgh Kernow* leaves the Tamar Valley AONB. Keep ahead and after a climb there are wide views to the left over the valley of Lowley Brook to the eastern edge of Bodmin Moor; especially noticeable are Caradon Hill with its mast and the high points of Brown Willy (the highest point in Cornwall) and Rough Tor.

Carry on to reach the B3362 Launceston–Tavistock road, with the outskirts of Launceston now visible ahead. Carefully cross the B3362 and onto the road opposite, signposted to Lawhitton. Cross the stile next to a private drive a little way up on the right (8), and head across the field parallel to the telephone poles to a gateway in the far corner. Go through and ahead, aiming for the stile between the two buildings. Cross the stile and go down the drive to the road. Bear left then right to Lawhitton church.

Lawhitton (D) has early associations with Saxon bishops. In AD830 King Egbert gave the manor to the Bishop of Sherborne, who at that time had responsibility for Devon and Cornwall. In AD909 the manor, and the episcopal responsibility, devolved to the Bishop of Crediton and a base established so that he might 'every year visit the Cornish race to extirpate their errors'. It seems that this referred to the desire of the Saxon kings to bring Cornwall from the Celtic to the Roman form of Christianity. The property and responsibility then in turn devolved to the Bishops of Exeter. It is said they used to visit by crossing the Tamar from Lifton by a chain bridge, then enter the village along the line of the road ahead. This became known as the 'Bishop's Road' (E).

The present church is old, mainly 13th century, and of unusual plan with a Norman south tower, but there has been a church here since the 9th century. To accommodate the visiting bishops a house was erected for them next to the church. Rebuilt much later this still stands, its original purpose still marked by a mitre on a chimney.

Lawhitton, Bishop's church

Lawhitton, Bishop's House with mitre on chimney

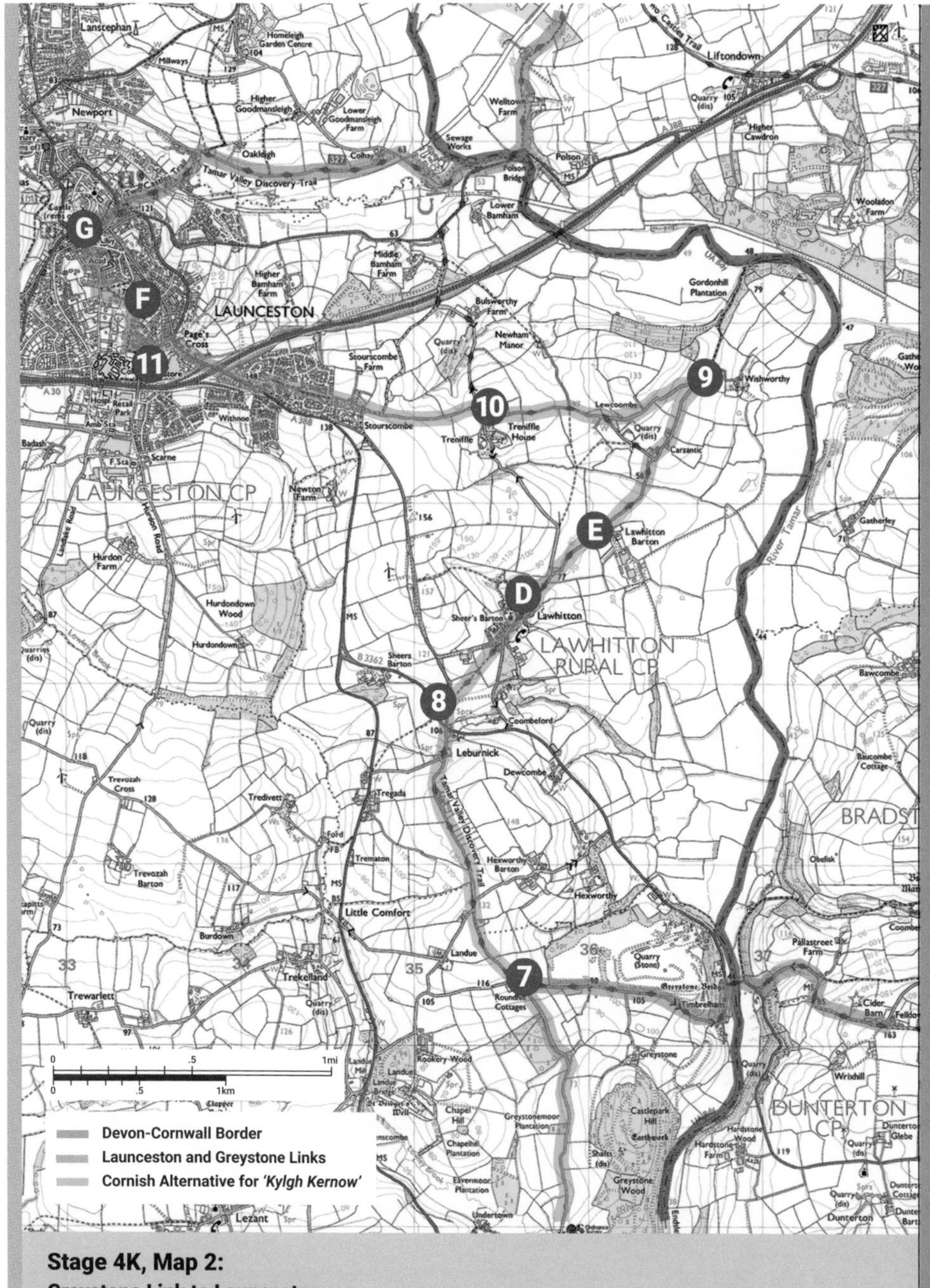

Stage 4K, Map 2:
Greystone Link to Launceston

There are no facilities in Lawhitton other than a bench on the green outside the church.

Continue along the lane through Lawhitton (on the line of the 'Bishop's Road), descending to the floor of the Tamar Valley.

Keep ahead at the first junction on the left and on to the second junction, immediately before Carzantic House. For the most direct route onward turn left here, but to stay closer to the Tamar on the 'Bishop's Road' for slightly longer continue ahead and turn back sharp left at the 'No Through Road' sign (9).

The 'Bishop's Road' continued ahead to the Tamar from this junction, on the line of a current public footpath. The path is now a cul-de-sac, ending at the Tamar.

Both this route and the shorter option climb, then come together again at Luccombe Cottage. The route continues to climb steadily west, out of the Tamar Valley. At a T-junction at Treniffle House turn right, then follow the road round to the left (10).

Go ahead at the next junction (signposted Launceston) and immediately after the Stourscombe sign continue straight ahead on a public footpath through a residential area which eventually ends at a road (Robin Drive – the second time this name is encountered). Continue ahead then fork right at the 'No Through Road' sign to arrive at a main road (A388).

Continue on the footway next to the A388, crossing the A30, then at the junction at Tesco's turn left (signposted Okehampton and Holsworthy). Now look out for a tarmac path on the right, immediately after Clarence Lodge (11). Follow this path as it zigzags round hard sports pitches then turns right to pass to the right of school buildings. Follow the obvious path uphill to pass by the reservoir on the right, on the top of Windmill Hill.

There are wide views over the Tamar Valley and far beyond from here, in most directions. As the name suggests, this was once the site of a windmill but has for many years been a **public park**. It was also the site of a Civil War battle (1643). Its high location made it the ideal site for the town's domestic water supply reservoir, set up here in 1885 (F). It is also a good spot to sit for a break, with numerous benches and some picnic tables.

Keep on the path as it curves round to the left and then emerges onto a road. Turn right here and go steeply downhill to arrive at the Westgate Inn.

Launceston was the only walled town in Cornwall, the walls being built in the 13th century, and this is the site of the town's West Gate. There is no sign of it today.

Turn right at the Westgate Inn to arrive at the town's main square, formed by High Street and Broad Street.

Launceston's origins lie in an early Christian church which was established at St Stephen, to the north of the modern town centre on the other side of the River Kensey, probably in the 5th century. From the dedication of the church, it became known in Cornish as Lann Stefan – the holy enclosure of St Stephen. Later, a monastery and a market were established there.

When the Normans arrived they built their castle on the strategically important hill south of *Lann Stefan*, at what was then called *Dunheved*, Middle English for 'end of the hill', and positioned to keep watch over the main Tamar crossing into and out of Cornwall at Polson to the east. As the castle gathered population and trade around it, in 1155 Lann Stefan's monastery (which had now become a priory), also moved and brought the name with it. With the addition of the English ending '-ton', or settlement, it became Lanstefanton, then Launceston (usually locally pronounced Lanson).

(Left) Launceston Castle

Launceston town centre

Launceston is a fascinating little town to explore, and has been described as 'retaining the air of the ancient border town that guarded the gateway to medieval Cornwall' (Beacham 2014, in his update of Pevsner's definitive work on Cornish buildings). Its most prominent feature is the castle on its distinctive mound (G).

Established by the Normans in the 11th century it was greatly enlarged to become the power base of the Earls of Cornwall in the 13th century. The castle is on the left from the main square.

Also of great interest is the 16th-century church – its exterior walls covered in sculptures – also off to the left of the square. Further on, down by the River Kensey beyond the castle, is the site of the priory next to St Thomas Church, which has the largest Norman font in Cornwall. Next to the church is the quaint 15th-century packhorse bridge which was built to allow access to the priory. The town centre square, dominated by the war memorial which was built on the site of the old Butter Market, is surrounded by some nice Georgian buildings.

From being the most important town in Cornwall, Launceston has slowly relinquished its responsibilities; the earldom moved its centre to Lostwithiel in the 13th century and the town lost its status of county town and centre of the assizes to Bodmin in 1838. It remains, however, an absolutely fascinating place to wander around and explore, a good place to break a journey on the *Kylgh Kernow* for a day or two.

As well as the full range of facilities Launceston has buses to and from Bude, Plymouth, Bodmin, Liskeard and Camelford.

To continue on the *Kylgh Kernow/Tamara Coast to Coast Way* follow the Launceston Link (see page 147) to meet the primary route of the Way at Heale Bridge north of Lifton.

Launceston Link

The Launceston Link (*Kevren bys Lanstefan*) provides the option for those on the primary route to walk into Launceston – which offers a wider range of facilities than Lifton – at the end of Stage 4. It will also be used by those who use the *Kylgh Kernow* Cornish alternative from Horsebridge to Launceston (Stage 4K) to re-join the main *Tamara Coast to Coast Way* near Heale Bridge (Stage 5), north of Lifton.

Distance:	2.6 miles/4.2km between Launceston and Heale Bridge
Total ascent:	195ft/60m
Estimated walking time (without stops):	1hr 10min

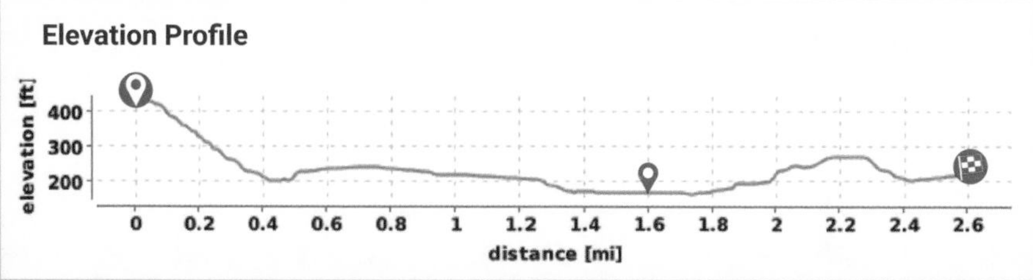

Start / 0m:	**Launceston**
1.6 miles:	**Polson Bridge**
End:	**near Heale Bridge**

Launceston to Heale Bridge

Leave Launceston's main square along Broad Street. then turn right along Southgate Street to the South Gate.

Launceston was the only walled town in Cornwall, the walls being built in the 13th century, and the gate is first mentioned in 1381. Only the South Gate (A) remains, the others being demolished in the early 19th century. The walls were described as still being in good condition by travellers in the 18th century, and although now incomplete there are substantial lengths remaining.

Launceston, South Gate

Go through the pedestrian arch (1) and turn left immediately afterwards, down steep Angel Hill. At the junction go straight across, and down the narrow hill opposite.

Difficult to believe now, **Angel Hill** was once one of the most important routes into and out of Launceston. As the route descends into the valley of the River Kensey, a tributary of the Tamar, it crosses two former railway bridges and then the river in the valley bottom.

Two railway lines entered Launceston from the east. The first was the GWR line from Plymouth, operating from 1865 to 1962, and the second was the London and South Western Railway's North Cornwall line, in use between 1886 and 1964 and which carried trains of the Atlantic Coast Express between London Waterloo and Padstow. Launceston had two adjacent and separate stations but is no longer on the rail network. However, the narrow-gauge Launceston Steam Railway uses the LSWR's alignment for a couple of miles west of the town.

Arriving at a T-junction turn right (2).

Ahead **Brentor church** is distinct on the skyline. This is a prominent landmark on the western edge of Dartmoor. At 1100ft/335m above sea level, the church is said to be the highest, and some say the smallest, complete parish church in England. It was built in 1130 and there are various legends associated with its construction. Whatever the truth of its origin, it makes for a dramatic silhouette over a wide area.

Looking over to the right, there is a viaduct which carried one of the railways over the River Kensey.

The link reaches another T-junction where it turns right, again crossing the line of the LSWR railway on an old bridge.

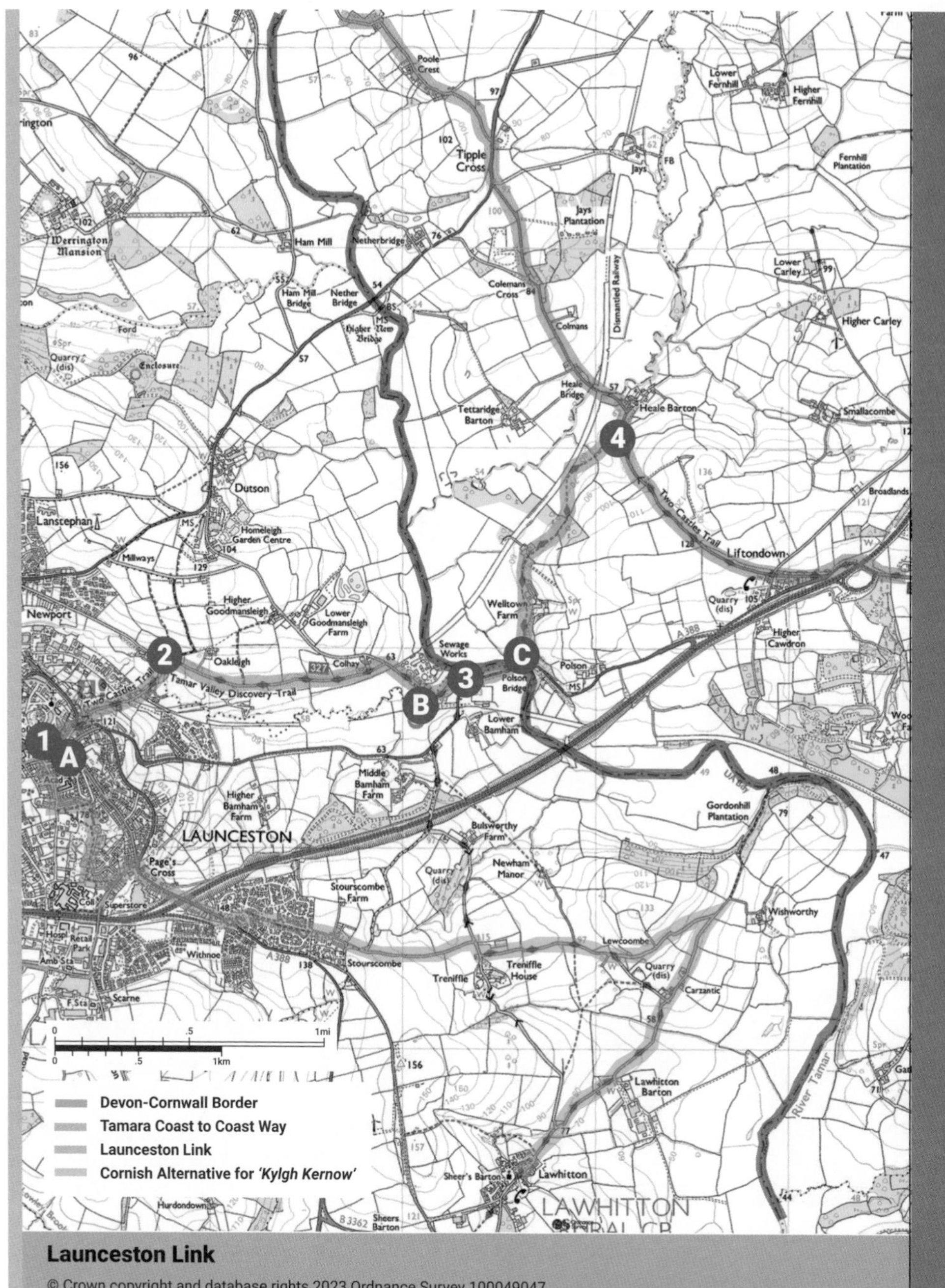

Launceston Link

Note on the right, just after the entrance to the wastewater treatment works, the **medieval packhorse bridge** (B) which crosses the Kensey. (The bridge can be crossed by taking the narrow path parallel to the road from opposite the works entrance.)

The bridge, which has a single pointed arch 8ft/2.5m in height, was probably built about 1580, but the abutments appear to belong to an earlier bridge. Before that date this area, **St Leonards**, had been the site of an important leper hospital. The hospital was founded in 1257 by Launceston Priory and situated on a peninsula between the Tamar and its tributary River Kensey, perhaps so that the rivers could provide a form of barrier. Although Launceston Priory was dissolved by Henry VIII in 1539 it appears the hospital continued until the end of that century.

After human remains had been found in 1995, assumed to belong to lepers buried on the site, it was excavated by Channel 4's Time Team in 1997. Their work suggested that the site of the hospital buildings unfortunately lay under the modern wastewater treatment works.

Continue past the equitation centre and turn left at the junction with a more major road, opposite Launceston Rugby Club (3). (Be careful: this road is busier.)

On the left here is the confluence of the River Kensey with the Tamar. The Kensey, whose valley has been followed from Launceston, rises on the eastern edge of Bodmin Moor and flows east for about 10 miles/16km.

St Leonards Bridge

Polson Bridge

A little way along here the link crosses the Tamar into Devon at Polson Bridge (C).

Historically **Polson Bridge** carried the main road into and out of Cornwall. In medieval times Launceston was the capital of Cornwall and any dignitaries – royalty or their representatives, or leading clergy – would have visited Launceston and crossed the Tamar here. It was probably the most prominent of the roads maintained by the Launceston Turnpike Trust when it was set up in 1760. Into the modern era the line of the road became the A30, the road from London to Land's End, until it was superseded by the new, current A30 in the 1970s.

While the earliest stone bridge was probably erected soon after the Norman Conquest, it is likely that there was a bridge here in Saxon times. Lifton, just over the border in Devon, was a significant royal West Saxon estate, its importance stemming from its proximity to Cornwall, and presumably there must have been a recognised crossing point.

After various rebuilds, by 1809 it is recorded still as being only 9.5ft/3m wide, but very long, with causeways on both approaches. The bridge was then completely rebuilt in 1833, then the main span again rebuilt, using the same materials, in 1934 – this is the current bridge, which is listed. Note that there is still a causeway on the Cornish side, reflecting the ongoing flood risk that can sometimes occur here, as seen by the depth gauge back by the road junction.

Immediately after crossing the bridge go left into the drive of Welltown Farm. Go left through the metal gate, then turn right along the edge of the field next to the hedge.

Cross the stile at the far end and then a little further on cross a stile on the right to a tarmac track. Follow this for 275yd/250m then, just before a stone building ahead, cross a stile on the right. Continue ahead next to the fence on the left then, when the fence goes sharp left, continue straight ahead, left of the hedge, to a metal gate on the far side.

Follow the path through the trees then cross two stiles on the left. Head diagonally down across the field to a gate then ahead a little above the fence to another gate in the far corner. Continue ahead alongside the hedge to a gate onto a road (4).

The *Kylgh Kernow* option re-joins the primary route of the *Tamara Coast to Coast Way* here. To continue north on the Way turn left here.

***Kylgh Kernow* walkers now continue north on Stage 5 (page 156), crossing into Cornwall a little way further on.**

Heale Bridge to Launceston

Leaving the primary route just south of Heale Bridge (4), go through the gate and walk alongside the hedge on the right. Keep ahead, then go through a small wooden gate in the far corner.

Continue ahead into the next field, keeping a little above the fence on the right, and go through the wooden gate in the fence ahead. Bear diagonally left over the next field, then cross two stiles in the top corner. Turn right on the path through the trees, through a metal gate then through the next field, first next to a hedge on the left then a fence on the right. Cross the stile onto the tarmac track and continue for about 275yd/250m.

Leave the track at the stile on the right. Continue next to the track to another stile, then ahead next to the hedge to a metal gate on the left. Go through and on to the road, turning right.

Be careful on this length of road, which can be a little busy. Almost immediately the Launceston Link crosses the River Tamar into Cornwall at Polson Bridge (3). A short way after the bridge turn right, signposted St Leonards.

Continue along the road then turn left along the lane just after the brick bridge. Heading west along this lane, the silhouette of Launceston Castle becomes very prominent ahead.

Take the next lane on the left, at a small hamlet of cottages (2), descending slightly to cross the River Kensey and then the two former railways. Climb steadily uphill, cross at the junction and continue uphill to arrive at Launceston's South Gate.

Turn right, through the pedestrian arch in the gateway and a little further, on the left, is Launceston's main square (1), formed by High Street and Broad Street.

Stage 5

Lifton (or Launceston) to Bridgerule

Due to the lack of public rights of way close to the river, this stage is on roads – mostly quiet country lanes, with lovely views. Early in the stage the *Tamara Coast to Coast Way* first meets the heritage feature of the Bude Canal, which will be encountered on numerous occasions further along the route. Most of the stage runs through a quiet and relatively remote landscape, with long-range views to both Dartmoor to the east and Bodmin Moor to the west.

Distance:	17.1 miles/27.5km between Lifton and Bridgerule; 19 miles/30.5km between Launceston and Bridgerule
Total ascent:	1458ft/444m
Estimated walking time (without stops):	7hr 40min
Car parks:	Launceston, North Tamerton

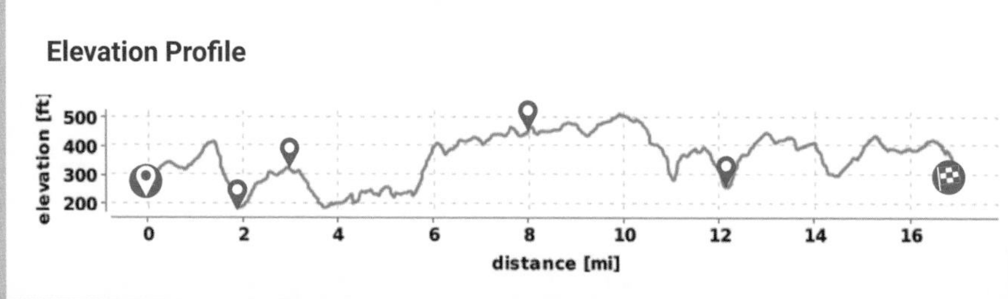

Start / 0m:	**Lifton**
2 miles:	**Heale Bridge**
3.5 miles:	**Druxton Bridge**
8 miles:	**Boyton**
12 miles:	**Tamerton Bridge**
End (17 miles):	**Bridgerule**

Public transport & shorter options: Launceston and Lifton are well served by bus services. For a shorter walk, the best option is to divide Stage 5 in two at Boyton, close to half way. A bus runs between Launceston, Boyton and North Tamerton a few days each week, and there is a regular and relatively frequent service bus between Launceston to and from Bude which stops at Bennacott (1.25 miles/2km from

Boyton – see page 163/164) and at Borough Cross on the B3254 just outside Bridgerule.
Link route: Launceston Link to/from Heale Bridge.

This stage of the *Tamara Coast to Coast Way* has two start point options: Lifton or Launceston. Those walking the primary route will have used the Devon side of the Tamar on Stage 4 and so start Stage 5 at Lifton. Those who have stayed on the Cornwall side for the *Kylgh Kernow* option (Stage 4K) will start Stage 5 at Launceston, following the Launceston Link to the primary route at Heale Bridge.

Some walkers following the primary route may wish to divert to Launceston for its wider range of facilities; for a description of the route between the *Tamara Coast to Coast Way* and Launceston see the Launceston Link description (page 152).

Starting from outside the Arundell Arms Hotel in the centre of Lifton (1), walk up the main road through the village, passing the Lifton Community Centre.

For many centuries, probably since Saxon times at least, this has been the main road in and out of Cornwall. When the Launceston **Turnpike Trust** was set up in 1760 to maintain the main roads into the town it took over the maintenance of this road as far as Combebow, to the west of Okehampton, and also erected milestones along its length (see opposite).

Leaving Lifton the route passes the distinctive terrace of **Westend Cottages**, built in 1866 by the Bradshaw family, Lords of the Manor, for their estate workers.

Keep ahead on the footway next to the road, ignoring the right turns, passing a bench on the outskirts of the village and another a little further along, then Strawberry Fields Farm Shop and Restaurant (A).

Milestone near Liftondown

Approaching the underpass beneath the modern A30 there is a **milestone** in the verge on the right, seemingly indicating 8 miles to Launceston and 13 to Okehampton, though it's not totally clear and could conceivably read 3 and 15 (B). This appears to be one of the Launceston Turnpike Trust milestones. Since this location is indeed about 3 miles from Launceston presumably the second of the readings is the true one.

Continue under the modern A30 to Liftondown, turning right at the junction next to the bench, signposted to Holsworthy (2).

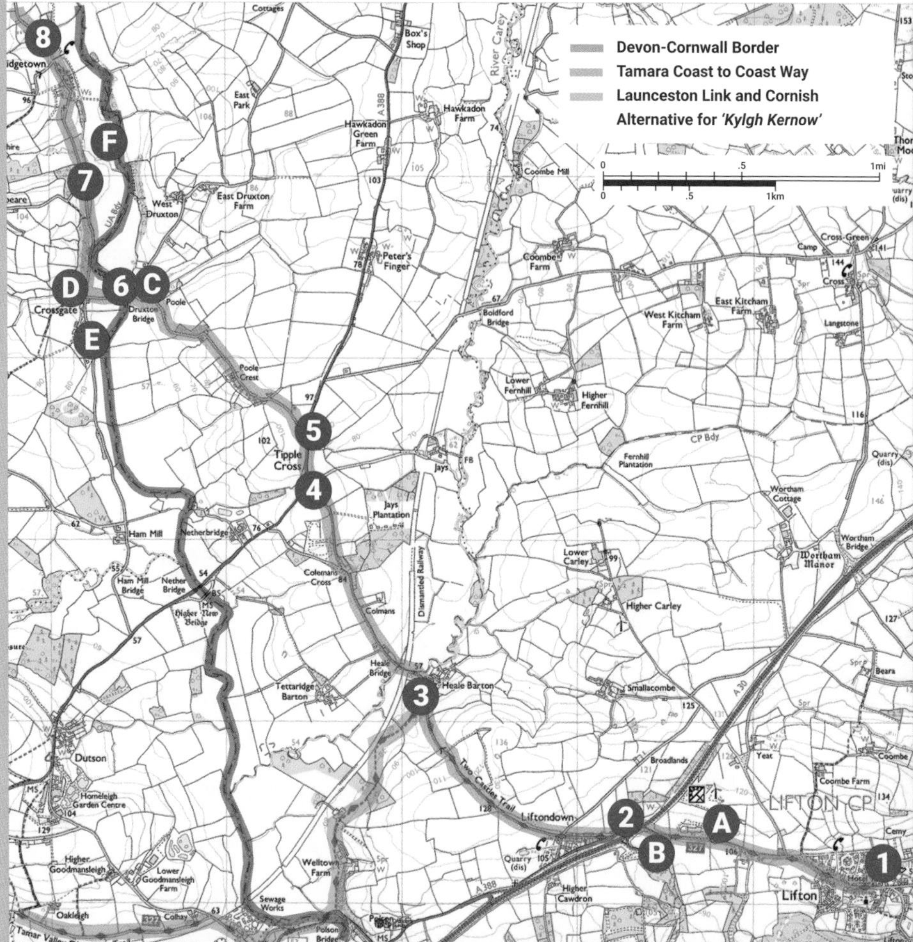

Stage 5, Map 1:
Lifton to Druxton Bridge

Liftondown is a relatively new settlement, there being nothing other than open land shown on the first edition OS map of 1809. There are no facilities here.

Follow this road through, then out of, Liftondown. Note that it's probably best to keep to one side of the road as it can be used as a cut-through by local traffic.

The route rises gently, giving views to the left to Bodmin Moor, with Caradon Hill and its masts, Brown Willy (the moor's, and Cornwall's, highest point) and Roughtor all visible; behind and to the right Dartmoor can be seen as a continuous skyline. There then begins a descent into the valley of the River Carey, a tributary of the Tamar. There are wide views ahead over both the Carey and Tamar valleys and into Cornwall.

Near the bottom of the hill, at the sign for a left-hand bend, and where the word 'Slow' is painted on the road, a signed public footpath goes off to the left (3). This is the route of the Launceston Link (3 miles/5km to Launceston). It is also where walkers who have followed the *Kylgh Kernow* option re-join the primary route of the *Tamara Coast to Coast Way* (see Stage 5, page 151).

The Launceston Link leaves and joins the *Tamara Coast to Coast Way* here.

***Kylgh Kernow* walkers who have come from Launceston, as well as those who have used the Launceston Link, turn left on arriving at the road here and join the primary *Tamara Coast to Coast Way*.**

Continue down the hill to pass a stone buttress on the left.

This carried an old railway line over both the road and the River Carey. The railway formed part of the London and South Western Railway's **North Cornwall line** and carried trains on the Atlantic Coast Express from London Waterloo to Padstow, as well as local services. The line opened in 1886 and closed in 1964 as part of the Beeching cuts.

The *Tamara Coast to Coast Way* continues on to cross the River Carey at the narrow Heale Bridge, then climbs gently away from the valley bottom. At the fork keep right. The route then arrives at the A388 Launceston–Holsworthy road at Jays Cross (4).

Approaching the A388 be sure to keep children and dogs under close control, as the road can be fast and busy, and be careful on this next roadside length of about 120yd/110m.

There is a relatively distant view of Launceston from here to the left, the outline of the castle being particularly prominent.

Turn right, signposted to Holsworthy, and walk along the verge. When safely away from the bend cross to the verge on the far side then take the first turning on the left, Tipple Cross (5), signposted to Crossgate and Bridgetown.

A little way along this road, if the conditions are clear, look back to the right and it should be possible to pick out the distinctive landmark of **Brent Tor**, with its crowning church. This is a prominent landmark on the western edge of Dartmoor. At 1100ft/335m above sea level, the church is said to be the highest, and some say the smallest, complete parish church in England. It was built in 1130 and there are various legends associated with its construction. Whatever the truth of its origin, it makes for a dramatic silhouette over a wide area.

Continue ahead and shortly after passing Poole Farm the Way forks left to cross over Druxton Bridge (6) and the Tamar into Cornwall (C).

There has been a bridge on this site since at least the 14th century, and the current bridge dates from the 16th century, though rebuilt in the 19th.

In 1814, J.M.W. Turner visited southwest England and completed many paintings, drawings and sketches, a number of which were on the Tamar, although the precise location of many is uncertain. One sketch was of Druxton Bridge, which seems to be the furthest north he ventured.

Although the crossing of the Tamar here marks the move of the *Tamara Coast to Coast Way* from Devon into Cornwall, for much of history this would not have been the case. The parish of Werrington – which the Way now enters – together with the neighbouring parish of North Petherwin, formed an anomalous 'finger' of Devon west of the Tamar. This area was some 7 miles/11km east–west and between 2 and 3 miles/3 and 5km north–south. It had been part of Cornwall in Saxon times, following King Athelstan's declaration that the Tamar would be the Devon–Cornwall boundary, although it seems to have been in the ownership of the family of the Saxon King Harold. It was then given by Gytha, mother of King Harold, to Tavistock Abbey.

There is some doubt about how it later became part of Devon. A possible explanation is that after the Norman Conquest, abbey lands came under the ultimate control of the Sherriff of Devon, who paid rent to the Crown for the land he administered in Devon and would have had to pay extra for land outside Devon. He therefore arranged for the area to be included as part of Devon in the Domesday Book of 1086 and so it remained for almost 900 years, until the Tamar again became the boundary and thus the two parishes restored to Cornwall in 1966. However, other abbey lands existed west of the Tamar which never became part of Devon, so there may be another explanation.

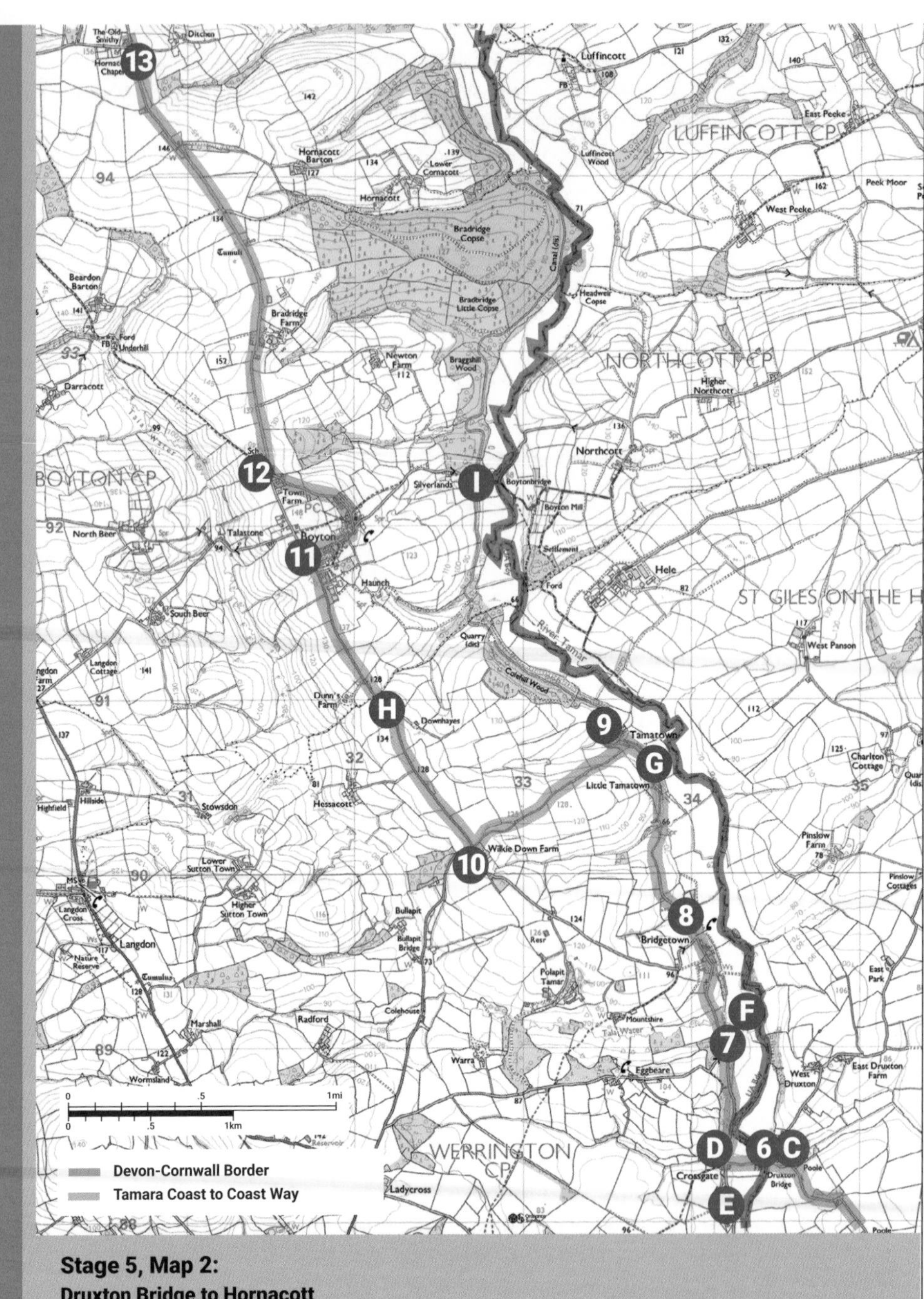

Stage 5, Map 2:
Druxton Bridge to Hornacott

Keep ahead to reach the T-junction at Crossgate (D).

Here the Way first encounters the Bude Canal. This was a product of what was called the 'canal mania' of the late 18th and early 19th centuries. Over much of the country canals revolutionised the transport system, making it easier and cheaper to move goods around. In the southwest, however, they had less impact. There had been grand plans for a canal to link the north and south coasts of the peninsula, using the tidal reaches of the Tamar, but they never materialised, apart from a short length passed on the Way near Gunnislake (Stage 3). But in 1819 an Act of Parliament authorised the building of a canal from Bude to Launceston, with a branch to Holsworthy in Devon. In fact, the canal never reached Launceston, ending about 3 miles/5km north of the town here at **Crossgate**. In addition to the two main lines of the canal, a third branch was constructed from the newly-built reservoir of Tamar Lake to feed water to the system. This was known as the 'Aqueduct branch'; a little later most of this branch was also used as a transport link. The canal opened for operation in 1823.

The canal's main use was to transport sea sand from the beaches at Bude to 'sweeten' the heavy and infertile soils of the region. In addition, coal, bricks and other materials were brought in, all almost unknown locally previously, and agricultural goods taken out. With a total length of some 36 miles/58km over its three branches it was Cornwall's biggest and most important canal by far, although some of this length was in Devon. It was described by Professor Roger Kain, editor of the Historical Atlas of South West England, as 'one of England's most remarkable engineering achievements'.

The Bude Canal was very unusual in that over most of its length, to achieve changes in level, it used inclined planes rather than locks. These were steep slopes fitted with rails; the small barges used, known as 'tub boats', had wheels fitted at each corner and were hauled up and down the slope on these. Power was provided by water-wheels attached to an endless chain, or by a system utilising the weight of water in a giant bucket.

A number of these features meant that the Bude Canal became of especial heritage significance: the first canal in the world to use wheeled tub boats; the first use of water power on inclined planes; and the longest canal in the world to be worked by tub boats. It was renowned for using the designs of Robert Fulton, American artist and inventor, for its water power; its engineer was James Green, a pioneering civil engineer much admired at the time. It was the longest canal scheme in Cornwall and the longest tub boat canal in Britain. The canal ceased to be used in 1891.

The next stretch of the *Tamara Coast to Coast Way* parallels the Bude Canal. The canal becomes a frequent companion of the Way from here on, towards its northern end actually running alongside it until reaching the water supply reservoir at what is now called Lower Tamar Lake.

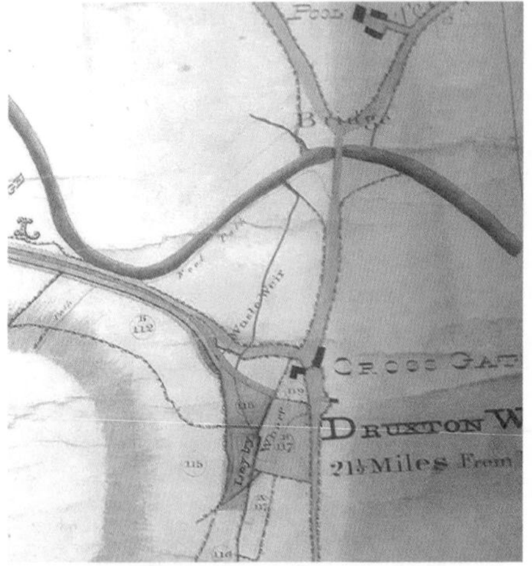

Mid-19th-century map of Druxton Wharf, Crossgate *(Map courtesy of Kresen Kernow)*

The adjacent map has north to the left. It shows the Tamar running left–right, crossed by Druxton Bridge. The wharf area is shown in yellow, with the canal's end basin and layby for barges in blue. The canal is then shown running off to the left (north), next to the road.

Arriving at Crossgate most of the buildings on the opposite side of the road were originally associated with the canal and its terminus, **Druxton Wharf**. These included store houses, stables for the towing horses and a wharfinger's house.

By the mid-19th century it was accepted that the canal would not be extended any further south. There was, however, a plan to construct a railway line from here south, next to the Tamar on the Cornwall side (E), to meet the railway from Plymouth to Launceston which was built in 1865. An Act of Parliament was prepared for this link line, but it was never built.

Coming from Druxton Bridge, at the T-junction turn right, parallel to the Tamar on the right (and also the canal which ran through the woods on the left, though little now remains of it here).

The Tamar comes alongside the Way for a short way and a little beyond, at the end of the wood on the left, the canal crossed the road and headed towards the Tamar, still roughly parallel to the road. There is no sign of the crossing now, but the line of the canal can be seen continuing as a line of woodland on the right.

Continue ahead at a junction, signposted to Bridgetown (7).

A little beyond the junction the Way crosses a small Tamar tributary, **Tala Water**. It is just possible to make out the aqueduct which carried the canal over the stream, through the trees on the right (F). It was rebuilt in its current form in 1835 after flooding destroyed the original construction. Unfortunately there is no public access.

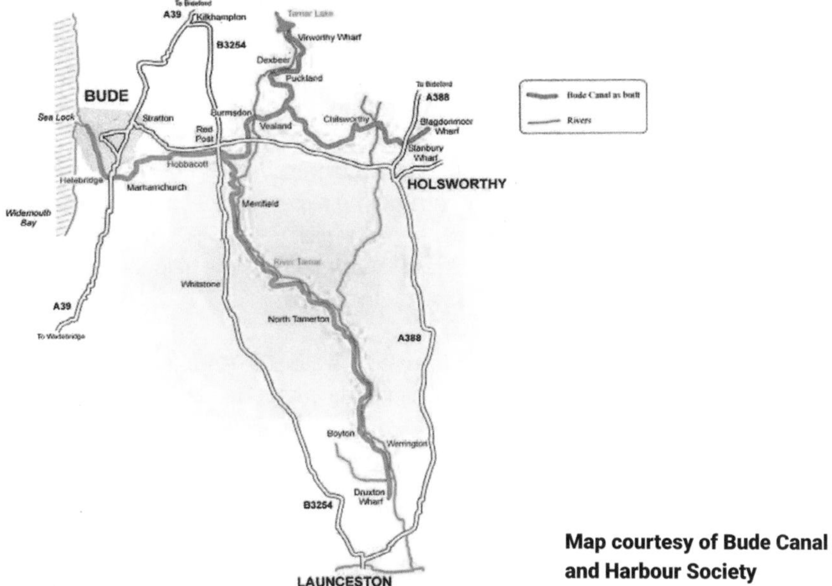

Map courtesy of Bude Canal and Harbour Society

Map of the Bude Canal System

The map above shows the line of the Bude Canal as originally built.

The short length between Bude and Helebridge was known as the 'Barge Canal' and is the only length which had locks. This included the sea lock at the mouth of the canal, one of only two such locks in the country.

Over the rest of the system changes in height were dealt with by the use of 'inclined planes'. These were at Marhamchurch, Hobbacott (the highest in the country apart from Ironbridge), Vealand, Merrifield, North Tamerton and Tamartown. Most of these are close to the Coast to Coast route.

The two main lines of the canal went from Bude to Crossgate and east to Holsworthy. The third branch linked the system to the water supply reservoir at what is now Lower Tamar Lake, although this branch was also used to transport sand and other goods in common with the rest of the canal system.

Carry on past Bridgetown Methodist Church and then a farm to arrive at a junction (8). Continue ahead on the road signed with a low bridge warning and pass through the farmstead of Bridgetown.

Despite the name of **Bridgetown**, there is no bridge over the Tamar here now, nor even in the first edition of the OS map in 1809. There were later bridges over the canal but as the name is first recorded in 1629, long before the coming of the canal, there must presumably have been a river bridge at one time.

The *Tamara Coast to Coast Way* continues north parallel to the Tamar and the canal. At the next farmstead, **Little Tamartown** (incorrectly spelt as Tamatown on Ordnance Survey maps), the canal left the river and crossed the road to a higher level on an inclined plane.The archway carrying the plane, known as the **Werrington Inclined Plane**, is still in place (G). As mentioned earlier, the Bude Canal was highly unusual in using inclined planes rather than locks to gain or lose height over most of its length. This is the first one to be passed on the Way.

The Werrington Inclined Plane raised or lowered the canal 51ft/15.5m over a length of 259ft/78.5m. Note that the road here is slightly lowered. Nearby, the wharfinger's house is still in place, now a farm building.

Continue ahead under the arch. At the next farmstead, Tamartown (9), the Way bears left away from the river and continues along the road, steadily climbing out of the valley.

At the next right-hand bend the road passes between two stone buttresses. These carried the canal on an overbridge. The canal's route can still be seen as a private track on the right as it continues parallel to the river.

The Way now turns west to climb away from the floor of the Tamar Valley, giving views up the valley, then later down.

Reaching a junction (Wilkie Down Farm), turn right, signposted to Boyton (10).

The *Tamara Coast to Coast Way* turns north again, parallel to the Tamar and now on the western lip of the valley.

After 0.6 mile/1km look out for the entrance to **Danesfield Farm** on the left, on a right-hand bend (H). This is the parish boundary from Werrington into Boyton and marks the Way leaving the historic incursion of Devon west of the Tamar, as described earlier when crossing the Tamar at Druxton Bridge (page 157).

Arriving at Boyton turn right at the junction (11), signposted to Boyton and Holsworthy, to the village centre, passing a bench opposite the Methodist Church.

In the early 20th century **Boyton** had a pub, the Duchy Arms, as well as carpenter's shops, an undertaker, a blacksmith, grocers, shoemakers, a tailor and a butcher. Clues to some old uses are seen in the house names 'The Old Smithy', 'Forge House' and 'The Old Post Office'. All are now gone, including the pub, but the village still has a primary school (which will be passed on the way out of the village), serving the whole surrounding rural area. Otherwise the main facilities are the village hall and, opposite it, the parish church.

The church, like many in this part of Cornwall, is mainly 14th and 15th century, although there are earlier elements, including an early Norman font. Prior to 1066 the church and lands at Boyton belonged to Tavistock Abbey but by 1540 it had come into the ownership of the Duchy of Cornwall in a land exchange arranged by Henry VIII. The Duchy disposed of the land in 1947.

The parish of Boyton, like Werrington, historically extended across the Tamar, where it included the hamlet of Northcott and its surrounding land east of the river. However, the Tamar has always been the Devon–Cornwall boundary here, so the parish was partly in Cornwall and partly in Devon. The situation has been regularised with Northcott now forming its own parish in Devon. It is one of the smallest parishes in the county, in both area and population.

Northcott parishioners reached Boyton by crossing the Tamar at **Boyton Bridge** (I). This can be visited by continuing ahead in the village centre, signposted to Northcott. There was a bridge here, probably built early in the 17th century, which seems to have been in some disrepair in the later part of that century. The modern bridge, based on the earlier one, was rebuilt in 2005. The Bude Canal, which has closely followed the Tamar since Tamartown, passed close by the bridge and there was a canal wharf here. Part of the canal has been retained as a private ornamental feature on one side of the road. On the other side of the river is the old mill, now a private residence. It is about 0.5 mile/0.8km from the village to the bridge.

It has been 8.5 miles/13.5km since leaving Lifton (and a couple of miles more for walkers starting from Launceston), and is a further 9.5 miles/12.25km to Bridgerule. If planning to catch the bus from Boyton to Launceston or North Tamerton (this only runs on certain days of the week), continue straight ahead at the earlier T-junction (before turning right into the village), signposted to North Tamerton and Week St Mary, and the bus stop is opposite Beacon Park. (There is another bench near here.)

Alternatively, if you plan to use the much more frequent Launceston–Bude bus, the bus stop is c. 1.25 miles/2km away on the B3254 road at Bennacott. The link route between Boyton and Bennacott is described below.

From Launceston follow the *Tamara Coast to Coast Way* as far as Boyton, arriving at a T-junction. Continue ahead here (the Way turns right), signposted to North Tamerton and Week St Mary, past Beacon Park then left at Queen's Acre. After descending to cross Tala Water, a Tamar tributary, turn right, signposted North Beer, and pass that farm, continuing on to reach the B3254 and the bus stop at Bennacott.

In reverse, the link route from the bus stop at Bennacott to Boyton is:

Go down the side lane opposite Bennacott and follow past North Beer to descend to a junction. Turn left, signposted to Boyton, and cross Tala Water, a Tamar tributary, then climb ahead to a T-junction and turn right here. At the next junction arrive at the *Tamara Coast to Coast Way*, turning left for Bridgerule or continuing ahead for Launceston.

To continue on the *Tamara Coast to Coast Way* turn left in the village centre, signposted to North Tamerton, passing the church. At the T-junction at the end turn right (12), again signposted to North Tamerton. Pass the village school and continue along the road, again heading north, parallel to the Tamar Valley over to the right.

On the skyline on the right-hand, or eastern, side the outline of Dartmoor can still be intermittently seen.

The Way continues ahead on the road, climbing gently and passing the entrance to Hornacott Manor.

Continue ahead, parallel to the Tamar Valley on the right, keeping straight on at the next junction at Hornacott (13), signposted North Tamerton.

As the Way descends to cross a small tributary of the Tamar it passes the entrance to the Eastcott pub. Originally set up as a facility for the holiday lodges here, it is now a public hostelry but is only open during the evening – see www.northtamerton.com/eastcottarms.

Behind **Eastcott** and next to the Tamar is another canal inclined plane with an existing underground waterwheel pit. However, there is no public access.

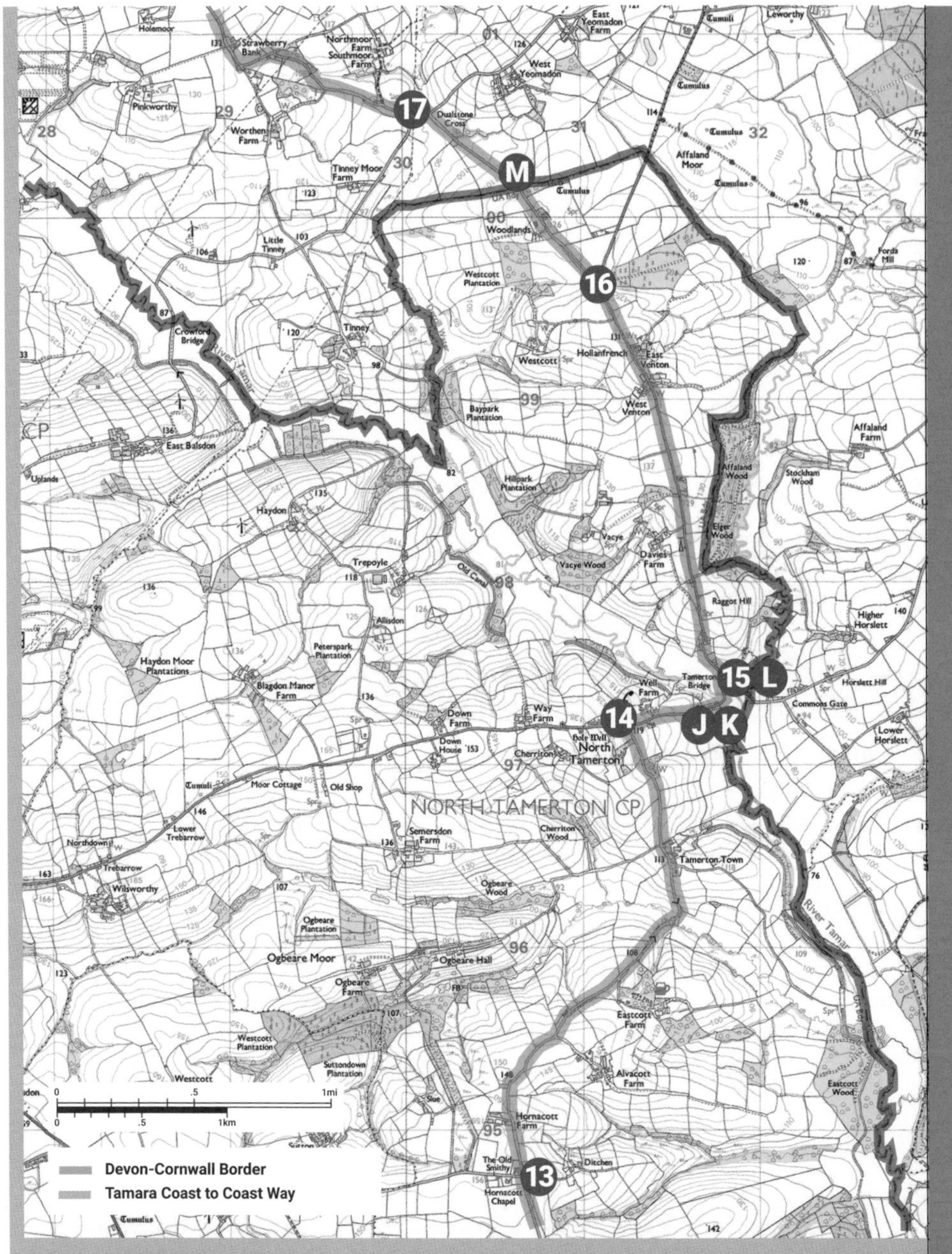

Stage 5, Map 3:
Hornacott to Strawberry Bank

The Way crosses the tributary stream then climbs, passing the farmstead of Tamerton Town, to arrive at the village of North Tamerton (14).

North Tamerton church and Church House

North Tamerton is a small village above the Tamar. There are no facilities, apart from occasional buses (to and from Launceston) which only operate on certain days of the week; check details beforehand if this is an option being considered.

The obvious feature of the village is the **church**, with its prominent tower a landmark in the surrounding district. Like many churches in the Tamar Valley it dates from the 1400s in its present form. Inside it has an unusual colourful screen as well as a 13th-century font. Next to the church is Church House, of the late 16th or early 17th century. Church houses were typically built for parish festivities and later often used as almshouses or schools.

The Revd R.S. Hawker was vicar here in the 19th century before moving to Morwenstow, where he will be encountered by *Tamara Coast to Coast Way* walkers at the end of their journey. North Tamerton church tower features as part of his design for Morwenstow's vicarage. Hawker is perhaps best known for being the writer of Cornwall's unofficial anthem, 'Trelawney'.

Until the 19th century North Tamerton is normally referred to simply as 'Tamerton', and there is no South Tamerton. One supposition is that the 'North' was added to distinguish the village from Tamerton Foliot near Plymouth, although confusion seems unlikely because of the distance between the two. Other possibilities are that it was added to distinguish it from the farm of Tamerton Town, passed a little to the south, or after the establishment of Tamartown even further to the south, which is not recorded until the 18th century and is shown on a map as Little Tamerton in 1809.

To continue on the Way turn right at North Tamerton, signposted to Holsworthy.

As the Way descends towards the Tamar it passes the entrance to **Well Farm** on the left. The buildings can just be glimpsed along its drive. This was probably originally a medieval longhouse, modernised later and with a datestone of 1660 on one end.

Approaching the bottom of the hill the Way again encounters the line of the Bude Canal. The canal crossed the road on an aqueduct where there is a short levelling (J). **Canal Farm** is just below this crossing point and was once the storage buildings for canal cargoes, especially sand and wood. The nearby cottages were built for canal workers.

Just before the left-hand bend at the bottom there is a slate stone (K) in the verge on the right marked with a 'C' (see Stage 4, page 112). Most of these bridge stones have now been lost but some, as here at **North Tamerton Bridge**, survive, the first on the Way since that passed at Horsebridge. Incidentally, this is a slightly unusual one in being a slate stone, where most of these bridge stones in Cornwall and also West Devon were granite.

Continue on to cross North Tamerton Bridge (L).

The boundary between Devon and Cornwall here was originally the Tamar, but part of North Tamerton parish was always on the east side of the river. This meant that, like Boyton, the parish was mostly in Cornwall but partly in Devon. In 1844 the Devon–Cornwall boundary was moved to coincide with the parish boundary, thus uniting the whole parish in Cornwall. Crossing the Tamar here does not therefore involve crossing the county boundary.

County bridge stone, North Tamerton Bridge

It seems that this was quite an important crossing point in medieval times, and that a *Pons Magnus* (great bridge) recorded as being over the Tamar between Kilkhampton and Launceston in 1478 refers to this location. It was also the site of a significant Civil War battle. The current bridge is a rebuilding after a flood in 1847.

North Tamerton Bridge

Continue ahead at the junction (15), signposted Holsworthy and Bridgerule.

The road climbs away from the Tamar, bending gradually to the left to be roughly parallel with the river valley and on its eastern flank.

Approximately 1.5 miles/2.5km after crossing North Tamerton Bridge the road forks (16). Bear left here, on the more minor road signposted Bridgerule.

Pass 'Woodlands' on the left and then, just under 0.25 mile/0.5km later, the Way crosses from Cornwall into Devon, at the far end of the woodland on the right ('Shepherd's Bush') (M).

There now follows some 4.25 miles/7km within Devon; there is no Cornish alternative for Kylgh Kernow walkers. Any alternative still requires some walking in Devon; in addition, part of this Devon length is actually west of the Tamar and is historically within Cornwall, having been moved into Devon only in the 19th century.

In any event, the route is always close to the Tamar, often giving views of the valley, whereas any alternative has to stray some way away and any sense of the Tamar Valley or the Devon–Cornwall boundary is lost.

Continue ahead at the next junction (Dualstone Cross), signposted Bridgerule and Whitstone (17) then cross a small tributary of the Tamar, Derril Water, then ahead again at the next junction (Moor Cross), signposted Bridgerule.

Continuing ahead the Way remains parallel to the Tamar, which is just over the ridge line to the left.

Keep ahead at the next junction (Bounds Cross), signposted Bridgerule (18).

A little after Bounds Cross the Way reaches an **old railway bridge**, the line marked by trees in both directions. This is the line to Bude, opened in 1898 principally for the tourist trade but also of importance in bringing in and taking out goods. Its arrival was probably the main reason why the canal lost trade and was closed. The tourist trade was given a boost in the 20th century when Bude became an element of the London and South Western Railway's Atlantic Coast Express, with fast steam expresses passing along this line. This was discontinued in 1964 and soon afterwards, in 1966, the line was closed as part of the Beeching plan.

At the next junction (Furze Cross) turn left, signposted to Bridgerule and Bude (19).

Ahead can be seen Bridgerule church (N), which is a little way out of the village.

The *Tamara Coast to Coast Way* descends to Bridgerule and the Tamar Valley. The Tamar is crossed at Bridgerule Bridge (O).

Bridgerule (20) has a pub, the Bridge Inn (01288 381316), and some accommodation, although there is no shop. It also has a bus service, but this is rather limited, so it is recommended that those wishing to use public transport to access accommodation should continue for a further 0.5 mile/0.8km on Stage 6 to Borough Cross, where there is a regular and relatively frequent bus service to Bude or Launceston.

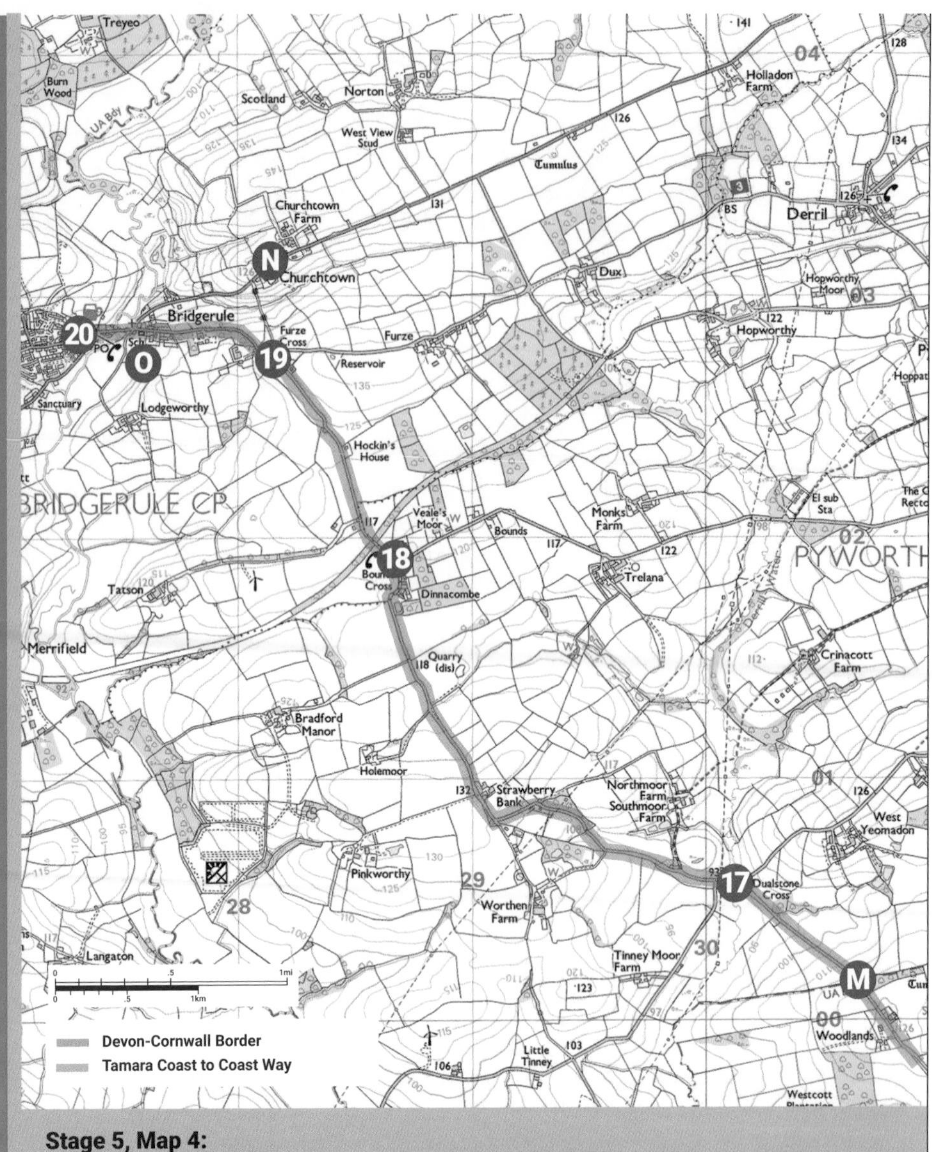

Stage 5, Map 4:
Strawberry Bank to Bridgerule

Bridgerule is recorded in the Domesday Book of 1086 as simply *Brige*, so there must have been an early bridge over the Tamar here, in Saxon times. The original centre of the manor was at Tackbeare, a little way to the southwest, and this manor was granted by William I to one of his Norman followers, Ruald. His name became added to 'Brige', presumably to distinguish it from any other bridges, and so the location became in time Bridgerule. There are 12th-century charters referring to it as *Pons-ruwold-on-Tamera*. While the site of a very ancient bridge, the current one dates from 1923, as noted by the date stone on the parapet.

Traditionally, the boundary between Devon and Cornwall was fixed as the Tamar by the Saxon King Athelstan in AD936. While as early as the 11th century variations in this had occurred, it remained the boundary at Bridgerule. The river was also a parish boundary and so two parishes, Bridgerule West and Bridgerule East, existed side by side, the former in Cornwall and the latter in Devon. As there was only one parish church, on the Devon side, it was eventually decided to regularise the situation and in 1844 Bridgerule West was transferred to Devon, although it was west of the Tamar. Oddly, though, the two parishes remained separate until 1950. So although the Tamar is crossed here, the Way remains in Devon, if historically in Cornwall.

The first edition OS map, dated 1809, shows the centre of the local population at that time being around the church, east of the bridge, with very little development around the bridge itself. This may have been because of the danger of flooding, a risk which can still arise. Nevertheless, by the end of the 19th century the inn had appeared together with other development and the village centre had gravitated here. Further residential development has now occurred over to the west.

St Bridget's Church (a short way off the route). Photographer: J. Guffogg

Stage 6
Bridgerule to Upper Tamar Lake (or Kilkhampton)

This stage is a mixture of footpaths and quiet lanes. Stage 6 leaves the Tamar Valley for a stretch, reflecting the Devon–Cornwall boundary which also forsakes the river for a while. The historic Bude Canal is intermittently followed, providing examples of a variety of heritage features on the historic waterway. It ends by passing Lower Tamar Lake, source of the canal's water supply, and the modern reservoir of Upper Tamar Lake.

Distance:	13.8 miles/22.1km between Bridgerule and Upper Tamar Lake; 18 miles/28.75km between Bridgerule and Kilkhampton
Total ascent:	1408ft/430m (to Upper Tamar Lake)
Estimated walking time (without stops):	6hr 15min (to Upper Tamar Lake)
Car parks:	Launcells church, Lower Tamar Lake, Upper Tamar Lake

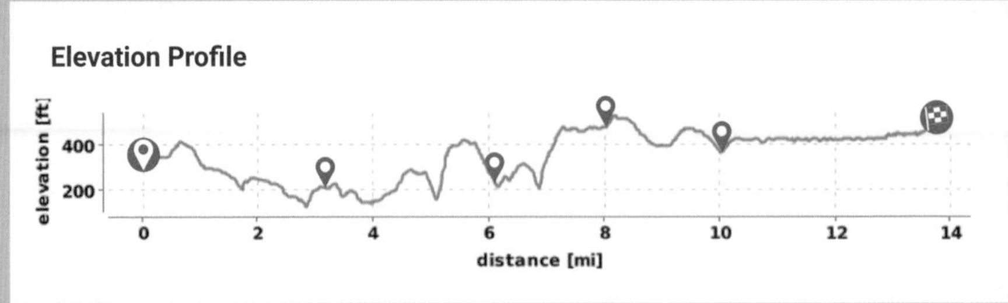

Start / 0m:	**Bridgerule**
3.3 miles:	**Marhamchurch**
6 miles:	**Launcells**
8 miles:	**Hersham**
10 miles:	**River Tamar**
End:	**Upper Tamar Lake**

Public transport & shorter options: Fairly frequent buses between Bude and Launceston stop at Borough Cross just outside Bridgerule. Relatively little accommodation on this stage, but a good range of accommodation and facilities in Marhamchurch (just off route) and especially in Bude (see Bude Link, page 188). From Bude buses run to and from Marhamchurch, Launcells, Hersham and Kilkhampton. There is a car park and seasonal café and toilets at Upper Tamar Lake; most people will need to walk the link route into Kilkhampton (see Stage 7, page 200), where there are bus services and accommodation.

Link route: Bude Link to/from a point near Marhamchurch.

For background information on Bridgerule, see the end of Stage 5, pages 169 -171.

From Bridgerule Bridge (1) walk through the village, past the Bridge Inn, straight on and up the hill.

Just past the house on the right part-way up the hill, the *Tamara Coast to Coast Way* crosses the line of the Bude Canal (A), now only identified by a raised grassy bank in the field on the left as it heads to and from the Launceston direction.

Keep on and the Way reaches the B3254 Bude–Launceston road at Borough Cross (2).

From Borough Cross there is a regular and relatively frequent bus service to Bude or Launceston.

To continue on the Tamara Coast to Coast Way go straight across, signposted to Marhamchurch, and through the hamlet of Borough.

This is an appropriately named settlement, as it is from the Old English for 'hill' – most often a fortified hill, although there are no old fortifications to be seen here.

Descending from **Borough** is a first distant view of the sea off the north coast ahead. After passing the white house on the right at the bottom of the hill, 'Kents', the Way is now actually on the line of the Devon–Cornwall border, which follows this road: Cornwall on the right and Devon on the left.

About 0.3 mile/0.5km after 'Kents' look out for a wide track on the right signed as a public footpath, by a sign for Great Beer Farm (3). Turn right along this track, entering completely into Cornwall, towards the farm.

The farm's name sounds like an advert for a good pint but actually comes from the Old English bearu, a grove or small wood. Walkers will not be able to get any ale here.

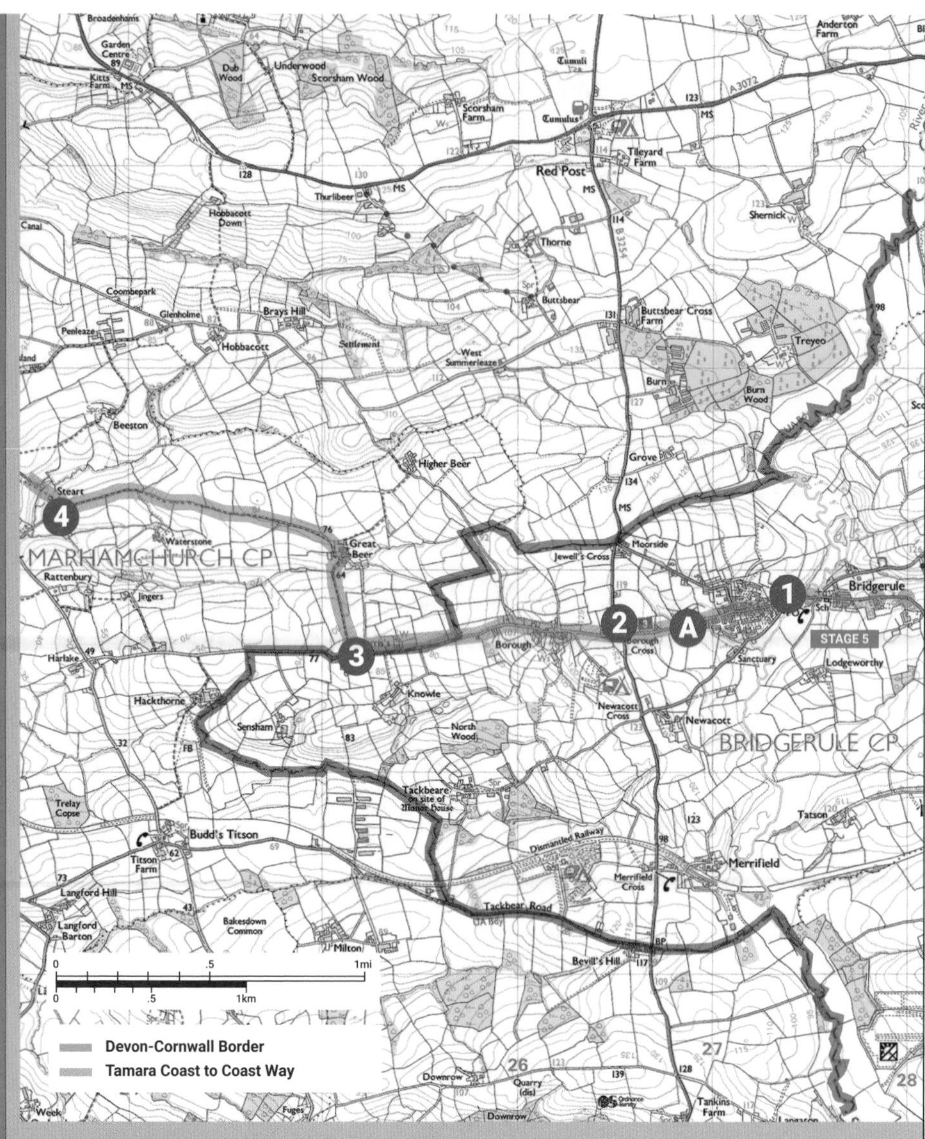

Stage 6, Map 1:
Bridgerule to Marhamchurch

At the farmyard bear left next to the farmhouse, then immediately sharp left, then right onto a track leading away from the farm. Follow the track to the end, go through the gate

and continue ahead on the right-hand side of the bank. The Way passes through another field gate, a kissing-gate and over three stiles to arrive at a tarmac lane. Follow this ahead. As the lane descends, look out for the entrance to Steart Farm on the right (4). Turn right here, on the right-hand of the two tracks. Bear left next to a greenhouse and along a hedged path, keeping left at a fork to descend to a footbridge. Cross this, and a stile, and follow the field edge up ahead then round to the left to a stile in the hedge.

Cross this stile into the next field and head for the top left-hand corner. Cross the stile here onto a track then go over another stile to reach a road (5). Turn right here, signposted to Stratton.

A little way along here the Way arrives at a crossroads at a hilltop (6).

The Tamara Coast to Coast Way is now close to the village of Marhamchurch. It has been 3.5 miles/5.5km from Bridgerule and there is a further 11 miles/17.5km to Upper Tamar Lake and 14 miles/22.5km to Kilkhampton. Marhamchurch has regular services to Bude and Kilkhampton. Turning left here, Marhamchurch is 0.5 mile/0.75km along the road.

The Tamara Coast to Coast Way has a further link beyond Marhamchurch to Bude, enabling a variety of circular walks incorporating the Way and the South West Coast Path – see page 188. It also gives access to Bude and its facilities. It is 3 miles/4.75km to Bude from here; directions for this link are found at the end of Stage 6 (page 188).

There is a bench a little way along the road towards Marhamchurch. The village has a pub (Bullers Arms Hotel, 01288 361277) and a village store, www.marhamchurchvillageshop.weebly.com.

The Bude Link leaves and joins the *Tamara Coast to Coast Way* here, going left at the crossroads.

Since crossing the Tamar at Bridgerule the Way has come some way west, partly because of the lack of suitable access nearer the river and partly because the Devon–Cornwall boundary leaves the Tamar in this area. Now, however, the Way starts to turn back to the east, towards the Tamar.

To continue on the *Tamara Coast to Coast Way*, carry on ahead at the crossroads, signposted to Stratton. After about 0.5 mile/0.8km look out for a wooden gate on the right

signed 'Planekeepers Path' (7). Turn along here (if you arrive at Cann Orchard you've gone too far; go back up the hill about 50yd/m to the next wooden gate, now on the left).

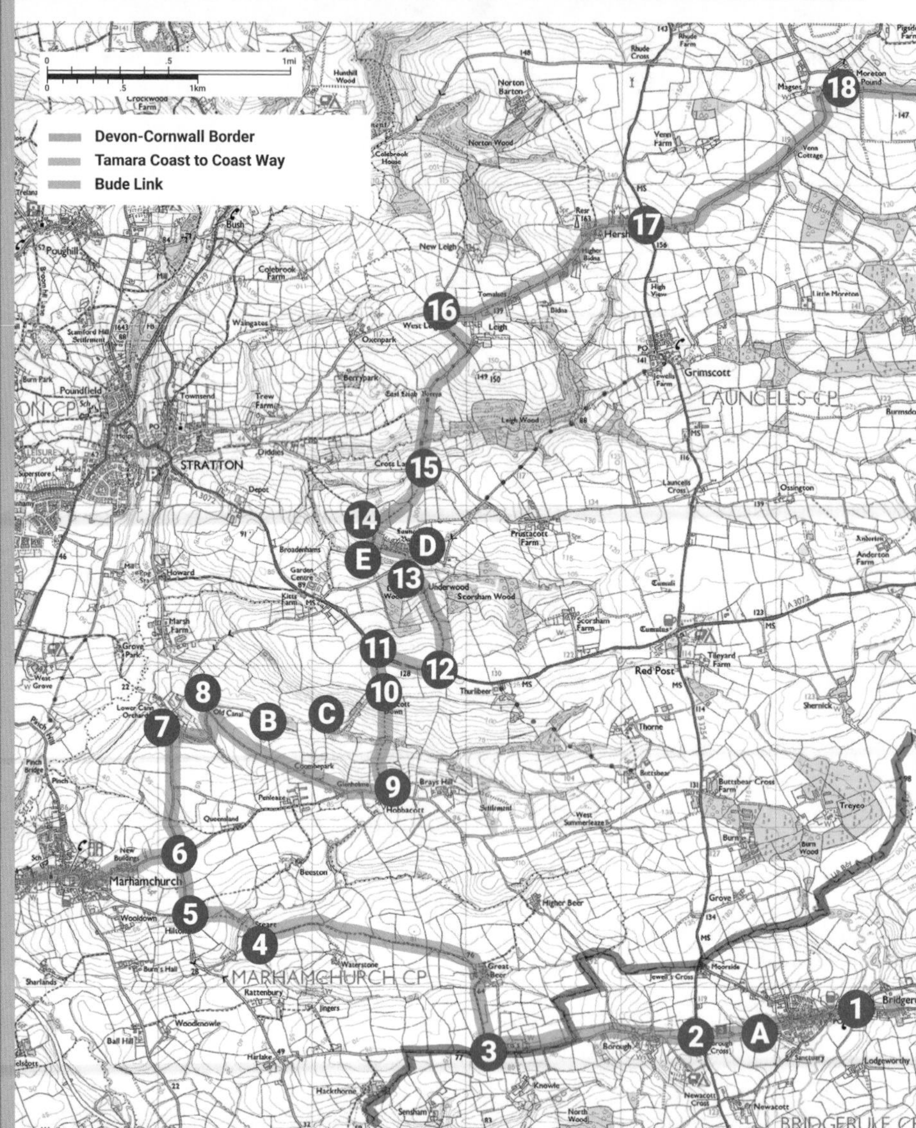

Stage 6, Map 2:
Marhamchurch to Hersham

This is the old towpath for the Bude Canal, and the canal profile is seen alongside on the right. This is part of the so-called 'main line' of the canal, where the branches from near Launceston, Holsworthy and Lower Tamar Lake have come together for the leg into Bude. Note the metal mileage post a short way along on the left, indicating 3¼ miles to Bude.

Follow the path to arrive at a road (8). Turn right here.

The canal continued into the field opposite, scarcely discernible here now. It then followed the valley (B) to arrive at the foot of one of the canal's celebrated inclined planes (C) – Hobbacott or Thurlibeer – (see historical background on page 159, Stage 5).

At the junction by the small post box bear left to reach Hobbacott Farm (9). Here turn left through the gate on the signed public footpath, going straight ahead to join a track which is followed down into a field ahead.

From here the line of the Hobbacott or Thurlibeer Inclined Plane on the Bude Canal is seen as the line of trees ahead and left climbing the hill.

Cross the field to the gate seen in the hedge at the bottom. Go through the two gates then head steeply uphill over the next field, aiming for the power supply pole to the right of the farmhouse. Go through the gate and over a stile then ahead to cross a bridge.

From the top of the field there are superb views back over the valley and Marhamchurch and along the north Cornwall coast.

Leaving the field the *Tamara Coast to Coast Way* has reached the Bude Canal again as the track crosses the line of the canal. On the left is the area at the top of the Hobbacott Inclined Plane and one of the canal buildings. On the right the canal continues on its way to Launceston and Holsworthy and also on to Lower Tamar Lake.

Follow the track to the left to arrive at a junction.

On the left is the top of the **Hobbacott Inclined Plane** (sometimes called Thurlibeer), one of the canal's celebrated features. This one was particularly notable, being the second highest inclined plane in the country at 225ft/68m, only that at the nationally important industrial archaeology site at Ironbridge in Shropshire being higher.

The system for raising and lowering the tub boats here used two wells sunk into the top of the plane, in each of which was a giant bucket, suspended on a double chain wound over a geared drum. Each bucket could contain 15 tons of water and the two were counterpoised so that the weight of water in the bucket at the top caused the bottom bucket to ascend while the top bucket sank down its shaft, the movement turning the gearing to haul the tub boats up and down. When the full bucket reached the bottom a valve opened and its load of water was discharged.

The wells and shafts were under the grassy area on the left of the path. Also here are some of the canal buildings. This location also had a steam engine for use when the water system failed and a blacksmith's shop, powered by a waterwheel. There were also bays for the parking of the tub boats while they awaited lowering or were made ready for their onward journey. These still exist at the bottom of the plane but unfortunately there is currently no public access to them.

Top of Hobbacott Inclined Plane

Barge bays, bottom of Hobbacott Inclined Plane (not accessible to public)

At the next path junction (10) bear right and go along this track to the gate at the end. Make sure children and dogs are under control at this point as the *Tamara Coast to Coast Way* here reaches the A3072 Bude–Holsworthy road, which can be fast and busy.

There are more panoramic views down the coast of North Cornwall from this high vantage point.

Go through the gate at the end (11) to a layby and turn right to the A3072. Carefully cross to the verge on the other side and walk for about 0.25 mile/0.4km to a gate on the left (12) – there is a Planekeepers Path sign opposite– it's the second gateway on the left after joining the road.

Go through the gate and follow the hedge on the right, descending to a track leading to a stile in the bottom corner. Cross the stile and continue ahead through gates to

a tarmac drive. Arriving at a road (13) turn right, then first left up a concrete drive and immediately left again, to pass Launcells Barton (D).

Launcells Barton

The earliest building on this site was the country retreat of the Abbot of Hartland. The land here was granted to the Abbot around 1200 by the wife of the then lord of the manor, perhaps to assure her of entry into heaven. The current building has Tudor elements but is mostly of the 1700s and is used as a wedding venue.

Pass Launcells Barton then go down the left-hand, narrower path to arrive at Launcells church (E). Follow the path on the left to the front of the church.

This charming **church**, in its equally charming setting, is mainly 15th century, but is presumably on the site of an older church, as it contains a Norman font. Its earliest known dedication is to St Andrew, but in 1321 it was rededicated to St Swithin (also spelled Swithun) – and is now dedicated to both. But there may be even older origins – the name Launcells seems to come from the Cornish lann seles, which is likely to mean the holy place of Seles, perhaps an early monk or hermit. Nearby, by the car park entrance, is a holy well, often associated with ancient religious sites. Now dedicated, like the church, to St Swithin, it is likely to have very early origins.

Launcells Church

The church is worth exploring; the least spoilt church in Cornwall, according to Sir John Betjeman. There are excellent old carved bench ends, 15th-century tiles in the chancel, 18th-century box pews and a 17th-century wall painting. As the church has not been restored since the 18th century, its original features are particularly well preserved.

In the churchyard is buried **Sir Goldsworthy Gurney**, a 19th-century inventor. He has been referred to as 'the father of incandescent light' and invented a successful navigation light, known usually as the 'Bude Light'. He also invented an early steam jet engine, which he used to power coaches. In 1829 he drove such a coach between London and Bath at an average speed of 14mph/22.5kph – a prodigious speed for the time. He is mostly associated with Bude, where he built his house, now known as Bude Castle, on a raft on the sandy beach.

It has been 6.5 miles/10.5km from Bridgerule, and is a further 8 miles/13km to Upper Tamar Lake and 11.25 miles/18km to Kilkhampton. There is the possibility of leaving the Way here by bus. There are regular bus services on the A3072 to and from Bude and these may be accessed by walking through the church car park to the road and turning right for about 0.25 mile/0.4km.

Follow the tarmac path up the left-hand side of the church. Go through two gates and then up to a kissing-gate into a field (14).

Climbing out of the valley it can be appreciated how secluded the church is. There is no village here.

Go through the metal gate and cross the field diagonally right, passing through a gate in a fence and then aiming for a gate on the right-hand side of a clump of trees on the far side.

Go into the next field and through a wooden path gate to follow a fenced path on the left-hand field edge and round to a kissing-gate in the far right-hand corner. Follow the track down to Cross Lanes (15) and go straight across, descending to cross a stream then climbing steeply on a sometimes wet and slippery length.

Looking back and left from this track there are more views down the North Cornwall coast, including views over Bude and the coastal landmark on Compass Point, known as the 'Pepper Pot'.

Keep climbing on the track through two gates and at the top turn left just before the farmyard. Keep ahead on this track then, when it finally goes left into a field, go through the gate on the right and past the buildings at West Leigh to a tarmac road (16). Turn right here. Follow this quiet road through the hamlet of Hersham until it arrives at the B3254 Launceston–Kilkhampton road (17).

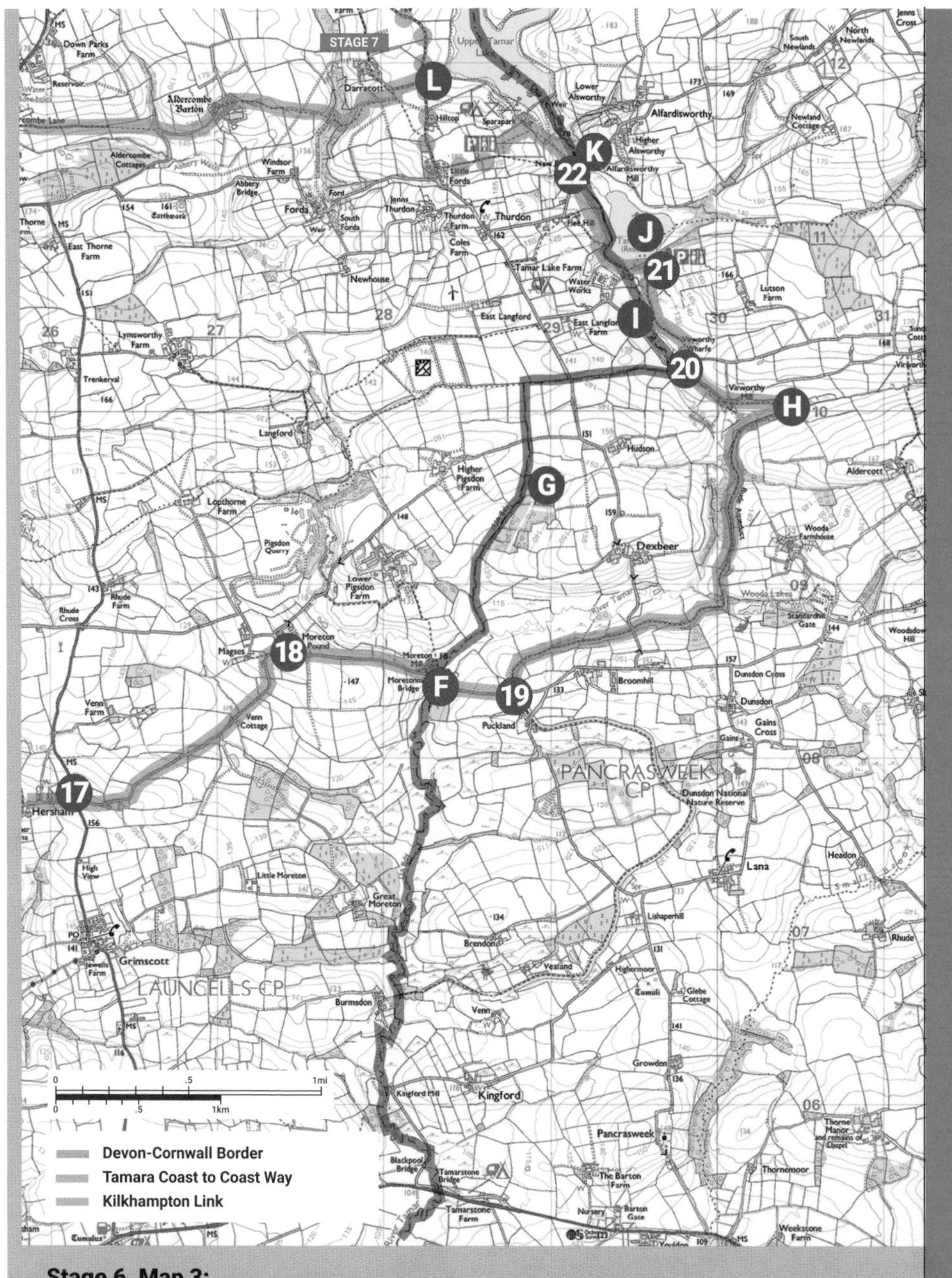

Stage 6, Map 3:
Hersham to Upper Tamar Lake

The Tamara Coast to Coast Way has now come 8.75 miles/14km from Bridgerule. There is still another 6 miles/9.5km to Upper Tamar Lake or 9 miles/14.5km to Kilkhampton. There is the possibility of picking up a bus here, linking to Kilkhampton or Bude along the B3254.

Cross the B3254 and follow the road ahead, signposted to Bradworthy. The road descends then climbs to the hamlet of Moreton Pound.

Moreton Pound

A little beyond Moreton Pound the *Tamara Coast to Coast Way* crosses into Devon. For those walking Kylgh Kernow there are local roads which stay in Cornwall for much of this next section, but there is still a length which crosses into Devon and runs alongside the Bude Canal, passing a canal wharf with an information centre in an old canal building. The cultural importance of the Bude Canal to Cornwall is such that *Kylgh Kernow* walkers are strongly recommended to walk this next section along the canal, regardless of its location.

Continue ahead at Moreton Pound, still signed to Bradworthy (18). The road descends to pass the buildings at Moreton Mill then crosses the Tamar at Moretonmill Bridge (F), taking the *Tamara Coast to Coast Way* into Devon.

This is the first sight of the Tamar since the Way left Bridgerule and followed its westward deviation. The river is smaller now it is reaching its upper stages, but still a river rather than a stream.

Continue and a little further on the road crosses the Bude Canal at Moreton Bridge (19).

This part of the canal is known as the **Aqueduct branch**. It was originally constructed to supply water from the reservoir on the Tamar to the canal system. After a little while, however, this branch was also used to transport goods, except for the extreme end length.

Like most of the road bridges over the canal, Moreton Bridge has been rebuilt for modern traffic but the original cast-iron support arches have been retained and the 'lead-in' walls have been rebuilt, although without the original capping stones. The **Bude Canal Trust** own and maintain the whole 5 mile/8km length of the Aqueduct branch, the longest continuous stretch of the canal remaining. For further information about the Trust see www.bude-canal-trust.co.uk. The Trust are always grateful for any help, practical, financial or otherwise, in maintaining this important heritage feature.

Bude Canal, Moreton Bridge

Next to the towpath on the right-hand side of the road is a convenient picnic site and table, maintained by the Bude Canal Trust. This is dedicated to a local councillor, the late Des Shadrick, who worked hard to ensure the survival and maintenance of this part of the canal.

The canal towpath continues to the right past the picnic site for a further 2.5 miles/4km to an aqueduct bridge which crosses the River Tamar, where it now ends as a cul-de-sac.

To continue on the *Tamara Coast to Coast Way* turn left from the road along the towpath, signed to Tamar Lakes. After a little more than 0.5 mile/1km the canal reaches another road, at Dexbeer Bridge. Continue ahead.

The Tamar is closely parallel to the canal along this section, and is occasionally seen on the left, but this is one of the short lengths where the Tamar and the Devon–Cornwall boundary do not coincide, the boundary being a little further over (G). The Tamar was established as the boundary as early as the 10th century for most of its length, but there seem to have always been some exceptions. Early maps are not clear, but certainly by the 1500s the boundary was west of the Tamar here. It has been suggested that this related to church land, as the earliest form of the name of this location, recorded in the 12th century, appears to mean 'deacon's wood'. This whole section has a quiet and remote character, the often unchanged landscape giving an idea of what the local area would have been like in the canal's heyday. An important part of its modern value is as a wildlife habitat, forming a conservation corridor through the countryside and linking the reservoir at Lower Tamar Lake, a National Nature Reserve at Dunsdon and a Local Nature Reserve at Vealand (the latter two a little further back along the canal, just beyond where the Way joins).

A little further along there are concrete constructions in the canal profile. These date from the early 20th century after the canal was no longer in use and Lower Tamar Lake became used for Bude's water supply. The water was carried along this part of the former canal and in places, such as here, controls were installed. This use of the canal ceased in the 1970s.

The canal had to meander somewhat in order to maintain a constant height. About 0.25 mile/0.4km after passing the demolished remains of an old bridge the canal swings to the east and then sharply back west. The relatively sharp left turn was known to the bargemen as Cape Horn because of the abrupt change of direction (H). Even with this meander, a culvert was needed for the canal to cross a tributary of the Tamar.

Pass through three gates next to the farm at Virworthy Mill then continue on to arrive at Virworthy Wharf (20).

Canal milestone, Virworthy

On the far side of the wharf is the canal repair and storage building, dating from the building of the canal, and maintained by the Bude Canal Trust. This now contains a display of information material and some old canal items.

Leaving the canal building notice the rescued abutment from one of the canal bridges. On returning to the path on the far side will be seen a canal milepost, indicating 13 miles to Bude. Next to it is an Aqueduct marker stone.

This was the furthest point used by the tub boats for transporting cargo on this branch. The wider area of canal here was used for loading and unloading.

Having crossed back over the canal from the workshop, turn right along the towpath, cross the footbridge and then the road. Continue ahead along the path.

Just to the left along the road at Virworthy can be seen the county boundary sign at the bridge over the Tamar. The boundary reverts to the Tamar near here, having left the river for a length near Moreton Bridge.

Above **Virworthy Wharf**, this length was only ever used for water supply for the canal system. After a while, more water control constructions from the early 20th century are seen in the canal profile.

Along this section some metal plaques will be seen, and also some little wooden boat models (I). These were installed when improvement works were undertaken on the path in the 1990s. On the far bank is an old canal boundary stone, marked BHC for Bude Harbour Company.

Shortly afterwards the canal ends, at a culvert ahead and on the right. This was the original supply source from the reservoir lake just ahead for the whole canal system. And so here the *Tamara Coast to Coast Way* leaves the Bude Canal for the last time, having accompanied it off and on since shortly after Launceston.

Virworthy Wharf

Lower Tamar Lake Dam

Follow the path up ahead to a footbridge (21) and turn left over the bridge.

The bridge crosses the outflow spillway from Lower Tamar Lake. The outflow forms the River Tamar, reborn after it had been subsumed by the lake into which it flows at its top end. The river being the Devon–Cornwall boundary, the Way re-enters Cornwall here.

Lower Tamar Lake (J) was constructed in the 1820s, for the purpose of supplying water to the new venture of the Bude Canal. Originally it was called Alfardisworthy Lake, after the nearby hamlet. The name, incidentally, was locally shortened to 'Alsworthy' or even 'Alsery' – it is West Saxon in origin, being 'Aelfheard's farm'.

When the canal ceased to be used at the beginning of the 20th century the lake's use was changed to provide a public water supply for Bude. The line of the canal was used to carry the water down to the town. This continued until the 1970s, when a new and larger reservoir, Upper Tamar Lake, was built specifically for that purpose. The old lake then became known as Lower Tamar Lake and used purely for low-key recreation and as a wildlife habitat.

Lower Tamar Lake has a quiet character. The only facilities are a small car park and seasonal toilets, and the only activities are bird-watching, coarse fishing and walking. There is a path all the way round the lake and a number of bird hides.

Bear left over the earth dam at the end of the lake then at the end follow the lakeside path round to the right. Just beyond the end of the lake the path arrives at a road. Cross to the access road to Upper Tamar Lake almost immediately opposite.

During the 19th century the Devon–Cornwall boundary was changed at Lower Tamar Lake. Instead of following the old line of the river along the middle of the lake it was moved to the west bank, meaning the whole of the lake is now in Devon. The boundary actually follows the line of the path. It reverts to the river on the stretch between the two lakes and a little way down the road to the right is Alfardisworthy New Bridge, which crosses the short length of the Tamar between the Upper and Lower Lakes. Just beyond the bridge is the historic boundary stone at the site of the old bridge over the Tamar (K). The stone does not name the counties but the two parishes, Bradworthy (Devon) and Kilkhampton (Cornwall). Similar stones will be seen towards the head of the Tamar.

Keep ahead on the main track (22) for the Upper Tamar Lake car park, café and toilets. For those continuing on towards Morwenstow, or for an overnight stop at Kilkhampton, turn left on the public footpath just before the car park and follow the directions set out in Stage 7 (see page 212).

Upper Tamar Lake has a car park, seasonal café and toilets, as well as an Activities and Angling Centre (www.swlakestrust.org.uk/upper-tamar).

Upper Tamar Lake is operated by the South West Lakes Trust. Work started on the lake in 1973 and it was completed in 1977. It was created by building a concrete dam across the Tamar, resulting in the river's valley, and part of a tributary valley, being flooded. Its purpose was to provide a reservoir for water supplies to the area, especially Bude.

It is a popular feature in the area, providing opportunities for sailing, windsurfing and kayaking, and is the base for the Upper Tamar Sailing Club. There are also camping facilities. In addition, it is an Area of Special Protection for Birds with over 200 species of nesting and migratory birds having been recorded here.

The Devon–Cornwall boundary still follows the original line of the Tamar here, meaning that it runs along the middle of the lake, then continues along the Tamar when the river enters the lake at its higher end.

Upper Tamar Lake

There is no public transport here and very little accommodation in the immediate area, although there is a camping site at the lake. For other facilities walkers should continue on to Kilkhampton by following the first part of Stage 7 (page 212) to pick up the Kilkhampton Link (see page 200). It is a further 2.75 miles/4.4km to Kilkhampton from here.

Bude Link (*Kevren bys Porthbud*)

The Bude Link (*Kevren bys Porthbud*) allows for a variety of circular walks incorporating the *Tamara Coast to Coast Way* and the South West Coast Path, including the link at Duckpool (see page 209) and the end of the Way at Morwenstow (see page 230). It also gives access to Bude and its shops, accommodation and other facilities. It also – although omitting part of the Devon–Cornwall boundary – provides the shortest route to and from the north coast.

Distance: 3 miles/4.8km between Marhamchurch and Bude Wharf
Total ascent: 21ft/6m
Estimated walking time (without stops): 1hr 15min

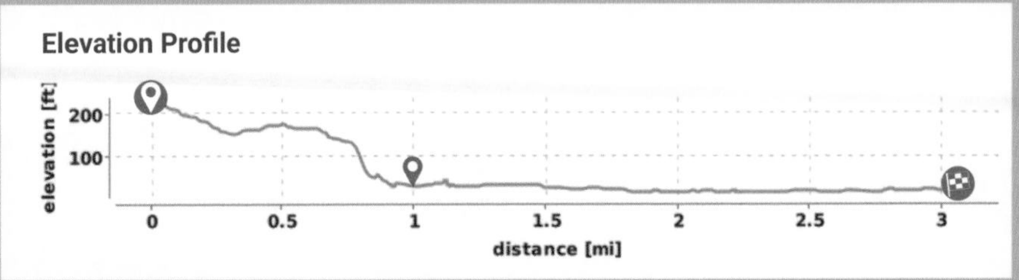

Start / 0m: ***Tamara Coast to Coast Way* Crossroads, Marhamchurch**
1 mile: **Hele Bridge**
End: **Bude**

Leave Stage 6 of the *Tamara Coast to Coast Way* at the crossroads (1) at the top of the hill (page 175), turning left along the lane. Follow this for 0.5 mile/0.75 km to arrive in the village of Marhamchurch. Turn right at the junction (signposted to Bude) and follow the road round to the left to the village centre, passing the Buller's Arms Hotel on the left and the Village Shop on the right.

Marhamchurch offers the facilities of its general stores, the 'Village Shop' (www.marhamchurchvillageshop.weebly.com), its pub and the Buller's Arms Hotel (01288 361277). Next to the shop are seasonal toilets. Buses to Bude and Kilkhampton leave from near the church.

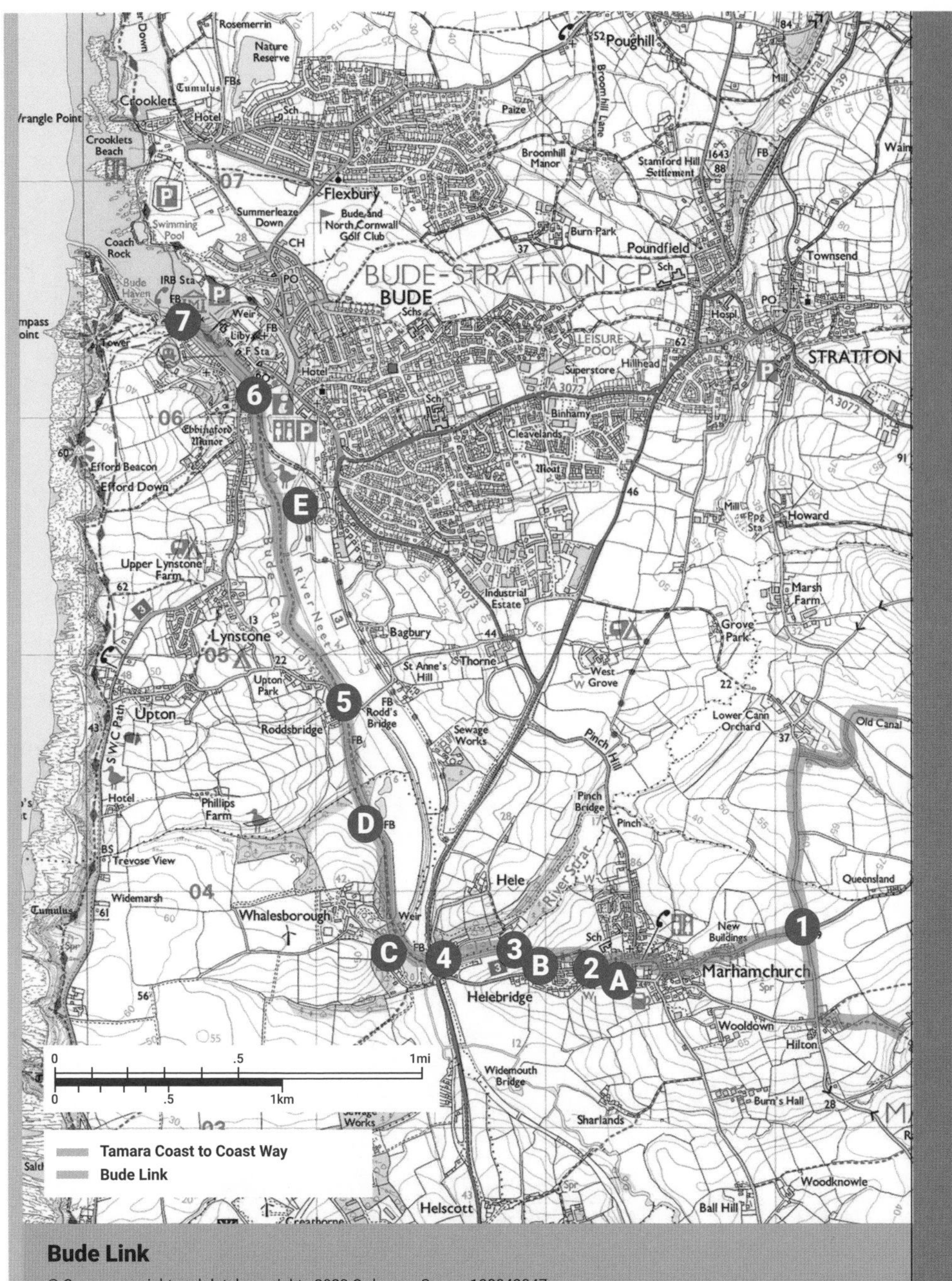
Rosemerrin
Nature Reserve
Poughill
Broomhill Lane
Cumulus
FBs
Crooklets
Wrangle Point
Hotel
Sch
Paize
Crooklets Beach
Broomhill Manor
Stamford Hill 1643 Settlement
88
FB
Mill
River Strat
A39
07
Flexbury
Summerleaze Down
Bude and North Cornwall Golf Club
Swimming Pool
Burn Park
Coach Rock
CH
37
Poundfield
Townsend
Bude Haven
IRB Sta
PO
BUDE-STRATTON CP
Sch
BUDE
Schs
Hospl
PO
Compass Point
FB
Weir
7
Tower
Liby
FB
F Sta
LEISURE POOL
Hillhead
62
STRATTON
Superstore
Hotel
A 3072
6
06
Sch
Binhamy
A 3072
Ebbingford Manor
Cleavelands
60
Efford Beacon
Moat
91
Efford Down
E
46
Mill
Ppg Sta
Howard
Bude Canal
River Neet
Upper Lynstone Farm
A3073
Marsh Farm
62
Industrial Estate
3
13
Bagbury
Grove Park
Lynstone
44
05
22
St Anne's Hill
Thorne
West Grove
Upton Park
22
5
FB
Lower Cann Orchard
Upton
Rodd's Bridge
Old Canal
43
Roddsbridge
FB
Sewage Works
37
SWC Path
Pinch Hill
Hotel
Phillips Farm
Pinch Bridge
28
D
FB
Pinch
BS
Trevose View
Hele
River Strat
Queensland
Widemarsh
04
Tumulus
61
Whalesborough
Weir
Sch
1
New Buildings
C
FB
4
3
B
2
A
Marhamchurch
Helebridge
Spr
56
Wooldown
55
12
Hilton
0
.5
1mi
0
.5
1km
Widemouth Bridge
Burn's Hall
28
Sewage Works
03
Sharlands
Tamara Coast to Coast Way
Bude Link
Woodknowle
Helscott
Ball Hill
Creathorne

Bude Link

Not so long ago **Marhamchurch** had a number of shops, including a baker, butcher, blacksmith, cobbler and even a wheelwright. Information about these old businesses, and a very interesting general history of the village and parish, is found in a locally produced book, *Marhamchurch Parish History and Heritage*, compiled by local resident Sue Proudfoot. This book also contains some fascinating old photographs of the village, and is available in the Village Shop. Marhamchurch occupies a prominent place on an east–west ridge a little inland from the coast. Its church tower (A) has traditionally been used as a landmark for shipping. There was a Norman church here, and a few Norman elements are found in the current building, although it is largely 14th and 15th century. As the place name, including the element 'church', is recorded in the Domesday Book of 1086, there was presumably a church here by at least the 11th century.

The current dedication is to St Marwenne, from whom the village gets its name. Marwenne is usually thought to have been a 5th-century daughter of the Welsh King Brychan. He is said to have had 24 children, many of whom sailed to Cornwall and established Christianity, initially by setting up hermitages or other religious settlements. Many have subsequently become villages bearing their names, including St Issey, St Mabyn, St Keyne and St Clether. Given the similarity of the name, Marwenne may possibly be the same as another daughter of Brychan, Morwenna, who established Morwenstow, at the end of the Way. However, another possibility, although less widely accepted, is that the name celebrates St Marwenn, a 10th-century Abbess of Romsey Abbey in Wessex.

The large building on the right is the Bray Institute, built in the Arts and Crafts style in 1913 and now used as the village hall. Just beyond, also on the right, is the old National School, built in 1873 and incorporating two 17th-century granite doorways from old almshouses demolished in the 19th century.

Marhamchurch

The Bude Canal passed close to Marhamchurch, skirting the village on its northern side.

Continue through the village passing between the church and the modern village school, then turn right along the signed public byway (2) a little after the school. This leads back to the line of the canal and the top of what was the Marhamchurch inclined plane (B).

The **canal and inclined plane** were over the hedge to the left of the track. This inclined plane carried the tub boats up and down 120ft/36m over a length of 836ft/250m. The plane was worked by a large overshot water wheel at the top, which operated an endless chain over a winding drum. The chain engaged with chain wheels at the top and bottom, mounted at right angles to the plane. Also at top and bottom were two channels with a central stone pier. A bargeman stood on the pier with a boathook and guided the tub boats to and from the chain and the rails on the plane.

Half-way down the inclined plane on the right-hand side the brick building was **Box's Iron Foundry**. This made and repaired the rails for the planes as well as other metal equipment for the canal. It was powered by a waterwheel fed by a leat from the canal at the top.

Near the bottom of the hill (3), turn off the track through a gate on your left between a South West Water building and the old foundry onto the tarmac path.

Soon the canal below the inclined plane appears on the left. There is an information board next to the path, which now arrives at the canal wharf at **Hele Bridge**. There was a large basin here associated with the main barge workshops on the wharf. This building still stands on the far side of the canal, now used as a museum by the Bude Canal and Harbour Society and open on summer Sundays (visit www.bude-canal.co.uk). This was the top end of the wide section of the canal, referred to as the Barge Canal. A metal name plate at the end of the path commemorates renovation work in 2008.

At the end turn left over the bridge (4). Almost immediately turn right, then right again along a footpath which follows the canal under the modern A39 and onwards towards Bude.

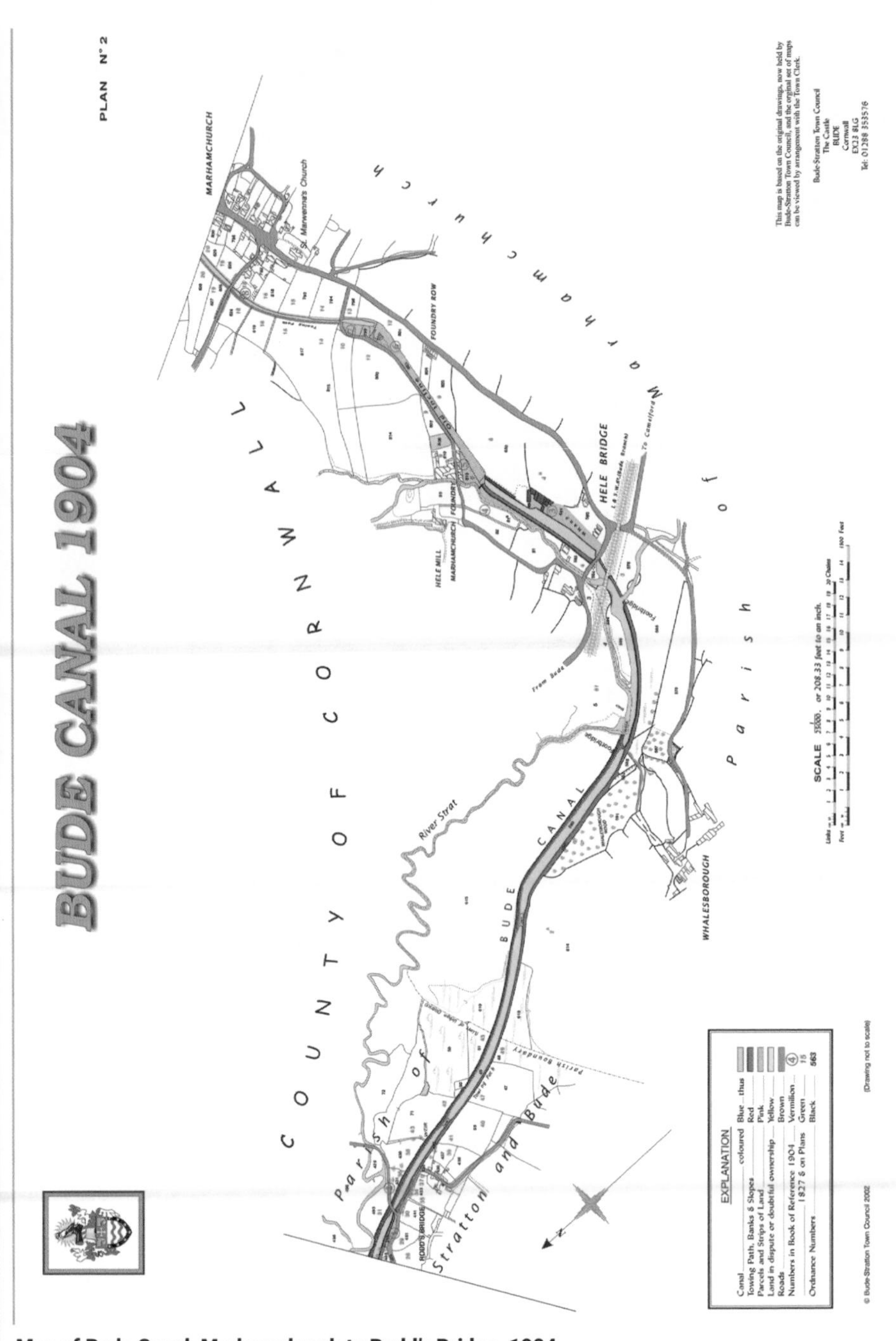

Map of Bude Canal, Marhamchurch to Rodd's Bridge, 1904
(Map courtesy of Bude-Stratton Town Council)

The road bridge is Hele Bridge, which carried what was then the main road between Bude and Camelford over the canal.

The canal is joined here by two rivers, one on each side of the path, the Strat from the north and the Neet from the south; the footbridge crosses the Neet.

Hele Bridge

On the far side, if in need of refreshment turn left then right a little later to reach 'The Weir' restaurant and tea room – www.whalesborough.co.uk/weir-restaurant (C).

This is the lowest length of the Bude Canal. The 2-mile/3.25km length between Hele Bridge and Bude is the widest part, both historically and currently. It was known as the **Barge Canal** although even on this length traffic was usually confined to tub boats. For a short time initially larger barges were used but soon abandoned, and very occasionally small coastal vessels which had entered the canal via the sea lock at Bude might reach Hele Bridge.

The two rivers, Strat and Neet, originally came together here to flow into the sea at Bude but when it was built the canal used both rivers to help supplement its flow over its lower length.

Much renovation work was undertaken here in 2008, including the installation of public art works. A series of such works, depicting giant chain links and designed as resting posts, had Cornish inscriptions, but the first one passed here has now lost its inscription which once read *Skathow Kibel*, meaning 'tub boats'.

A little further on the towpath passes a weir which marks the exit of the River Strat/Neet from the canal. Note the fish pass alongside the weir. All this was modernised in 2008. There is an information board next to the path.

A little further on the towpath reaches **Whalesborough Lock** (D), renovated as part of the 2008 works. While the majority of the canal achieved its changes in height by the use of inclined planes, locks were used on this lowest length between Hele Bridge and Bude. This one raised and lowered the water level 5.5ft/1.6m.

The lock gets its name from the nearby Whalesborough Farm. Until the 19th century this was spelled 'Walesborough' and it is probably the case that the first part of the name is identical to Wales, the country. In this part of Cornwall place names of Cornish language origin, like the well-known *tre-, pol- and pen-* names, are rare. It seems likely that, although west of the Tamar, there was quite extensive English settlement in this area in the 10th century. Some have suggested that for a while the boundary was effectively the River Ottery, a tributary of the Tamar some way to the south, rather than the Tamar itself. The name Walesborough probably reflects a settlement of *Wealas*, the Saxon word for Celts, in a largely English area.

Beyond the lock is another piece of canal-side public art, previously inscribed *Gwydhyel*, or 'wooded', descriptive of the locality, although again the inscription has been lost. A little further on is **Rodd's Bridge Lock**. This raised and lowered the canal height by a further 5.5ft/1.6m.

Continue and cross the canal at the road bridge (Rodd's Bridge) to the footpath alongside the canal on the far side (5).

A little way further is another artwork, this time with its inscription intact – *Avon*, or 'river'. Just beyond is an original cast-iron canal mileage post '1 Bude'.

The canal and towpath now continue next to marshland, part of the **Bude Valley Marshes Nature Reserve** (E), and another artwork, inscribed *Nans Bud* or 'Bude Valley'. This is an area of wet grassland and reeds – some 9 acres/3.6ha of reed beds, one of the largest in Cornwall. It is used by many species of migratory and resident birds, with chiffchaffs, sedge warblers, sand martins, reed buntings and willow warblers all found. In winter there are sandpipers, snipe, teal, widgeon and moorhen. This valuable habitat is also populated by otters and water voles.

More artworks are passed, inscribed respectively *Krowshyns* – 'crossroads', *Godhvewnans* – 'wildlife' and *Lestriva* – 'shipyard'.

Approaching Bude the canal widens further, with modern development on the opposite bank. This was the private wharf of Sir Thomas Acland, a local landowner and prime mover behind the development of the canal.

Next to the car park by the Tourist Information Centre are two more, larger, public artworks. These also have inscriptions, the upright one in English and the horizontal one in Cornish. The latter translates as *Don't be afraid of the sea, respect it. If a man*

could have the strength of the sea, he'd be a strong man.

Canal approaching Bude

Continue to the road bridge (6) and cross to the other side.

This is **Falcon Bridge**, named after the nearby hotel, which first developed with the coming of the canal. The bridge was originally a swing bridge, allowing access to the higher wharfs for larger vessels.

Bude Lower Wharf

Bude Lower Wharf, 1875
(Photo courtesy of Kresen Kernow)

Go down to the Lower Wharf and follow the canal seawards to the sea lock (7).

On the **Lower Wharf**, the so-called 'Company Wharf', the café and brasserie was originally a warehouse and coalyard. Beyond here is the Bark House, used for storing bark for the tanning trade. The ice-cream kiosk further on was the Harbour Master's office and the long low building further on again was the blacksmith's shop.

Towards the end of the canal are the sand rails, used by trucks to tip sand from the beach into the tub boats on the canal. Finally, at the mouth of the canal is the sea lock. This is one of only two in the country and is a Scheduled Ancient Monument. It was constructed in 1835 and allowed ships of up to 300 tons to enter the canal. It has been renovated several times since.

Bude Sea Lock

Note beyond the lock out towards the sea is the breakwater. This stretches from the shore to **Chapel Rock** to protect the sea lock and shipping in the haven. Destroyed by storm in 1838, it was rebuilt in 1839. Chapel Rock gets its name from a chapel, or hermitage, said to have been there in medieval times. It is described in 1602 as 'decayed'. One theory of the origin of Bude's name is that it is derived from 'Bede's' (or holy man's) haven, perhaps based on the legend of this hermitage.

Alternatively, the town's name may come from an older name of the river, a Celtic word – *Budr* – probably meaning 'muddy'. (Interestingly the river at Bude is now called both the Strat and the Neet!)

Bude Sea Lock and shipping, 1905
(Photo courtesy of Kresen Kernow)

The town centre is most easily accessed through one of the canal-side car parks. Historically it was a very minor settlement, although by the 18th century it had become a small-scale port, based in the mouth of the river, dealing mostly in limestone and coal from Wales. Its main development started with the building of the canal in the early 1820s and it was then given a boost when the railway arrived in 1898, and with it the tourist industry. This was further helped when it received a direct service from London Waterloo in the 20th century as an element of the London and South Western Railway's Atlantic Coast Express. This service was discontinued in 1964 and in 1966 Bude lost its railway completely. It now has the reputation of being the town in England (and Cornwall) furthest from a railway station.

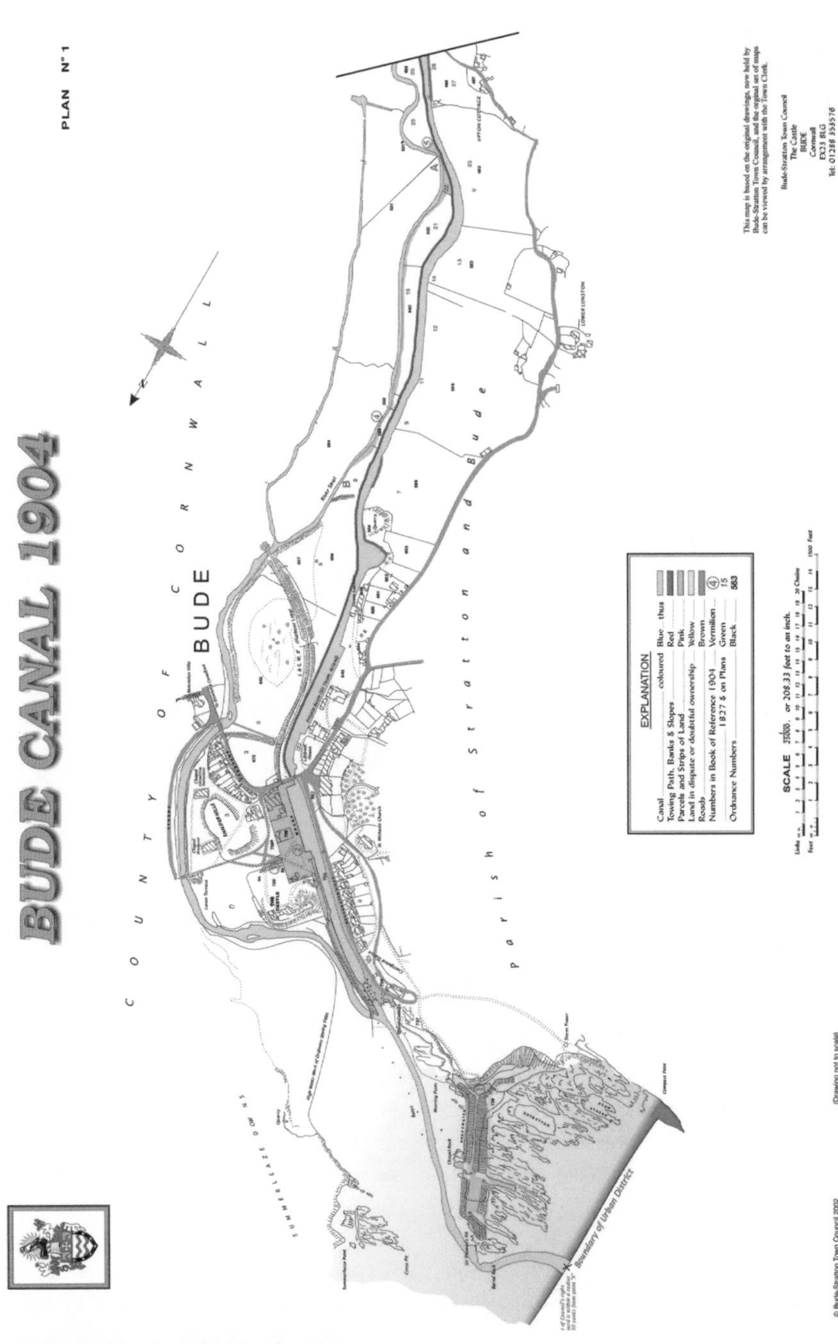

Map of Bude Canal, Bude Wharf, 1904
(Map courtesy of Bude-Stratton Town Council)

Being a relatively recently developed town, there is little historic building in Bude, other than those associated with the canal. Of major interest, however, is **Bude Castle**. This was built c. 1830 and was constructed on a raft built on the sand of one of the beaches. It was built by Sir Goldsworthy Gurney, a Victorian Cornish inventor. Known at the time as 'the father of incandescent light' he invented a successful navigation light, known as the 'Bude Light'. He also invented an early steam jet engine, which he used to power coaches. In 1829 he drove from London to Bath and back in one of his coaches at an average speed of 14mph/22.5kph – prodigious for road travel at the time. However, although technically successful he was less successful in commercially promoting his invention and he received powerful opposition from the horse-based stagecoach companies, and the project never progressed. Gurney later invented the lighting and ventilation system for Parliament and was knighted in 1863.

Gurney is buried at Launcells church a little to the north on Stage 6 of the *Tamara Coast to Coast Way*. Bude Castle is now the town's Heritage Centre and well worth a visit.

Bude to the *Tamara Coast to Coast Way* near Marhamchurch

For those who wish to access the *Tamara Coast to Coast Way* from Bude, a description of the link route (3 miles/4.8km) to is set out below.

Start at the Tourist Information Centre and go to the canal-side path on the edge of the adjacent car park. Walk along this path inland. After just under 1 mile/1.5km cross the canal at Rodd's Bridge and continue alongside the water on the other side. The path passes two locks and then a weir and fish pass where the river leaves the canal on the far side.

A little further on is a junction. Continue ahead, then turn right if in need of refreshment – there is a restaurant and tea room, 'The Weir', here. To continue on the link to the Tamara Coast to Coast Way turn left over the footbridge across the river then left alongside the canal under the A39. At the road turn left on the bridge over the canal (Hele Bridge) then go immediately right alongside the canal.

Continue up the path and then, after passing the old brick workshop, up the track next to the line of the inclined plane to arrive at the village of Marhamchurch. Turn left into the village centre then, after passing the Village Shop on the left and Buller's Arms Hotel on the right,

follow round to the right. At the junction turn left, signposted to Holsworthy and Bridgerule and follow the road (Hobbacott Lane) to a crossroads, where the link joins the *Tamara Coast to Coast Way*. Turn left to continue towards Morwenstow and the north coast or right towards Bridgerule (see Stage 6, page 175).

Compass Point, Bude. Photographer: David Geen

Kilkhampton and Coast Link

The Kilkhampton Link *(Kevren bys Kylgh)* is a useful option for *Tamara Coast to Coast* walkers at the end of Stage 6/start of Stage 7. Stage 6 ends at Upper Tamar Lake, where there is neither accommodation nor public transport. The link to Kilkhampton provides access to these facilities, plus refreshments and shops.

The link can be extended beyond Kilkhampton down to the coast at Duckpool, giving the possibility of circular routes combining the Way with the South West Coast Path.

Distance:	2 miles/3.2km between Upper Tamar Lake and Kilkhampton; 3.5 miles/5.7km between Kilkhampton and Duckpool
Total ascent:	Upper Tamar Lake to Kilkhampton 160ft/50m; Kilkhampton to Duckpool 140ft/43m
Estimated walking time (without stops):	Upper Tamar Lake to Kilkhampton 45min; Kilkhampton to Duckpool 1hr 30min.

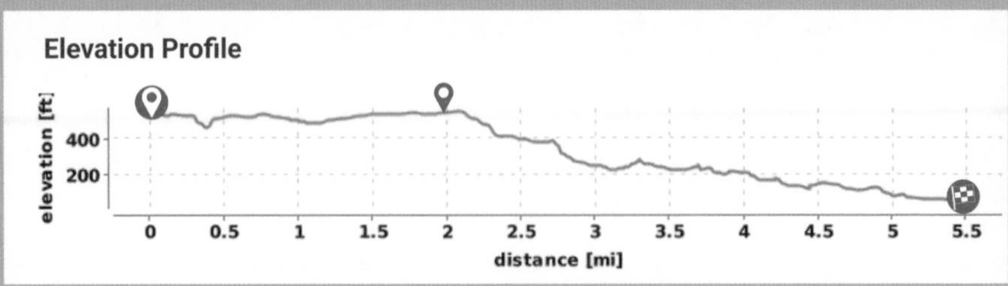

Start / 0m:	**Upper Tamar Lakes**
2 miles:	**Kilkhampton**
End:	**Duckpool**

Tamara Coast to Coast Way to Kilkhampton *(Kevren bys Kylgh)*

Leave the *Tamara Coast to Coast Way* north of Upper Tamar Lake (see Stage 7, page 214) (1). Follow the side concrete track for a short way until it turns sharp right. At this point, leave the track and turn back and left and through a gateway, then immediately turn right along a track heading towards Kilkhampton church on the skyline.

When this track goes right continue ahead alongside the field edge. Keep on to a stile on the right; cross this and descend on what can be a wet and slippery path to cross a stream (2). Cross a boggy area beyond and climb the other side, turning sharp left at a junction, to enter a field. Keep ahead along the field edge and on through gates and over stiles, always keeping to the hedge on the right, to arrive at a track. Go ahead on this track, pass a barn and skirt a farmyard to arrive at a concrete track. Turn left here to pass Aldercombe Barton, with its impressive gatehouse, on the right.

Aldercombe Barton (A) is regarded as one of the most complete early courtyard houses in Cornwall. It originated in the 16th century, with its most outstanding feature being the gatehouse, built around 1500. The pinnacles were added the following century. It had connections with Hartland Abbey in Devon, and may have been a farm, or grange, of the abbey. However in the 18th century the Sherriff of Cornwall, Paul Orchard, lived here and his wife's family owned the abbey after its religious days were over, so that may be the connection.

Aldercombe Barton

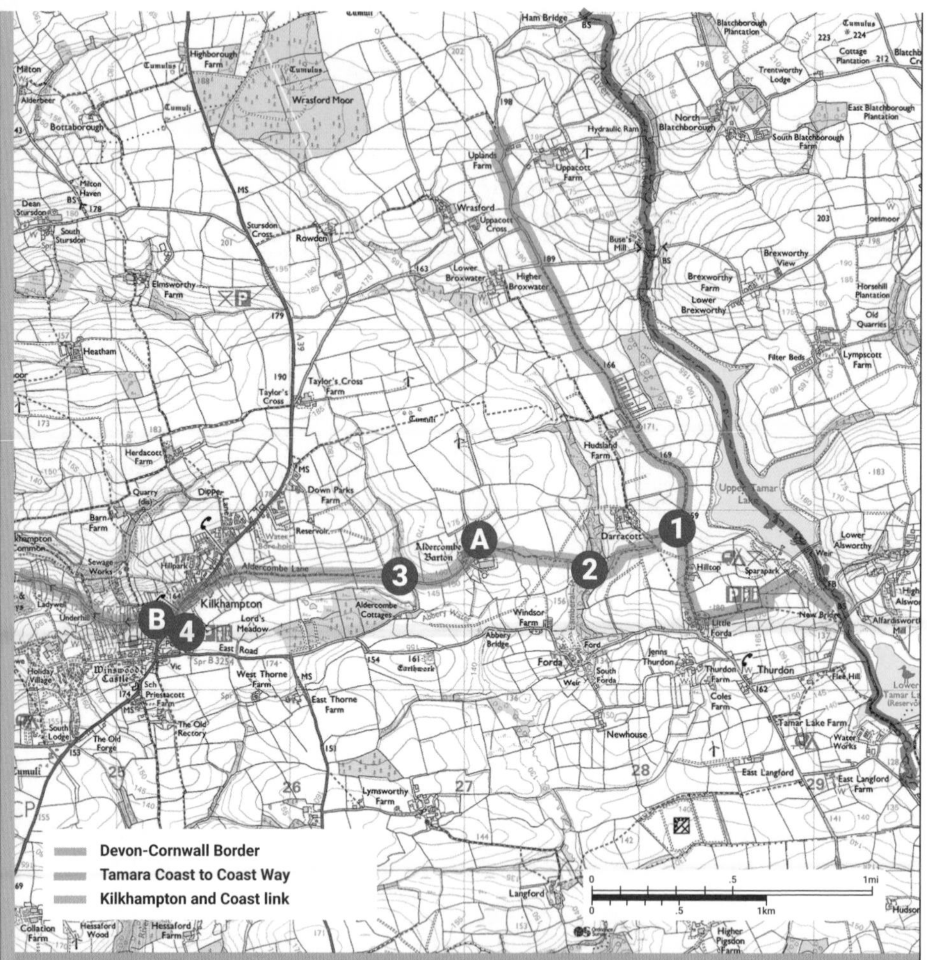

Kilkhampton and Coast Link, Map 1:
Tamara Coast to Coast Way to Kilkhampton

Continue along the lane until it turns sharp left and here continue on the public footpath ahead, through a kissing-gate and over a footbridge (3). Enter the field and go along the top edge, heading for Kilkhampton church tower (ignore the gates on the right).

Continue ahead onto a track and green lane which eventually becomes a surfaced lane into Kilkhampton. Go ahead to reach the centre of the village at the church and square (4).

There is an early reference to what is probably **Kilkhampton**, as *Kelk*, in AD839. It is certainly pre-11th century in origin, having been mentioned in the Domesday Book of 1086. During the 13th and 14th centuries it was a minor borough with a weekly market and three annual fairs. The market place was next to the churchyard.

After the Norman Conquest it came into the possession of the Granville, later Grenville, family. Kilkhampton still styles itself as 'the Grenville Country'. Among well-known members are Sir Richard Grenville, who died on the *Revenge* fighting the Spanish in 1591, and Sir Bevil Grenville, a Royalist general in the English Civil War.

Kilkhampton church (B) is largely 15th and 16th century but contains Norman elements, especially the main doorway, so there was clearly an earlier church here. The tower, very prominent for miles around, is also older than the bulk of the church. The dedication is to St James; there is a statue of him over the southeast door dressed in the style of a Tudor pilgrim. Pilgrimages to the tomb of St James in Santiago de Compostela in northwest Spain were highly valued at that time. It seems likely that Kilkhampton was on a cross-country pilgrimage route from Ireland and Wales to Spain, thus avoiding the tricky voyage around Land's End, and this prompted the dedication to St James.

Kylgh Kernow walkers will have already encountered such pilgrims at Landulph on the Tamar Estuary, a known embarkation point.

St James as a pilgrim, Kilkhampton church

The earliest form of the village's name, *Kelk*, seems to have been derived from the Cornish *kylgh*, a circle, although why this name was given is unknown. Later, the English endings '-ton', and then '-hampton' were added. It is usually referred to locally as simply '*Kilk*', and the modern Cornish version of the name is *Kylgh*.

Kilkhampton has shops, including a post office, pubs and refreshments, and also some accommodation; bus services to Bude.

Kilkhampton to the *Tamara Coast to Coast Way*

A description of the link route in the opposite direction is set out below.

From Kilkhampton square walk north along the A39, past the New Inn, then fork right, along the signed public footpath of Aldercombe Lane. Continue ahead when it becomes an unsurfaced green lane.

After about 0.5 mile/1km the lane emerges into a field. Continue along the top edge then, after passing two gates on the left, bear right downhill to a path that descends to a footbridge then a kissing-gate. This leads to a tarmac road which is followed ahead and left. The road then reaches Aldercombe Barton, with its impressive gatehouse.

Arriving at the farmyard just beyond, go left with the concrete track, then at the top of the slope turn sharp back right to skirt the farmyard, bearing left along a track at the far side of the yard. Where the track goes left into a field, fork right through a gate and continue ahead along the edge of the field. The path continues with a series of gates and stiles until it descends through woodland to a stream crossing.

Climb the other side to a stile into a field and go left along the field edge. On reaching a surfaced track continue ahead, then turn left at the junction shortly afterwards. This leads to a concrete track. Turn right here and follow to a T-junction. Here the link route arrives at the Tamara Coast to Coast Way. Turn left to Morwenstow, right to Upper Tamar Lake (see Stage 7, page 214).

Kilkhampton to Duckpool *(Kevren bys an Arvor)*

It is a further 4 miles/6.5km from Kilkhampton to the coast at Duckpool.

Leave Kilkhampton along West Street, the road between the war memorial and the Spar shop.

Follow the road as it descends out of the village for 0.6 mile/1km. Immediately after 'Wildgates' go left through the gate on a public footpath at the National Trust land 'Castles' (5). Immediately ahead is the mound of a medieval motte and bailey castle (C).

This is known locally as **'The Castles'**. There is no reference to it in medieval documents, although its design puts it firmly in the 12th–14th centuries. It has been suggested it was erected without royal assent during the wars for the crown between Stephen and Matilda in the 13th century, although most such castles were later destroyed by Stephen. Presumably it was built by the Grenvilles as the local lords. It consists of a motte (the mound, which would have been fortified with timber fencing) and two baileys (outer courtyards, which would have contained timber buildings). It has an atmospheric character.

The Castles, Kilkhampton

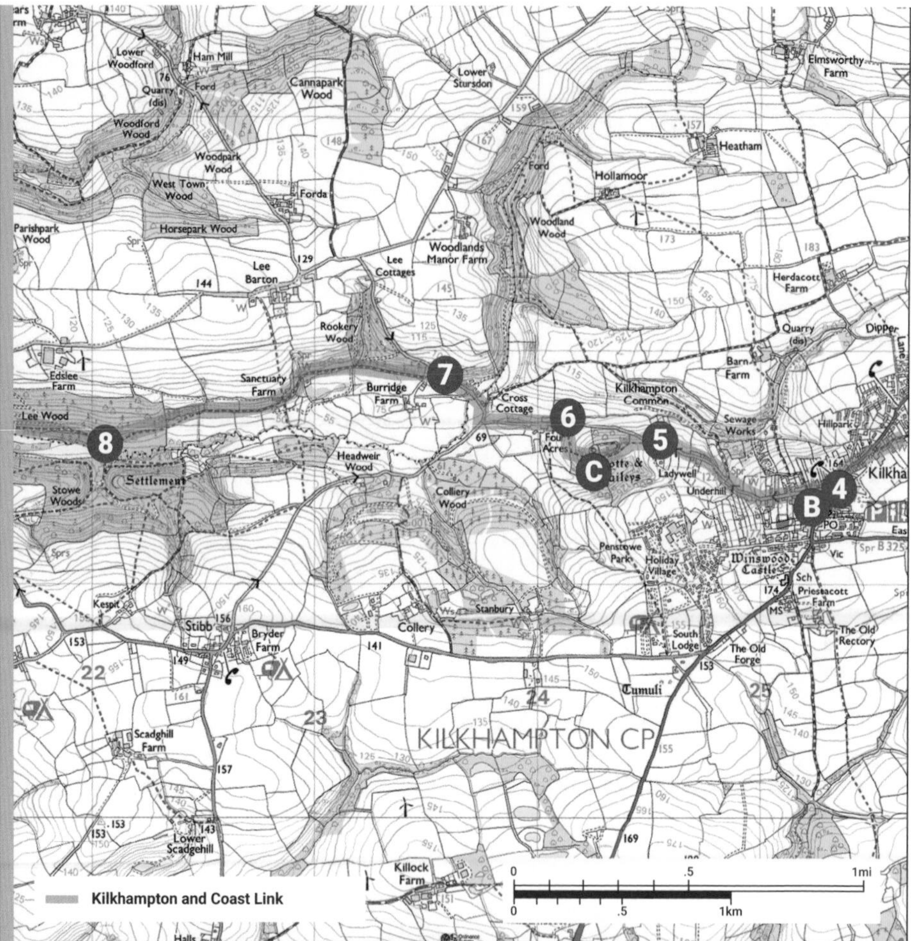

Kilkhampton and Coast Link, Map 2:
Kilkhampton to Coombe Valley

Go through the gate ahead and right to access the top of the motte and its surrounding defensive ditch. To continue on the link, take the path which runs along the left-hand side of the castle, outside the fence, over a stile and ahead before bearing left through the woods to come out into a field. (Alternatively, from the motte it is possible to walk along the defensive ditch on the left to a gate to join the main path in the woods.)

Cross the field slightly diagonally left to reach a stile to the road (6). Turn left and at the

T-junction soon afterwards turn right, signposted Woodford.

The lane crosses a stream then passes the track to Burridge Farm, then after climbing slightly turn left along a track signed to Sanctuary Farm and North Park House, and as a public footpath to Duckpool (7). Almost immediately fork right, towards Sanctuary Farm.

This takes the route along the beautiful Coombe Valley, 'so good they named it twice'. 'Coombe' is the old Celtic word for valley and in modern Cornish komm is a small valley, so strictly speaking Coombe Valley means 'valley valley'.

Pass to the left of Sanctuary Farm then descend a grassy track. When the track arrives at a field keep along the top edge then bear left to a kissing-gate into woods. When the woodland path forks bear right (8). Keep going until the path arrives at a lane at the very picturesque hamlet of Coombe (D).

Coombe

Kilkhampton and Coast Link, Map 3:
Coombe to Duckpool

On the left, just before the stream, is the old **water mill**, dating from the 1840s. Some of the old mill stones are in the garden. The mill was powered by water from a leat off the main valley stream.

At Coombe there are buses to and from Morwenstow and Bude.

Turn left along the lane and cross the footbridge.

The cottage on the right behind the hedge at the junction after the footbridge, which dates from the 17th century, was lived in for a while by the Revd R.S. Hawker, vicar of Morwenstow in the 19th century. He lived here while the vicarage at Morwenstow was being built (see the end of Stage 7, page 228).

Continue to a junction and go straight ahead here. At the next junction immediately following turn right, signposted to Duckpool (9).

On the road straight ahead is **King William's Bridge** over the stream (E). This was built in 1836 by subscription which was organised by Hawker. He approached the king, William IV, who started the fund with a contribution of £20 and the bridge was named in his honour. A stone on the bridge wall commemorates its building.

Follow the lane down the valley to arrive at the coast at Duckpool (10).

This scenic location is at a gap in the very imposing cliff coast here. Quiet and fairly remote now, with no facilities, it may once have been an important location, as archaeological excavations have found evidence of a Romano-British metallurgy site and possibly an early medieval port.

From here the Coast Path can be followed north to Morwenstow to create a long, exciting and very scenic circular walk. Alternatively, head south to Bude. In either direction, the coast is extremely scenic but quite tough walking, with numerous climbs and descents.

Duckpool to Kilkhampton

A description of the link route in the opposite direction is set out below.

Walk up the lane from Duckpool, inland. At the T-junction turn left, then immediately fork right to the hamlet of Coombe.

Cross the footbridge then bear right on to the signed public footpath up a slope and onto a path through woodland.

Keep ahead on the path until it forks, and here bear left. Emerging into a field head for the gate in the far top left-hand corner. Go through the gate onto a track. Continue ahead, passing to the right of Sanctuary Farm and then go ahead on the farm track to reach a tarmac road.

Turn right and at the next junction take the road to the left, signposted Kilkhampton. After passing 'Four Acres' ignore the first public footpath on the right, but cross the stile onto National Trust land to follow the second one. Head uphill across the field, to the right-hand side of the wooded mound, to a waymark post pointing the path into the woods. (The mound is a medieval motte and bailey castle: there is access via a gate above a waymark post in the woods.) Continue parallel to the fence to a stile then on alongside the fence to reach a gate to emerge into a field.

Follow the left-hand side of the field to reach a gate at the far corner. Go through and continue up the road, which climbs steadily to arrive in Kilkhampton.

Marsland Mouth beach and cliffs

Stage 7
Upper Tamar Lake (or Kilkhampton) to Marsland Mouth and Morwenstow

After leaving Upper Tamar Lake the route runs parallel to the Tamar as its valley becomes ever shallower and less of a major feature in the landscape. After eventually passing the river's source on an area of wet highland, the route turns west towards the coast and then follows a largely wooded valley to reach the coast at Marsland Mouth. The last part of the Way follows the spectacular coast to Morwenstow.

Distance:	11.8 miles/19.1km between Upper Tamar Lake and Morwenstow; 13.8 miles/22.2km between Kilkhampton and Morwenstow
Total ascent:	2033ft/620m
Estimated walking time (without stops):	Upper Tamar Lake to Morwenstow 5hr 50min
Car parks:	Upper Tamar Lake, Kilkhampton, Morwenstow

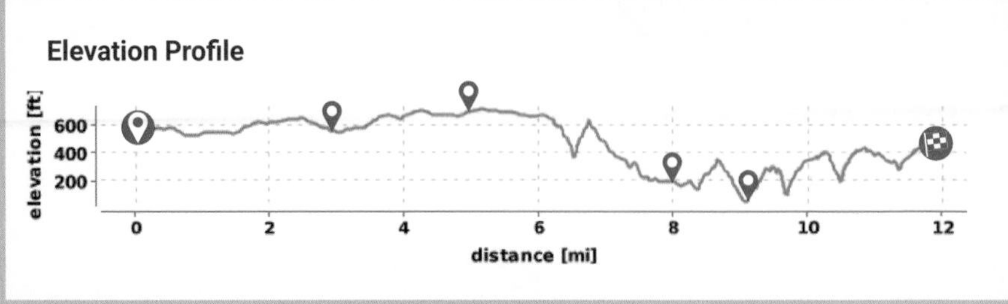

Start / 0m:	**Upper Tamar Lake**
3 miles:	**Youlstone Bridge**
5 miles:	**Woolley Moor**
8 miles:	**Gooseham Mill**
9 miles:	**Marsland Mouth**
End:	**Morwenstow**

Public transport & shorter options: There is a regular bus service along the A39 between Bude and Hartland. The nearest bus stop to the start is at Kilkhampton, 2.25 miles (3.5km) away (see Kilkhampton Link on page 200). To shorten the walk,

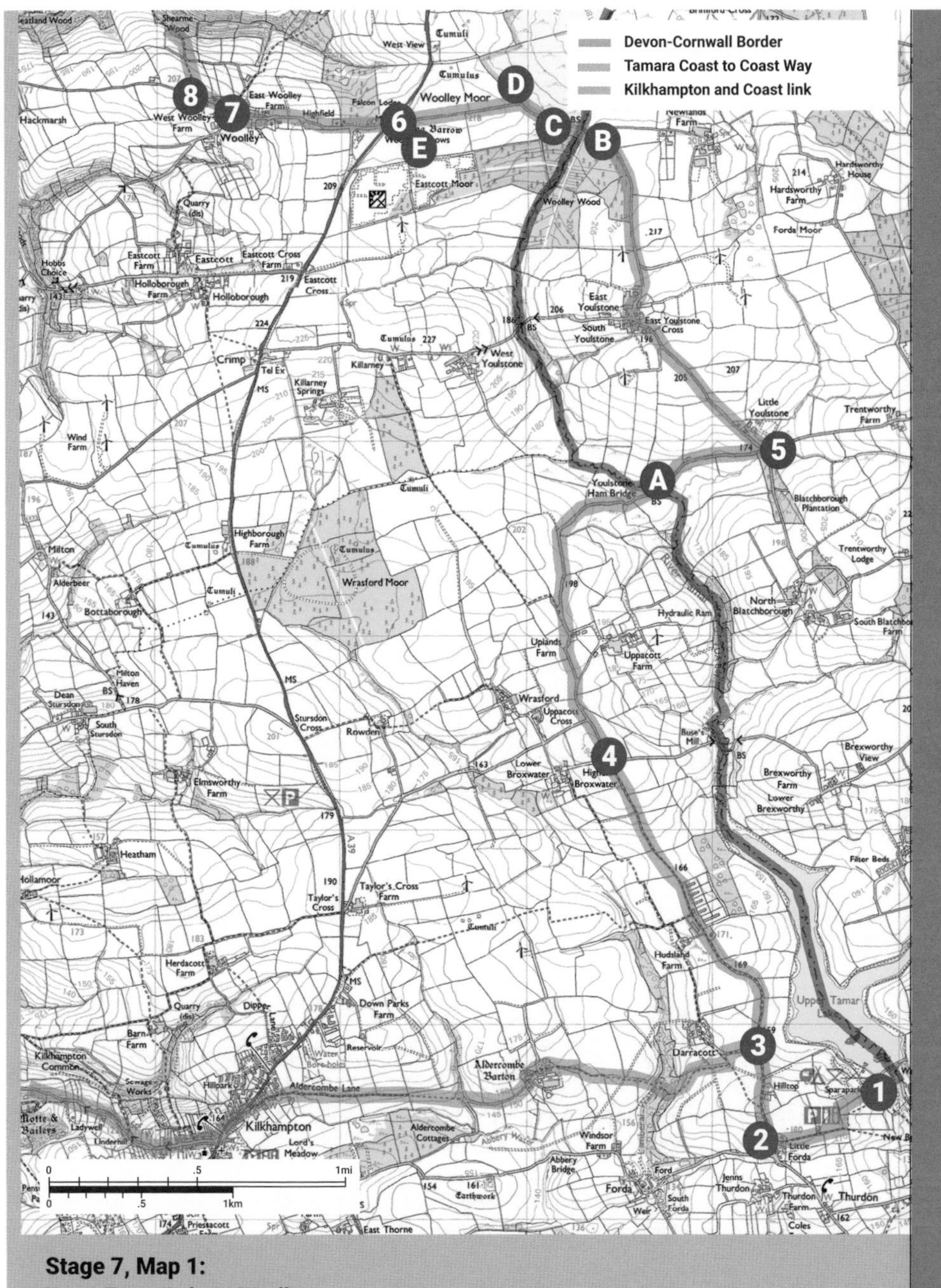

Stage 7, Map 1:
Upper Tamar Lake to Woolley

catch the bus back to Kilkhampton from where it crosses the A39 near Woolley. From Morwenstow, there are regular buses to Bude, from where you can get buses to the train stations at Okehampton or Exeter.
Link route: Kilkhampton and Coast Link to/from a point near Upper Tamar Lake.

The Devon–Cornwall border reaches the north coast at Marsland Mouth, a small, picturesque, but remote cove at the mouth of the Marsland Water, the stream which forms the border at this point. Although an atmospheric spot, there is no road access, no facilities and of course no accommodation. For practical purposes the route of the T*amara Coast to Coast Way* therefore ends at Morwenstow, a settlement 2.5 miles/4km south of Marsland Mouth along the South West Coast Path, and the Way follows the Coast Path for this last stretch.

Note that although spectacular, the length of coast between Marsland Mouth and Morwenstow is tough walking, with a number of steep gradients, both up and down. Make sure you are prepared for this stunning but demanding finale.

From Upper Tamar Lake car park go down the access road for a short way and turn right into a field on the signed public footpath (1). (Coming from Lower Tamar Lake turn left onto the public footpath on the left just before the car park.) Go along the right-hand edge and over a stile in the corner, then cross a footbridge.

Go straight across the next field to the far hedge and cross a stile over a fence on the left. Go along the top of the next field, round a stone barn, then right on a track towards a wooden barn (NB ignore the kissing-gate ahead). Keep on ahead on the track to reach a concrete lane (2). Turn right here.

After a little while another concrete track goes off to the left, just before a gate and cattle grid (3).

***As there is no accommodation or public transport at Upper Tamar Lake, walkers need to go to Kilkhampton (2.25 miles/3.5km away) for facilities, following the Kilkhampton Link which starts from here. Turn left along the side concrete track at (3) and follow the directions on page 200.* The Kilkhampton Link leaves and joins the *Tamara Coast to Coast Way* here.**

There is an excellent view of **Upper Tamar Lake** from here, showing the flooding of a side valley on the far side.

Upper Tamar Lake

Last sight of the River Tamar: Youlstone Ham Bridge

To continue on the *Tamara Coast to Coast Way*, continue ahead on the concrete track. When this enters a farmyard on the right continue ahead on an unsurfaced track. When this track ends cross the stile ahead and continue along the narrow enclosed green lane.

At the far end of the enclosed green lane you reach a tarmac lane (4), where you continue straight ahead. When you reach the turn for Bude and Kilkhampton, continue following the road straight ahead, which soon swings right and descends to the Tamar.

This is the *Tamara Coast to Coast Way's* last sight, and crossing, of the Tamar, taking the Way from Cornwall into Devon for a short while. This bridge, **Youlstone Ham Bridge** (A), is regarded as the highest proper bridge over the river. Its name is not derived from a pig farm but from the Old English word for a water meadow, appropriately for its location. The river now is not much more than a wide stream, only a mile or so/1.6km from its source, although the valley is still an obvious feature, if quite shallow.

Note the boundary stone on the right-hand wall of the bridge; this early 19th-century stone marks the parishes, Kilkhampton (Cornwall) and Bradworthy (Devon), not the counties.

On the Devon side the lane arrives at a junction in a block of woodland – Trentworthy Water (5). Turn left here, signed to East Youlstone. At the junction at East Youlstone bear right, signed Wooley.

Continue along this lane past a plantation on the left.

At the end of the plantation the Way crosses back from Devon into Cornwall. Note the boundary stone on the left (B). As before, the early 19th-century stone shows the parishes, Bradworthy (Devon) and Morwenstow (Cornwall) here, not the counties.

Boundary stone, Woolley Moor

Source area of River Tamar

The *Tamara Coast to Coast Way* now approaches the **source of the Tamar**. There is no one single source, but a number of springs in the woodland and the wet and boggy land either side of the road (C), a surprisingly low-key location for the start of such a significant watercourse. As part of the Tamara project a marker stone has been installed on the roadside verge, adjacent to a tiny ditch in which a trickle can be seen starting its long journey south to Plymouth. The artwork on the stone showing the route of the Tamar as it flows down to Plymouth and some of the wildlife it supports was designed by Esmé Lawton and carved onto Delabole slate and granite from Bodmin Moor by Newquay stonemason, Patrick Morgan.

The Devon–Cornwall border leaves the Tamar here, continuing north to cross the *Tamara Coast to Coast Way* and then swinging left. The border continues still parallel to the Way and now heading west, along a low ridge intermittently seen from the route off to the right. There is now a change in the trend of direction, from south–north when following the Tamar to east–west as the Way heads for the coast.

This high borderland area has never been easy farming (D). It forms part of the geological area known as the Culm, characterised by shales and sandstones and giving rise to infertile, heavy, acidic soils. These in turn lead to a vegetation of purple moor grass, rushes and wet heath. On the other hand, these conditions have also been important for a wide range of often rare species, particularly of butterflies and other insects. Most of the Culm grasslands have been lost by drainage and improvement – 92% of them gone in the last 100 years. Here on **Woolley Moor** however, there are still areas of Culm alongside the road, although some has been drained and forestry plantations cover large areas.

Woolley Moor

The lane rises gently to a summit level of 720 feet/218m. This is the highest point on the entire Way, on the watershed between the valleys draining to the north coast ahead and the catchment of the River Tamar behind. This relatively short length of watershed is all that prevents Cornwall from being an island.

Keep ahead and the route then arrives at the A39 (6).

The raised and uneven area in the field on the left by the corner of the A39 is **Woolley Long Barrow** (E). This dates from the Neolithic period, between 3700 and 2500BC. While Neolithic remains are not uncommon in Cornwall, long barrows are very rare, although fairly widely found across the rest of southern Britain. They may or may not contain internal chambers, but no evidence has been found of any internal structure here. It is likely to be the only survivor of a larger Neolithic cemetery.

The significance of the location to the Neolithic population is unknown; perhaps being on the high land of a watershed above the sources of many rivers and streams was important.

Neolithic long barrows represent the burial places of Britain's earliest farming communities and, as such, Woolley Long Barrow is of national as well as local importance. Note that the barrow is on private land and there is no public access.

It may well be that the line of the A39 continues that of an early trackway. Certainly it would have been useful from early times for access parallel to the coast, but sufficiently inland to avoid the deep and wooded valleys closer to the coast and their dangers and difficulties. It may possibly have been incorporated into the Roman road system. Early maps of Cornwall do not show roads, but one of the first to do so, Bowles map of 1785, includes the line of the current A39, and by the first edition of the 1" OS map of the area, in 1809, it is clearly marked.

After having been looked after by the parishes from Tudor times, some central funding for what were defined as 'Main Roads' was made available under an 1837 Act. To achieve this status, roads had to be administered by a county highways board, and in the late 19th century the Stratton District Highways Board took over the road. Then, after the establishment of Cornwall County Council in 1889, the District Highways Board transferred responsibility to the county. Before doing so, they had to erect milestones, and granite stones were erected in 1890. One is seen on the left on the verge opposite the road to Woolley.

After a period in the 20th century of the whole length of the A39 between Bath and Falmouth being designated as a 'Trunk Road', administered by the Ministry of Transport, in 2002 it devolved again to the county council. More recently, the length in North Devon and North Cornwall has been promoted as the 'Atlantic Highway'.

There are buses from here into Kilkhampton or Bude.

Carefully cross the A39 (6) and go along the road almost opposite, signed to Woolley.

Milestone on the A39, Woolley

Woolley

The Devon–Cornwall boundary, parallel to the *Tamara Coast to Coast Way* to the right (north), now descends to follow a stream which runs down to the coast, Marsland Water. The Way will become well acquainted with this stream as it heads towards the sea.

Crossing the A39 takes the Way into the Cornwall Area of Outstanding Natural Beauty (AONB). Much of the early part of the route passed through the Tamar Valley AONB, and this part of the Cornwall AONB is primarily designated for its coastal landscapes and hinterland. As the Way descends towards the coast it will spend a short length in Devon, and here crosses into the North Devon AONB, designated for the same reasons.

The road soon reaches the attractive little hamlet of Woolley (7). Follow the main lane to the right, signed as a No Through Road.

It has been about 6.75 miles/11km since leaving Upper Tamar Lake (or 8.25/13km from Kilkhampton) and there is another 6.25 miles/10km to Morwenstow, so for those thinking about ending the walk here there is the possibility of a cut-off to a bus stop. This is a walk of 1.3 miles/2km from Woolley. Take the narrow lane that leaves Woolley on the left just before the green. Follow the lane then turn left along the side lane at the top of the hill. Go through the hamlet of Eastcott and turn left at the T-junction. Follow this lane to reach the A39 at Eastcott Cross, from where buses run every couple of hours to Kilkhampton or Bude.

Very soon after leaving Woolley, by a wide grassy verge, for the primary *Tamara Coast to Coast Way* go through a field gate on the right (8) on a signed public footpath, and crosses the field diagonally a little to the left, heading for a gate.

This gives a view of the sea off the north coast, still looking a little distant.

A little way beyond here the primary *Tamara Coast to Coast Way* enters Devon. This Devon length is relatively short, about 1.75 miles/2.8km, and is a very pleasant length of woodland, always very close to the stream of Marsland Water.

However, for those who wish to complete a *Kylgh Kernow* circuit, there is an alternative which remains in Cornwall. It does involve some road walking, all on quiet lanes. Details of this are given on page 222.

Go through the gate and over a stile, then continue over two further stiles, descending towards the wooded valley ahead.

The valley is that of **Marsland Water**, the stream which marks the Devon–Cornwall border to the north coast.

Enter the top of a wood, then follow the path down through the wood to a footbridge over the stream. This is Marsland Water, and the route here crosses into Devon. The path climbs steeply up the Devon side to arrive at a lane (9). Turn left down the lane then continue ahead on a track. Keep on and cross a bridge, then at a path junction continue ahead on the signed public bridleway. Go through a gate and turn left, downhill.

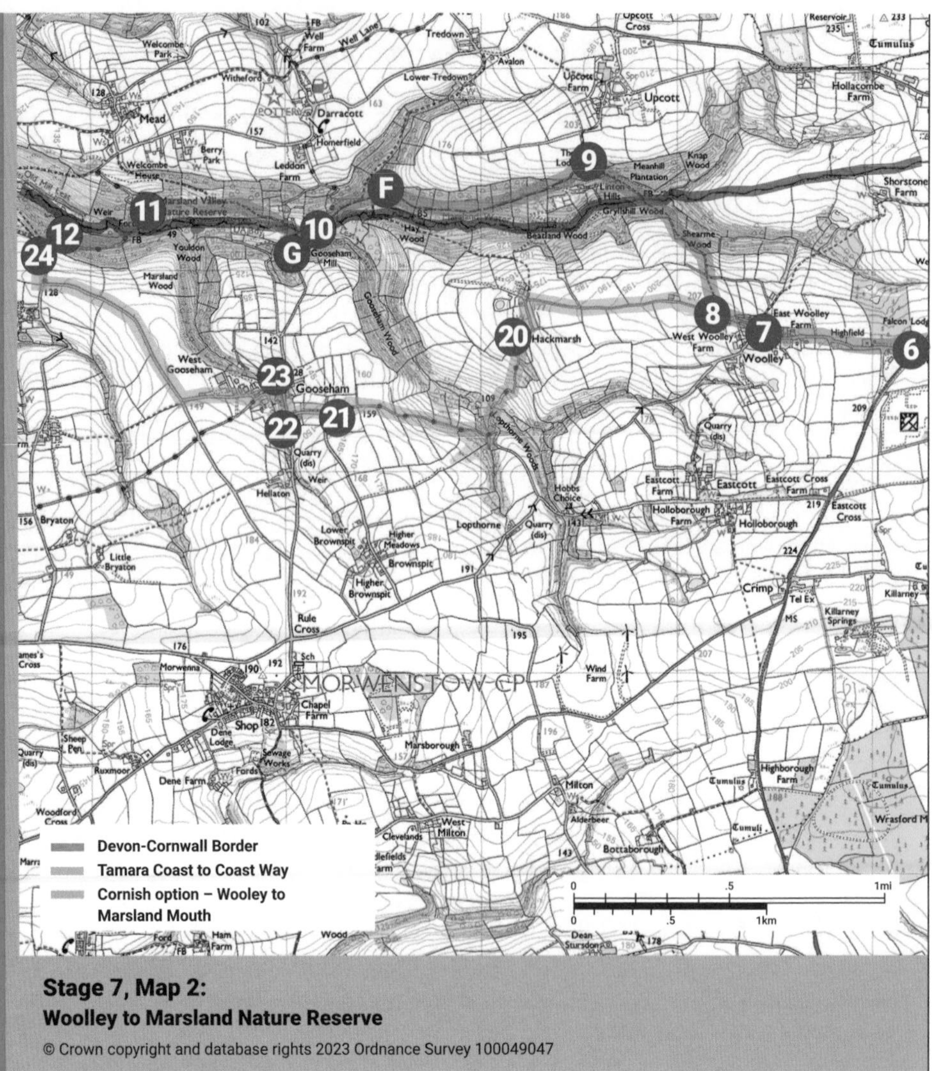

Stage 7, Map 2:

Woolley to Marsland Nature Reserve

This was the old road crossing the Devon–Cornwall border. Here, the *Tamara Coast to Coast Way* enters **Marsland Nature Reserve** (F).

The nature reserve owes its origins to Christopher Cadbury. A nature lover, he left his family's chocolate business and in the 1950s and 1960s he bought the land here to develop it as a nature reserve. The reserve covers the lower Marsland Valley, including its slopes, on both the Devon and Cornwall sides. He donated it to the Royal Society for Nature Conservation, of which he was president until 1988, and the Devon

Wildlife Trust took over the management of the site under a lease arrangement, in conjunction with the Cornwall Wildlife Trust.

The track continues for about 0.5 mile/0.8km and descends to cross Marsland Water (10) back into Cornwall, before passing Gooseham Mill. Continue ahead on the public footpath, passing the old mill house (G).

There is a nature reserve information board on the wall of the mill. **Gooseham Mill** is about 0.5 mile/1km from the hamlet of Gooseham, on what was an old road crossing the border to Welcombe in Devon. It used the power of the stream of Marsland Water, channelling the flow along a leat behind the mill. Gooseham Mill is now used as holiday accommodation, for those seeking peace, wildlife and remoteness.

The nature reserve has a variety of habitats. On the south-facing sunny slopes above the trees the grass is mown or grazed so that flowers and insects may flourish. This especially encourages butterflies. In the valley bottom is the woodland, largely oak, interspersed with ash, sycamore, beech, holly, rowan and hazel. Alongside the stream are alder and willow. This range of habitat supports many species of wildlife, including comparative rarities like otters and dormice. The range of habitats also attracts butterflies, and 34 species have been recorded here, including the rare pearl-bordered fritillary.

Gooseham Mill

Almost immediately after the track recrosses Marsland Water back into Devon (10) take the narrow public footpath on the left (do not continue on the concrete track ahead). The path enters woodland and after a while there is a fork. Bear left on the lower path, parallel to Marsland Water (this is a Devon Wildlife Trust permitted path). Keep ahead to reach a gate and a stile (11). Here turn left down the track to reach a footbridge crossing Marsland Water. Here the route returns into Cornwall.

These tracks, quiet and almost secretive now, formerly comprised part of the local road system linking Marsland and Morwenstow in Cornwall with Welcombe in Devon. The old road forded the stream at this point.

Crossing Marsland Water

Continue on the track as it climbs to reach a junction at a nature reserve information board. Turn right here (12). This is where the alternative Cornish route from Woolley re-joins.

Cornish option – Woolley to Marsland Mouth

For this *Kylgh Kernow* route, at West Woolley (8) do not use the footpath heading across the field, but instead continue on the lane ahead, eventually following it as it turns left. Keep on the lane and when it ends continue ahead and slightly left onto a track (20). This descends, steeply at times, to a bridge over a tributary of Marsland Water. Continue on the track, climbing to a fork a little way up and here bear right then right again, following the track until it meets a tarmac road (21). Go ahead on the road then, arriving at a T-junction by a 'Gooseham' sign, turn right into the hamlet (22).

If this is far enough to walk – about 9 miles/14.5km from Upper Tamar Lake (or 10.5 miles /17km from Kilkhampton) and another 4 miles/6.5km to Morwenstow – then it is possible to catch a bus at Gooseham. There are two or three buses a day to and from Bude or back to Morwenstow.

At the junction in Gooseham turn left (23), passing West Gooseham Farm then just after Higher Yeolden, at a T-junction, turn right.

Continue ahead then when the lane turns sharp left go right along a track, signed 'Unsuitable for Motors', at Little Marsland (24). Going down the track the route enters the Marsland Nature Reserve – for more information see the primary route description above. The track soon arrives at a junction by a nature reserve information board.

Here the route re-joins the primary *Tamara Coast to Coast Way* coming up from the right (12).

A little after this junction (12), at a gate, there is a fork. Those heading towards Morwenstow can fork left here, the path forming a short cut leading to the Coast Path on Marsland Cliff and avoiding a climb out of the valley.

However, for those wishing to go all the way to the coast at the county boundary at Marsland Mouth (13), and thus following the Devon–Cornwall border for its entire length, the *Tamara Coast to Coast Way* main route forks right. The route then follows the Coast Path from the mouth of Marsland Water up the cliff side and re-joins the short-cut route.

First close sight of the north coast

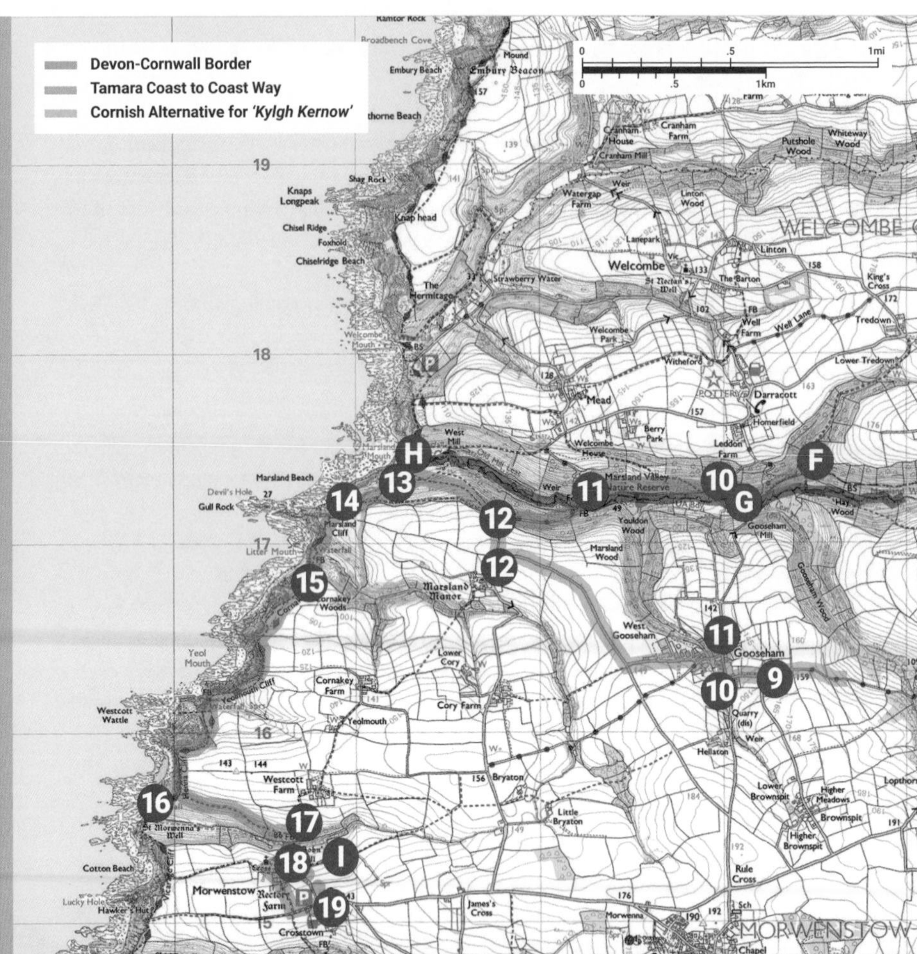

Stage 7, Map 3:

Marsland Nature Reserve to Morwenstow

Descending towards the coast the path passes on the right a memorial stone to Christopher Cadbury, the man responsible for this nature reserve. This part of the reserve is characterised by heathland and maritime grasses. Gannets may be seen out to sea and fulmars, shags and guillemots nest on the cliffs.

Towards the bottom of the path there is a Devon Wildlife Trust memorial bench. Although this is definitely Cornwall, the Devon Wildlife Trust owns both sides of the valley, Devon

and Cornwall, as a joint nature reserve. By the bench there is a junction with the Coast Path, which rises to the left towards Morwenstow. This is the onward route, but having come this far it is worth continuing the last couple of hundred yards to Marsland Mouth (13), where the Devon–Cornwall boundary reaches the sea. The footbridge over Marsland Water marks where the Coast Path crosses the boundary (H). It is generally possible to walk down the beach to the sea at low tide.

Those who started at the Tamar Estuary have now walked the complete Devon–Cornwall boundary. Congratulations – it will doubtless have been a memorable walk. Now you will need to reach facilities, so for most, it will mean continuing on the Coast Path to the nearest settlement, Morwenstow.

The contrast of the landscape of this end of the boundary, a wild and remote coast, with that of the start opposite Plymouth, is remarkable.

Above: Marsland Mouth. Inset: The Coast Path at Marsland Mouth

From Marsland Mouth retrace your steps past the Cornwall/Kernow sign and walk back up to the previous junction and turn right, following the Coast Path climbing to Marsland Cliff (the Coast Path is waymarked with an acorn symbol). Pass a footpath junction on the cliff top (14), where the short cut from inland arrives.

This is an imposing length of coast with impressive rugged cliffs. Looking out to sea from the cliff top it is usually possible to see Lundy on the far skyline behind. **Lundy** is situated where the Atlantic Ocean meets the Bristol Channel. It was a base for the Vikings, who gave it its name (Norse *lundey*, meaning 'puffin island'), and was later used by the Knights Templar and a variety of pirates. Later it became owned by a succession of eccentrics, including in the 19th century one William Hudson Heaven, who called it 'the Kingdom of Heaven'. In the 20th century the then owner issued currency and postage stamps using the denomination of 'puffins', a puffin being nominally worth an old British penny. These are now collectors' items. Lundy is now owned by the National Trust and managed by the Landmark Trust.

This length of coast is superbly attractive but not the easiest walking. After the climb out of Marsland Mouth it drops steeply then climbs equally steeply across two further valleys, at Litter Mouth and Westcott Wattle. After the first of these two big climbs, out of Litter Mouth on Cornakey Cliff (15), be careful not to keep too close to the cliff top as the old path has been lost to a cliff fall. Instead, bear to the left to a kissing-gate slightly inland then continue on the path to another kissing-gate on the cliff-top skyline ahead.

Typical of this length of coast are the knife-edged fingers of rock stretching out into the Atlantic. In the days of sail, the prevailing westerly winds frequently drove ships onto these rocks, earning the area the name 'Skeleton Coast'. As recently as 1982 a cargo ship, the *Joanna*, was driven aground near Hartland Point, not far north of here.

'Knife-edged fingers of rock stretching out into the Atlantic'

After the second of the steep climbs, out of Westcott Wattle, the Coast Path reaches the top of Henna Cliff.

At just over 450ft/137m **Henna Cliff** has the highest sheer drop of any cliff in Cornwall – more widely, only Beachy Head in Sussex has a higher sheer drop. Looking back, the line of the coast can be seen as far as Hartland Point, the far headland visible. Hartland Point, on the far northwest tip of Devon, marks a major change in the southwest's coastal alignment, from predominately east–west along the North Devon coast to north–south along this stretch. Its geographical significance was recognised long ago, when the Roman geographer Ptolemy called it the 'Promontory of Hercules'.

Ahead it is possible to see some of the domes and dishes of what is technically **Cleave Camp**, the listening station of GCHQ. Originally established as an RAF base for World War II, there were gun batteries positioned here and it was used to train anti-aircraft gunners. Later, its remote position on the west coast made it a good place to base air listening equipment. Inland, the church at Morwenstow can be seen, almost hiding in its picturesque valley.

Of possible interest to those doing the full *Kylgh Kernow* route around Cornwall, the Cornish coast continues ahead into the distance. In good conditions the view is as far as Trevose Head beyond Padstow, a distinctive hump-backed shape.

As the path begins to descend into the Morwenstow Valley, there is a kissing-gate on the left with a name plaque 'Henna Cliff' (16). Go through and follow the bottom edge of the field, parallel to the valley.

Morwenstow in its valley

Morwenstow is the northernmost parish in Cornwall and historically was one of the most remote. It gets its name from St Morwenna, to whom the church is dedicated, although dedication to St John the Baptist was added later. Morwenna was traditionally a daughter of the Welsh King Brychan, who reputedly had 24 children, many of whom sailed across to Cornwall and founded churches – further offspring are said to be St Clether, St Issey, St Keyne and St Mabyn, among others, all now Cornish parishes. Legend has it that Morwenna carried a stone for the font up from the shore on her head and pointed out the place for the church to be built. Presumably an early holy place, possibly a hermitage, was established here at this time.

Distant from any large settlements and with poor communications, the parish remained largely unchanged until the 19th century. In 1834 things began to happen when the parish received its most famous vicar, the Revd Robert Stephen Hawker. He repaired the church and also built a new vicarage, the old one having fallen into ruins.

Hawker was a real one-off, something of an oddity. He rarely wore traditional clergyman's clothing, preferring a fisherman's jersey and boots and a long purple coat. He is reputed to have smoked opium, which may have prompted one of his more bizarre actions of sitting on a shoreline rock pretending to be a mermaid!

But he had a more serious side too. As well as his work on the church and the vicarage he is renowned in Cornwall for writing the 'Song of the Western Men', or 'Trelawney' as it is perhaps better known. He is also credited with introducing the modern Harvest Festival into the church calendar. In addition, having seen the ship the *Caledonia* being wrecked offshore, he became concerned about the treatment of shipwrecked seamen and organised for them to be given a Christian burial (see below).

Cross a stile and continue along the bottom of the next field. Turn right at the end (17) and go down through trees to cross a footbridge. Keep on the path ahead to pass, on the right, Morwenstow's Old Vicarage (18).

This was designed by Hawker to replace the even older, derelict vicarage. Particularly notable are the chimneys. Hawker decided to create chimneys modelled on the towers of churches which had had an impact on his life. They are based on the towers at North Tamerton (passed earlier on the Way), Welcombe (just across the border in Devon), Magdalen College in Oxford and here at Morwenstow.

While the vicarage was being built Hawker lived in a cottage at Coombe, a little further down the coast. Walkers who took the Kilkhampton and Coast Link to Duckpool will have encountered this location (see page 209).

Note that the Old Vicarage is now a private residence so please do not trespass on its grounds. The stone building opposite the vicarage was once the stables.

Follow the path up into the churchyard.

Morwenstow, Old Vicarage

St John's Well

'Few churches can surpass Morwenstow in romantic situation or architectural interest' was the opinion of *The Parochial History of Cornwall* in 1928, and little has changed since. Its origins are Norman, and it has been described as one of the best-preserved Norman churches in Cornwall. The porch especially has retained Norman work; one of the inside arcades has been described as being one of the most exciting pieces of Norman work in the country, dating back to the 1130s. Whatever the truth of the Morwenna origin, it appears to have been a place of worship in very early times. Indeed, it is described as 'an old building' in 1248, and its font seems to be of Saxon age.

On arriving at the churchyard those interested can divert along the path to the left. This leads to **St John's Well** (I). This holy well is named after St John the Baptist, to whom the church was dedicated in addition to St Morwenna in 1290. The well is first mentioned at about the same time, 1296, but is doubtless much older. It is housed in a stone cover, of uncertain but later date. Water from the well is still used for christenings in the church.

Morwenstow has, or had, another holy well, named after **St Morwenna** and said to have been her favourite place. This was on the cliff face at the mouth of the stream valley west of the church, but it is no longer accessible or even recognisable (J). Nevertheless, the mouth of the valley remains an atmospheric location, and can be reached by following a permissive path which leaves the footpath followed by our route just before passing the vicarage.

Climb up the railed path to the top of the churchyard.

Note the white memorial on the right at the top of the churchyard. A painted ship's figurehead, it comes from the *Caledonia*, wrecked here in 1842. Her captain is buried beneath it. Other seamen from this and other vessels are buried nearby, marked by a tall granite cross inscribed 'Unknown yet Well Known'.

Go through the lychgate, or over the stile next to it.

Morwenstow church

Morwenstow, Crosstown

Up on the right outside the churchyard is Morwenstow's parking area. Behind are the Rectory Farm Tea Rooms (seasonal) – www.rectory-tearooms.co.uk.

As the name suggests, Rectory Farm has historic links to the church. The farmhouse is medieval in origin with a roof reputed to be one of the oldest in the country, including 14th-century work.

Follow the tarmac lane ahead. This leads, after a little less than a quarter of a mile, to a green next to the road.

Alternatively, for an off-road option if conditions are not wet, go up the track immediately next to Rectory Farm, through the wooden gate to a stile, signposted 'Footpath to Tidna Valley'. Cross the stile and continue alongside the hedge to a gate and a large stone stile. Cross this to the track beyond and turn left, signposted 'Crosstown', which leads to Morwenstow's green (19) by its pub and bus stop.

This is **Crosstown**. Morwenstow is something of a scattered settlement and Crosstown consists of a large green part-surrounded by attractive old stone buildings, including the local inn, the Bush Inn, a building of 13th-century origin. Part of the inn was destroyed by a fire in 1968, but it has since been completely restored.

Crosstown is where the buses to and from Morwenstow stop. There are two or three buses a day to and from Bude, the main centre for this part of the coast.

So that's it. After 100 miles/160km the *Tamara Coast to Coast Way* has done just that – gone from coast to coast. The contrast in landscape and character between the start of the Way at the mouth of the Tamar and here at Morwenstow – or Marsland Mouth – could scarcely be greater, and perhaps epitomises the great range of landscapes and experiences encountered on the route. In any event, it should have been a memorable experience.

The Countryside Code

Your guide to enjoying parks and waterways, coast and countryside

Respect everyone

- be considerate to those living in, working in and enjoying the countryside
- leave gates and property as you find them
- do not block access to gateways or driveways when parking
- be nice, say hello, share the space
- follow local signs and keep to marked paths unless wider access is available

Protect the environment

- take your litter home – leave no trace of your visit
- do not light fires and only have BBQs where signs say you can
- always keep dogs under control and in sight
- dog poo – bag it and bin it in any public waste bin or take it home
- care for nature – do not cause damage or disturbance

Enjoy the outdoors

- check your route and local conditions
- plan your adventure – know what to expect and what you can do
- enjoy your visit, have fun, make a memory

www.countryside-code.org.uk

The Tamar Valley and Early Celtic Saints

One of the more obvious features that visitors to Cornwall and, to a lesser extent, West Devon, notice is the existence of unfamiliar saints' names in church dedications and village names. This dates back to the 5th to 7th centuries, a time sometimes referred to in English history as the 'Dark Ages', but often known in Cornwall as the 'Age of Saints'.

This was the time when Christianity was being introduced, or more accurately reintroduced, to the country, and reflects the fact that in the far southwest this happened in a different way from elsewhere. Generally, in England, Christianity was introduced from the east following the visit of St Augustine in AD595 and his conversion of the King of Kent, Aethelberht. As churches were established they were generally dedicated to Biblical saints or European martyrs who had been sanctified.

But in the far southwest, Christianity spread across the neighbouring Celtic lands of Ireland, Wales, Brittany and Cornwall, brought by missionaries, monks and priests travelling between them and converting the local populations. In the case of Cornwall and West Devon, the pattern was often one of a holy man or woman arriving and establishing a religious base which may often have been on an earlier holy site – sometimes a pagan one – and converting the local people to Christianity from there. This otherwise often obscure holy figure is now commemorated in the dedication of the church which became established at the site and, sometimes, in the name of the village which grew around it.

Walkers on the *Tamara Coast to Coast Way* will encounter numerous examples of these saints on their way from south to north coast.

The Tamar Estuary

The first time Way walkers will encounter one of these early Celtic saints is when passing through the suburb of St Budeaux in Plymouth when approaching the Tamar Bridge (Stage 1). Although looking like a French name, it is derived from an earlier version of a Celtic saint's name: St Budoc's. The story of **St Budoc** is that he was born in a cask off the coast of Brittany around the 6th century after family enemies had cast his pregnant mother adrift. Mother and child landed in Cornwall or Ireland, depending on the detailed legend, but later returned to Brittany where Budoc became Bishop of Dol-de-Bretagne. He sent monks to Britain to spread the Christian word, later accompanying some of them. He established an early Christian site by the banks of the Tamar, possibly near what is now Warren Point, near Ernesettle in Plymouth (Stage 2). An early farmstead belonging to the original religious site was then established at Budshead, meaning 'Budoc's land' (also in Stage 2). Later a medieval church was built away from the river for safety before the St Budeaux name became centred on the modern suburb when the railway arrived. As well as this Plymouth location, St Budoc also established a holy site near Falmouth in west Cornwall, now the church and village of St Budock.

As the Way leaves Plymouth on Stage 2 it passes through the village and suburb of Tamerton Foliot. This is associated with two Irish sibling saints, **Indract** and **Dominica**, who came up the Tamar Estuary and landed at Tamerunta (presumed to be Tamerton Foliot), traditionally in AD689. While this seems to have been their first landing place they also landed on the Cornish side of the estuary, at what is now Halton Quay (Stage 3K). St Dominica founded a small religious settlement close by, at what is still called Chapel Farm (where there is a holy well), before moving to found a church at the current village of St Dominick nearby. Later, Dominica became confused with the St Dominic who founded the Dominican friars, but originally they were recognised as quite separate.

St Indract remains commemorated at Halton Quay, where one of the old quay buildings was consecrated as a chapel dedicated to him in 1959.

Old port building, Halton Quay; now a chapel dedicated to St Indract

Also on the Cornish side of the Tamar Estuary, a little further down towards the mouth, the *Kylgh Kernow* option passes Landulph church (Stage 2K). This church, on a little headland overlooking the estuary, is now dedicated to St Leonard, a European saint, but the place name (the element lan) suggests it was an early Celtic holy site. The second part of the name presumably refers to the holy man or woman who established the holy site, although the early records vary in form – **Dylyk, Delek, Dilp** and **Dilph** are all found. Whoever this person was is now lost in time. However, it is recorded that Indract and Dominica were accompanied by seven companions when they landed, so it could be that this holy person was one of these, and Irish.

Between Landulph and Halton Quay the *Kylgh Kernow* option passes through St Mellion (Stage 2K/3K). This village gets its name from another Breton, a 6th-century Bishop of Rennes, recorded variously as **Melanius, Melanus, Melaine** or **Mellanus**. The current Cornish version is Melyan. He is not known to have visited the area so presumably his godly reputation in the Celtic world prompted his commemoration here.

The Middle Tamar

As the Way heads north into the middle section of the Tamar Valley, the *Kylgh Kernow* option crosses an important tributary, the River Inny, where it enters the parish of Lezant (Stage 4K). The village is about a mile west of the Way, and is another example of an early holy site; its name is first noted as Lan sant in the 12th century, or 'holy enclosure' in Old Cornish.

Who established this early holy site is not recorded. However, the dedication of the church is to **St Briochus**. He is said to have been born in Dyfed, Wales, in the 6th century and came to Cornwall where he established a mission at what became St Breock, near Wadebridge. He went on to Brittany and there founded a famous monastery at St Brieuc. His connection with Lezant is not certain, but he is known to have had numerous disciples in Cornwall – 84 in one record, 168 in another – and it seems likely that one or more of these founded the settlement here.

Launceston (Stage 4K), originally *Lan Stefan*, the main centre of the middle Tamar Valley, owes its name to the international martyr St Stephen, but there is evidence of Celtic saints nearby. The next parish to the west is Egloskerry, Cornish for 'the church of Kerry'. **St Kerry**, also recorded as **Kery, Keria** and **Keri**, was one of a large family of Celtic Christian missionaries involved in converting the local population in the 6th century. Head of this family was King Brychan of South Wales, who is said to have had 24 children, all of whom helped Christianise the southwest. They include a number of others who have given their names to Cornish parishes, such as **St Issey,**

St Mabyn, St Keyne and **St Clether,** all in east and north Cornwall, and other siblings the Way will encounter later, such as **Marwenne, Morwenna** and **Nectan.**

Lezant church

On the Devon side in this middle section the Way only encounters one Celtic saint. This is **St Non**, or **Nonna,** the church dedication at Bradstone. This parish is to the west of Milton Abbot (Stage 4), and the church is seen by those using the Greystone Link (between Stages 4 and 4K). St Non is a Welsh saint, best known as the mother of the patron saint of Wales, St David. One legend has her as the grand-daughter of King Brychan, although which of Brychan's children is her parent seems not to be recorded. She is presumed to have visited the southwest, where she established the holy site at Altarnun, on the eastern edge of Bodmin Moor and not too far away, and it may be relevant that nearby is the parish of Davidstow, commemorating her son.

The North

Towards its top end the Way arrives in the parish of Marhamchurch (Stage 6). The village is slightly off, though close to, the Way; its name commemorates the Celtic saint **Marwenne.** She is usually regarded as another of the 24 offspring of the 6th-century King Brychan who did so much to establish Christianity in this part of the world.

There is a Link from the Way at Marhamchurch to the town of Bude. There is some debate over the origin of the town's name, with perhaps a majority of authorities suggesting it comes from the old name of the river here, a Celtic word possibly meaning 'muddy'. However, another theory is that it derives from an Old English word *bede*, or 'holy man'. This idea springs from the fact that Chapel Rock, now incorporated into the town's breakwater, was once the site of a hermit's hut. When the Saxons arrived the settlement got its name from their word for what was presumably a Celtic holy man living a secluded life.

A little further along the Way (Stage 6) the secluded little church of Launcells is passed. The church is dedicated to St Swithun, or Swithin, the Saxon saint associated particularly with Winchester, but the location seems to be an early holy site pre-dating this dedication.

Bude breakwater with Chapel Rock at its end

The place name appears to be derived from the early Cornish 'lan seles,' where lan usually applies to a holy enclosure. Seles is likely to be a personal name, probably of an early monk or hermit who established a site for prayer here. There is a holy well in the church car park, now also dedicated to St Swithun, but which is likely to have provided the inspiration for the early holy site. The quiet and secluded nature of the location was also probably a factor. Who Seles was will never now be known, but his or her name lives on.

Launcells church

Morwenstow church

The last parish encountered on the Way is Morwenstow (end of Stage 7). **St Morwenna** was another daughter of King Brychan who established a holy site on these lonely cliffs (it has also been suggested that Morwenna and the Marwenne of

Marhamchurch are one and the same). Like most of these early sites, it is associated with a holy well. Close to the church is what is now called St John's Well, first recorded in 1296. There is also St Morwenna's Well, now in an inaccessible location on the cliff face near the mouth of the valley. As well as being holy Morwenna is also said to have been learned. One legend has her being the teacher of Edith, daughter of King Ethelwulf of Wessex – although the dates make this unlikely, as Ethelwulf was king in the 9th century and the children of Brychan are usually ascribed to the 6th century.

The eldest of the offspring of King Brychan was **St Nectan**. Although there is no parish named after him, he was much venerated throughout north Cornwall and northwest Devon. The church at Welcombe, the next parish to Morwenstow across the border in Devon, is dedicated to him. He is also commemorated at Hartland, the next parish north again. Here, a collegiate church was established by Gytha, mother of the Saxon King Harold, as a thanks offering for the escape of her husband from a shipwreck in the 11th century. She dedicated this church to St Nectan, suggesting he already had a local cult following. The current church is built on the same site and remains dedicated to Nectan. He is also remembered at other sites, notably St Nectan's Kieve, a waterfall near Tintagel. Tradition has it that he was visited at Christmas every year at Hartland by his 23 siblings, where they 'talked of the things of God'. He is said to have been martyred by being beheaded by cattle thieves he pursued after they took a couple of his best milkers. And one final legend has him picking up his head and walking following this incident – a holy man indeed!

It's pretty clear that many or most of these stories of the early Celtic saints owe more to legend than to history. Nevertheless, they do give a background to the very different way in which the start of Christianity and, in some respects, the modern world took place in the southwest compared with the rest of the country, and how and why this is reflected in the names of the saints encountered here.

Cornwall and West Devon Mining Landscape World Heritage Site

World Heritage Sites are unique features which have special cultural or physical significance on a world-wide basis, and are designated by UNESCO for their 'Outstanding Universal Value'. They include natural features such as the Galapagos or the Great Barrier Reef, historical features such as the pyramids of Giza and the Great Wall of China, and cultural features, of which the Cornwall and West Devon Mining Landscape is a prime example.

This World Heritage Site is defined by the mining landscape which was formed by the cultural tradition of non-ferrous hard-rock mining, especially during the 19th century. It contributed to developing the Industrial Revolution in Britain and pioneered its transfer overseas. Remains of mines, engine houses, smallholdings, ports, harbours, canals, railways, tramroads and associated industries, as well as distinctive towns and villages, all reflect the industrial expansion and innovation of the area. It greatly influenced 19th-century mining practice internationally and, arising from this, the course of the wider Industrial Revolution.

As well as the physical outcome, the culture of the area was distinctive and was, and still is, reflected in the architecture and landscape. All these factors have contributed to discernible landscapes and communities across the world, taken there by migration and expanded by imitation.

The World Heritage Site designation in Cornwall and West Devon covers 10 distinct areas, one of which is the Tamar Valley. The Tamara Coast to Coast Way enters the site on the Bere Peninsula on the primary route (Stage 3), and at Cotehele on the *Kylgh Kernow* option (Stage 3K). It exits the site on both options when leaving the village of Luckett (Stage 4). On this stretch the Way passes a range of mining heritage features, including old mines and associated buildings, miners' cottages, miners' smallholdings and inclined planes. Even the Tamar Valley branch line railway owes its existence to the mining industry.

Market Gardening in the Tamar Valley

Historically, one of the most important industries of the Tamar Valley, and especially its lower end, was the market gardening of fruit and flowers. The industry was developed as a result of both climate and location. The climate was favourable, being in the southern part of the country and with the topography of the valley affording protection from cold winds. And with the growth of Plymouth, the location was also favourable, with a large market almost on the doorstep, accessible by river transport. The development of the dockyard at Plymouth also boosted demand. In addition, street sweepings and other refuse were brought up from the town by river for use as fertiliser.

It may be that some form of market gardening started in the valley as early as the 16th century, but it really took off in the 19th century. By this time the area was specialising in soft fruit, particularly strawberries and cherries, as well as apples, and also flowers, especially daffodils. The produce was originally shipped to Plymouth by river transport but the situation changed when the Great Western Railway reached the town in 1849. In 1862 local strawberry grower James Lawry visited London and realised what a premium there was on market garden produce prices there, especially for early fruit. Prices at Covent Garden market could be up to five times that in Plymouth. This gave rise to what was called the 'Strawberry Rush', with fresh produce being sent to London from Plymouth by train, reaching the capital within 24 hours of picking.

In 1876 the London and South Western Railway reached Plymouth, and that company's route passed along the valley, with stations at Bere Alston and Bere Ferrers. This gave an even greater impetus to the trade. Growers on the Cornish side of the Tamar would send their produce across the river by ferry between Cargreen and Thorn Point near Bere Ferrers for transport by train from there, rather than sending it down river to Plymouth.

The area specialised in daffodils and also strawberries, the earliest in the country. It is said that daffodils were the first crop to be grown, especially the local Tamar Valley Double White. Producers would switch to strawberries as soon as the bulb fields in Lincolnshire produced their flowers. The cry of 'Spalding's in' would go up, a sign that the produce had to change.

The industry continued into the 20th century, and indeed may have reached its height in the 1950s when it employed perhaps 8000–10000 people. There are still people living in the area who can recall vast numbers of boxes of fruit and flowers on local station platforms, waiting to be sent to London. Associated industries developed alongside the growing, especially trades like basket and punnet making.

As well as soft fruit and flowers the lower Tamar was also a centre of apple growing. Many local varieties were grown – a list of around 80 has been recorded. They include some interesting names, such as Bottlestopper, Colloggett Pippin, Grow-bi-Nights, Lady's Fingers, Pig's Nose and Slack-ma-Girdle.

Since the mid-20th century the industry has declined greatly, largely as a result of competition from international, intensively farmed produce. There are still fruit and flower growers scattered throughout the area, and examples will be seen by walkers on the Tamara Coast to Coast Way. These days they are often represented by polytunnels, and by place names like Strawberry Hill.

Daffodils from the Valley

The Tamar Valley AONB and other Protected Landscapes

The purpose of an Area of Outstanding Natural Beauty (AONB) is to conserve and enhance the natural beauty of the designated area. AONBs are designated by central Government and are regarded as representing the highest level of landscape beauty the country has to offer, equivalent in status to the National Parks. They differ from National Parks only in that they do not have their own planning powers, tend to be smaller in scale and offer recreation as long as it is consistent with the conservation of natural beauty and the needs of agriculture, forestry and other uses. They enjoy the protection of specific policies of the local planning authorities to conserve and enhance the landscape, scenic beauty and character of the area.

At time of writing (May 2023) the Government is consulting on proposals to rebrand AONBs as 'National Landscapes' and along with National Parks to have a new core function to drive nature recovery.

The lower half of the Tamar Valley has been designated as an AONB. It is defined by the River Tamar and its valley, and part of the tributary valleys of the Rivers Tavy and Lynher. The main features of the AONB include: a wide estuary landscape lined with wetlands; a tidal middle valley with creeks, wetlands and wooded sides; a short gorge-like section where it is crossed by a granite ridge; a mining heritage dating back to medieval times giving rise to distinctive architecture, including often prominent chimneys; a market garden and orchard legacy; and landscaped estates. It is an historic transport route, with quays, limekilns, old ferry points and historic stone bridges, and links with the arrival and settlement of early medieval saints. Walkers on the Tamara Coast to Coast Way will experience many examples of these features, both natural and man-made.

The Way enters the Tamar Valley AONB when leaving Tamerton Foliot on the primary route (Stage 2), or when leaving Carkeel, north of Saltash, on the *Kylgh Kernow* Cornish option (Stage 2K). It leaves the AONB north of Milton Abbot on the primary route (Stage 4) or at the end of the Greystone Link on the *Kylgh Kernow* option (Stage 4K). The Tamara Coast to Coast Way passes through two further AONBs, if more briefly. These are the Cornwall and North Devon AONBs, which are entered when approaching the north coast (Stage 7).

The Cornwall AONB is unusual in being divided into a number of sections, encompassing long stretches of the Cornish coast and its hinterland, inland areas of the Penwith and Lizard peninsulas in the west of the county, the Camel Estuary and the whole of Bodmin Moor. The Way passes through the AONB in its most northerly subdivision, known as the Hartland section. This area is characterised by dramatic coastal scenery, with coastal heathland meeting granite cliffs, and secluded and intimate valleys such as that of Marsland Water, which the Way follows to the coast.

In addition, the primary route of the Way crosses into Devon for a short while, where it enters the North Devon AONB. This AONB is also largely concentrated on the dramatic coast and secluded coastal valleys, a direct reflection of the landscape of the Cornwall AONB in this part of the county.

The Cornwall AONB is entered by the *Tamara Coast to Coast Way* on crossing the A39 near Woolley (Stage 7). After passing through the North Devon AONB when descending the Marsland Water valley it re-enters the Cornwall AONB and continues along the coast to the end of the Way at Morwenstow.

Cornwall also has a local landscape designation: Area of Great Landscape Value (AGLV). These are areas of high landscape quality with a strong and distinctive character which make them particularly sensitive to development. The primary objective in these areas is conservation and enhancement of their landscape quality and individual character. The majority of the *Tamara Coast to Coast Way* in Cornwall (between the AONBs) falls into the AGLV designation.

Devon no longer has the AGLV designation but aims to protect all its individual landscapes by identifying the essential landscape characteristics of its various Landscape Character Areas and protecting and enhancing these. Cornwall has a similar approach, in addition to its AGLV protection policy. Historically, Devon also used AGLVs, and these included the area immediately north of the Tamar Valley AONB.

In summary, walkers on the *Tamara Coast to Coast Way* will experience a landscape and environment of the highest quality, and one that is appropriately protected.

The Cornish Language

Part of Cornwall's perceived sense of difference from the rest of the country, and even of its being perhaps 'exotic', derives from the survival and use of the Cornish language. *The Tamara Coast to Coast* project refers to this in its use of the term *Kylgh Kernow* – 'circuit/circle of Cornwall' – for the Cornish option of the route, and has also referred to the name of the route in its Cornish form: *Hyns Tamara Arvor dh 'Arvor.*

It will be appreciated from these examples that Cornish is not merely a local dialect of English, but a fully-fledged language in its own right. It is descended from the Celtic language spoken over much or all of the country until and through Roman times. Then, from the 5th and 6th centuries onwards, Britain was invaded by Saxon and Anglian settlers from what is now northern Germany and southern Denmark, bringing their language with them, which became the earliest form of English.

There is much debate over whether this settlement, and its westward spread, was physical, with the new settlers driving out the original inhabitants, or whether it was cultural, with the local inhabitants gradually taking on the language of the new arrivals. Whatever the process, the Celtic British language retreated west where it became confined by the time of the Norman Conquest to Cumbria, Wales and Cornwall.

Throughout the Middle Ages the use of Cornish gradually continued to retreat westwards under the cultural and economic pressure of the English language. As far as the Tamar Valley is concerned, the language had probably disappeared from daily use shortly after the Normans' arrival in 1066. It continued to retreat until the 18th century when tradition has it that the last speaker of Cornish only, Dolly Pentreath, died in Mousehole in west Cornwall. There are, however, records of people able to speak Cornish well into the 19th century, although generally their ability was confined to rhymes or short folk tales.

In the early 20th century the language was revived by Cornish academics, especially initially Henry Jenner and Robert Morton Nance, and this revival continues, with Cornish now taught in many evening classes throughout the county and in some schools as part of their curriculum.

Recently the Cornish revival has been taken forward by Cornwall Council, with the use of Cornish as a foreword in most of its official documents, and in bilingual public signage.

A bilingual sign in Torpoint (Penntorr) in Stage 1

However, in one sense Cornish never died, being represented in the majority of place names in Cornwall. The Tamar Valley differs a little from the rest of the county in this case: being the most easterly part it fell under the influence of English earlier than elsewhere. The result is that the valley contains many English place names, even on the Cornish side of the river, despite the boundary between Cornwall and Wessex being formally established on the Tamar (mostly) in the 10th century.

This is presumably due to an early English presence west of the Tamar, although whether this was due primarily to physical settlement or cultural influence is unknown. Particularly noticeable is the switch from English to Cornish place names in the north of the area, not at the Tamar but at the tributary River Ottery, raising the possibility that this was an important divide in the Saxon period.

Nevertheless, numerous Cornish place names are encountered along the Tamara Coast to Coast Way. Some of the more common place name elements found here and throughout Cornwall are:

Bal	mine
Bean, pean	small, little
Bod, bos	dwelling
Bre, vre	hill
Car, ker	fortification
Carn	rock outcrop
Carrack	rock
Chy, chi	house
Dennis, dinas, din	fort
Du	black
Eglos	church
Ennis	island
Gear	fortification
Goon, gun	downland
Gwyn	white
Hal	moor, marsh
Hen	old
Kelly	grove
Lan	holy enclosure
Les, lis	court
Mellan	mill
Men	stone
Mear, meor	big
Mor	sea
Nan, nans, nant	valley
Pen	head, top, hill
Pol	pool, cove
Pons, pont	bridge
Porth	cove, harbour
Red, res, rid	ford
Rose	heath, promontory
Towan	dune
Treath	beach
Tre	farm, settlement, village
Ty	house
Vean	small, little
Vear, veor	big
Vellan	mill
Venton	spring
Vounder	lane
Wartha	higher, upper
Wheal	working, workshop, mine working
Wollas	lower
Zawn	cleft in cliffs

The Tamara Landscape Partnership Scheme

The creation of the Tamara Coast to Coast Way is one of the first projects to be completed as part of The Tamara Landscape Partnership Scheme with support from the Heritage Lottery Fund.

This is a 5-year project, that aims to create a brighter future for the Tamar Valley and its communities, by creating opportunities and positive change through a programme of 10 exciting projects broken down into 4 themes. They are:

People and Communities

- **Celebrating Tamara:** an events timetable packed full of activities for individuals and families to connect communities and provide great experiences. This will culminate in a River Festival in 2024.
- **Natural Connections:** new events and activities to improve physical health and well-being. They include walks and talks; art therapy; bushcraft; tree planting and yoga.
- **Tamara Trainees:** over 20 apprenticeship, foundation and internships will be created.
- **River Explorers:** with The Westcountry Rivers Trust, recruiting volunteers to look after their local waterways and schools will take part in fun workshops.

Heritage

- **Small Detail Big Difference:** conserving and enhancing key historic sites, whilst helping local communities to identify, research and protect the heritage that matters to them.
- **Promoting our Produce:** with Tamar Grow Local, working to revitalise the Valley's market garden industry.
- **Heritage of Innovation:** preserving the history of the valley by creating a Heritage Hub that contains the oral, written and visual history of the Valley.

Access and Sustainable Tourism

- **Accessible Tamar:** we aim to improve sustainable and integrated transport in the Valley. Highlights include the creation of the Tamara Coast to Coast Way and a trial reinstatement of the Calstock Ferry.
- **Come, Visit, Stay Awhile:** with Visit Tamar Valley we are working to support the Valley to become a sustainable tourism hub.

Farming and Land Management

- **New Approaches / Making Connections:** providing support and advice to farmers, landowners and communities to create opportunities and mitigate challenges.

The Legend of Tamara

The origin of the legend behind the name 'Tamara' has been lost in time. It tells of a nymph called Tamara, who lived in the underworld. She wanted to wander free in the mortal world, against the wishes of her parents. But one day she managed to rise from the underworld and was wandering on Dartmoor where she met two giants, called Torridge and Tavy. They both became enchanted with Tamara and vied for her affections. Tamara would never let them touch her, darting out of reach whenever either came too close.

Eventually both giants caught up with her on the high lands near Morwenstow, just as Tamara's father, out looking for her, also found her. He became enraged with the giants and put a spell on both of them, sending them into a deep sleep. Tamara was upset at this and she refused to return to the underworld with her father.

Tamara's father became even more enraged at this behaviour and cast a spell on Tamara, turning her into a spring, which produced the River Tamar and flowed south all the way to the sea. When Torridge awoke from his spell-induced sleep he found that his beloved had become a river. He sought the advice of a magician, who in turn made him into a river so that he could reunite with Tamara. But the spell on Tamara was so strong that Torridge was never able to meet with her and instead he had to turn north, to flow to the sea at Bideford. This explains the different destinations of the two rivers, which rise so close to each other, less than a mile apart.

Tamara's other suitor, Tavy, also woke to find Tamara had become a river and asked his father, another powerful magician, to help, His father turned Tavy into a river as well, and he set off in pursuit of Tamara, eventually finding her and merging with her to form a large and beautiful estuary.

Tamara C2C
Plymouth 87m
TAMARA
COAST TO COAST
Coast Path
Plymouth 300m
Kylgh Kernow
Circuit of Cornwall